Live Tastefully

The Fresh Life Series

What people are saying about …

The Fresh Life Series

"What a great way for women to learn to study the Bible: interesting stories, thought-provoking questions, and a life-changing approach to applying Scripture."

Franklin Graham, president and CEO of Billy Graham Evangelistic Association and Samaritan's Purse

"Skip and Lenya Heitzig have been friends of my wife, Cathe, and I for more than twenty years. Lenya loves to study God's Word and teach it to women in a way that is both exciting and accessible. I trust her latest book will be a blessing to you."

Greg Laurie, pastor and evangelist of Harvest Ministries

"Discover the pathway to God through these in-depth Bible studies."

Kay Smith, wife of Chuck Smith (Calvary Chapel)

"The Fresh Life Series is an insightful and in-depth look at God's Word."

K. P. Yohannan, president of Gospel for Asia

"A wonderful Bible study series that invites participants to spend time in God's Word and then see the Word come to fruition in their lives. What a blessing! These studies are perfect for small groups or personal daily devotions."

Robin Lee Hatcher, women's event speaker and award-winning author

A
20-Minutes-a-Day
Study

Live Tastefully

Savoring Encounters with Jesus

Lenya Heitzig

David C Cook®

transforming lives together

LIVE TASTEFULLY
Published by David C Cook
4050 Lee Vance View
Colorado Springs, CO 80918 U.S.A.

David C Cook Distribution Canada
55 Woodslee Avenue, Paris, Ontario, Canada N3L 3E5

David C Cook U.K., Kingsway Communications
Eastbourne, East Sussex BN23 6NT, England

The graphic circle C logo is a registered trademark of David C Cook.

The website addresses recommended throughout this book are offered as a resource to you. These websites are not intended in any way to be or imply an endorsement on the part of David C Cook, nor do we vouch for their content.

LCCN 2012935338
ISBN 978-0-7814-0594-2

© 2012 Lenya Heitzig
Published in association with William K. Jensen Literary Agency, 119 Bampton Court, Eugene, OR 97404

The Team: Terry Behimer, Karen Lee-Thorp, Amy Konyndyk, Caitlyn York, Karen Athen
Additional material provided by Misty Foster, Maria Guy, Vicki Perrigo, and Christy Willis
General Editor: Laura Sowers
Copy Editor: Rebekah Hanson
Cover Design: ThinkPen Design, Greg Jackson
Cover Image: Shutterstock

Printed in the United States of America
First Edition 2012

1 2 3 4 5 6 7 8 9 10

032912

Contents

Introduction

GUESS WHO'S COMING TO DINNER?

Imagine planning a dinner party with Jesus as the guest of honor. Does your blood pressure rise at the mere thought? No doubt you'd agonize over the guest list and consider every detail to make this a very special occasion. Perhaps a sunny backyard barbecue with burgers on the grill suits your fancy. Then again, a formal affair might come to mind: filet mignon served in the dining room with candlelight. Either way, the fine dinnerware escapes the china cabinet as Great-aunt Helen's sterling silver gets a long-overdue polishing. Nothing but the best for the Savior, right?

Just picture Jesus sitting at the head of your table. Perhaps you ask Him to pray for a prodigal when He says grace. As dinner progresses, you might keep the conversation flowing by asking Him to share how it feels to perform miracles or transform a hardened heart. Picture Him taking a healthy bite of your entrée, smiling, and saying, "These are the best enchiladas I've ever eaten!" While your heart pounds with joy, you answer quietly, "Oh, it's nothing—just an old family recipe."

It's fun to envision such an easy interaction, but deep down, we know that such an experience would forever change the way we looked at the value of sharing a meal. In Scripture, this was traditionally the highest form of hospitality. If a traveler happened by a person's house, it was considered a sacred duty to invite him in for a meal. The host not only presented the guest with food and drink but also offered lodging and protection if needed.

People in that culture believed that partaking of the same food nourished each individual, while simultaneously creating a union. This dining experience often created bonds that reached to their descendants and future heirs. The connection was sometimes confirmed by the exchange of gifts, as in the case of King Solomon and the queen of Sheba: "Now King Solomon gave the queen of Sheba all she desired, whatever she asked, besides what Solomon had given her according to the royal generosity" (1 Kings 10:13).

The law of Moses elevated hospitality to a religious duty (Lev. 19:34). And we see the importance of hospitality in Jesus' description of those who would inherit the kingdom: "For I was hungry and you gave Me food; I was thirsty and you gave Me drink; I was a stranger and you took Me in" (Matt. 25:35).

In Genesis 18:1–15, Abraham enthusiastically entertained three strangers who arrived unannounced at his tent. Initially, he was unaware that his guests were far from common travelers. In the traditional Middle Eastern custom, Abraham lavished them with fine cakes, tender calf, butter, milk, and bread—a rich and delicious meal by any standard. The New Testament gives us further insight into these strangers' identities: "Do not forget to entertain strangers, for by so doing some have unwittingly entertained angels" (Heb. 13:2). Abraham entertained two angels—and the Lord Himself!

Today, Arabs still practice a form of hospitality similar to that of the ancient Hebrews. My son, Nathan, and I were strangers invited into a Jordanian bedouin tent to enjoy a special feast known as *mansaf*. Picture the desert version of a Hawaiian luau; rather than a pig on a platter, the tray was adorned with roasted lamb and all the trimmings. Nathan and I were greeted by a long line of local sheikhs who said, "You are among your family." The sheikh who owned the tent treated Nathan like a most honored guest. He patted him on the head, embraced his cheeks, and gave him double portions of the *mansaf*.

It is said that "a traveler may sit at the tent door of a perfect stranger and smoke his pipe until the master welcomes him with an evening meal, may tarry a limited number of days without inquiry as to his purposes, and may then depart with a simple 'God be with you' as his only compensation."[1] The Greek word for *hospitality* is beautifully translated as "love of strangers."

Extending hospitality is an integral part of living tastefully. Inviting unbelievers into our home and sharing a meal might be the first step to unlocking their hearts in preparation to receive the gospel. Paul recognized the value of this simple ritual when he reminded the Romans to be generous, "distributing to the needs of the saints, given to hospitality" (Rom. 12:13).

It's my prayer that as you dig into this study, you will also choose to live fully and graciously in the midst of a hungering world. Who knows? You might inadvertently offer Grandma's famous pot roast to an angel! Even better—the unbeliever you invite to dinner may one day be seated next to you at the marriage supper of the Lamb.

GUEST OF HONOR

In the course of this Bible study, we'll eavesdrop on meals shared with the Savior and see the vast variety of people He encountered. We'll meet peasants like the travelers to Emmaus, a spiritually dehydrated woman at a well, self-satisfied religious men, hungry sinners, outcast tax collectors, kings, and humble saints.

At some meals Jesus went unnoticed—slipping under the wire as just another wedding guest in the crowd. On other occasions, Jesus was the guest of honor—as at the Last Supper. Sadly, there was even a banquet where our Lord was treated with dishonor. At each and every repast, the Savior exemplified how to live fully and purposefully. We'll discover the intimacy that developed between Jesus and those with whom He dined—and we'll even take a look at their menus.

MENU PLANNING

Have you ever wondered what kind of food Jesus ate? I have. I envision Him having a sweet tooth just like me. He probably enjoyed honey-covered pastries layered with nuts (similar to Greek baklava). Perhaps He slathered his bread with butter and date or fig jam. How could He resist the variety of fruits that filled the Promised Land, from pomegranates to succulent grapes?

The Middle Eastern diet was comprised of more than just sweets. Meals varied from fish to cattle to quail. These were often rubbed with olive oil and seasonings and then boiled or roasted over an open fire. The spice trade ran through Israel's borders, so the area abounded with seasonings. They enjoyed cumin, saffron, and cinnamon, to name a few. Grains included barley and wheat, which supplied basic nourishment for the working class. Middle Easterners enjoyed a healthy diet of vegetables such as leeks, garlic, and onions, and legumes like peas, beans, and lentils. As you can see, their menu-planning possibilities were abundant and diverse.

Along the way, as we step into the Word to observe Jesus dining with others, I'll offer some sweet and savory Middle Eastern recipes that you may want to prepare and share with your own guests. Even if you're not "into" cooking, don't let doubts about your culinary abilities deprive you of the blessings of sharing your home and your gifts with others.

LEARN ABOUT ...

Authors: Matthew, Mark, Luke, and John.

Audience: Varied: the apostles, His mother and brothers, the crowd of five thousand, Zacchaeus, and ultimately the world.

Theme: John 6:35: "Jesus said to them, 'I am the bread of life. He who comes to Me shall never hunger, and he who believes in Me shall never thirst.'"

Date: Probably AD 65–95.

Setting: Varied: Cana, Jerusalem, Emmaus, and the Sea of Galilee.

Practice makes perfect—so I encourage you to practice hospitality. Each lesson will end with a sweet or savory selection so that you, too, can live tastefully.

Dear Reader,

When I was a young single woman living in Hawaii, I served the Lord with Youth With A Mission. To freshen up my quiet time, I departed from my trusty old King James Bible and purchased a New International Version Bible. As I read each passage, it seemed as though God was speaking directly to *me*, especially when I read Revelation 3:20: "Here I am! I stand at the door and knock. If anyone hears my voice and opens the door, I will come in and eat with him, and he with me" (NIV).

At that point, the Holy Spirit inspired a truly unique thought: *You should go on a date with Jesus.* Excuse me? A *date* with Jesus? So despite the fact that my mom taught me never to call the man first, I decided to ask Jesus out on a date! My heart pounded as I thought about it: *How do I ask the Lord over for dinner? What will He say? Will my dorm mates think I'm crazy? What will I say to the Savior? What will I serve the King of Kings? Oh my goodness—I need a new outfit!*

As you might expect, the Lord graciously accepted my invitation. And then my preparations began. I cleaned the room, rustled up some candles for a soft ambiance, and brought in plumeria blossoms from the garden to string into a beautiful lei necklace. Because I lived on a school budget, dinner from the cafeteria would have to do, but I ran to the bakery to find a delicious dessert to crown the meal. At last, I curled my hair, applied lipstick, and put on my best dress.

We sat at the table, talked, and ate. When an awkward silence filled the room, I opened up my photo album. I spent the rest of the evening introducing Jesus to my friends and family and telling Him all about their individual needs. Before I knew it, it was time to say, "Good night." I didn't want the evening to end. It was one of the most delicious moments of my life.

It is my prayer that as you partake in this Bible study, you, too, will meet Jesus over a meal. You might even be inspired to plan your own special date with the Savior. It might be your first—but I predict it won't be your last.

Jesus stands at your door, knocking. He wants nothing more than to reveal Himself to you and have a rich relationship with you. Indulge! This is one time you don't have to count calories, carbs, or points. Live fully with the Savior. Dine luxuriously on His Word. A banquet awaits.

Live Tastefully,

Lenya

How to Get the Most out of This Study

Has your life lost its luster? Perhaps the abundance of *things* has tarnished the abundant life God offers. The best way to polish your life is through the cleansing power of God's Word. That's why doing a Bible study like this is so vital—because God's Word has the power to do God's work in our lives. It's the catalyst that refreshes your heart, renews your mind, and restores your soul—His Word makes life worth living!

In this Bible study, we're going to sit down and dine with Jesus. We'll attend the wedding feast of an embarrassed host, drink water at a well with a wayward woman, see how Jesus dealt with hungry masses, eat with the undesirables of Jewish culture, and so much more.

We'll learn about God's compassion, His confrontations, and His miraculous creativity. Come. Sit down. Turn off all the competing distractions. It's time to dine with Jesus—taste and see that He is good!

Each week of the study is divided into five days for your personal time with God. Each day's lesson has five elements. They are designed to help you fully "live" as you apply the truths you learn to your life:

1. Lift Up … Here we ask you to "Lift Up" prayers to God, asking Him to give you spiritual insight for the day.

2. Look At … This portion of the study asks you to "Look At" the Scripture text using inductive questions. These questions help you discover *What are the facts?* You'll learn the basic who-what-when-where-how aspects of the passage as well as some of the important background material.

3. Learn About … The "Learn About" sidebars correlate to specific questions in order to help you understand *What does this text mean?* These sidebar elements offer cultural insight, linguistic definitions, and biblical commentary.

4. Live Out … These questions and exercises are designed to help you investigate *How should this change my life?* Here you're challenged to personally apply the lessons you have learned as you "Live Out" God's principles in a practical way. I encourage you to write out all of the answers to the questions in this study. You may want to write the answers to the personal application questions in a journal to ensure privacy. By writing your insights from God day by day, you'll have a record of your relationship with Him that you can look back on when you need a faith boost.

5. Listen To … We finish with inspiring quotes from authors, speakers, and writers. You'll be able to "Listen To" the wisdom they've gleaned in their lives and relate it to your own.

Live Tastefully: Savoring Encounters with Jesus is ideal for discussion in a small-group setting, as well as for individual study. The following suggestions will help you and your group get the most out of your study time.

PERSONAL CHECKLIST

- **Be determined.** Examine your daily schedule, then set aside a consistent time for this study.
- **Be prepared.** Gather the materials you'll need: the Bible, your Fresh Life Bible Study, and a pen.
- **Be inspired.** Begin each day with prayer, asking the Holy Spirit to be your teacher and to illuminate your mind.
- **Be complete.** Read the suggested Bible passage and finish the homework each day.
- **Be persistent.** Answer each question as fully as possible. If you're unable to answer a question, move forward to the next question or read the explanation in the "Learn About" section, which may offer further insight.
- **Be consistent.** Don't get discouraged. If you miss a day, use the weekend to catch up.
- **Be honest.** When answering the "Live Out" questions, allow the Lord to search your heart and transform your life. Take time to reflect honestly about your feelings, experiences, sins, goals, and responses to God.

- **Be blessed.** Enjoy your daily study time with God as He speaks to you through His Word.

SMALL-GROUP CHECKLIST

- **Be prayerful.** Pray before you begin your time together.
- **Be biblical.** Keep all answers in line with God's Word; avoid personal opinion.
- **Be confidential.** Keep all sharing within your small group confidential.
- **Be respectful.** Listen without interrupting. Keep comments on track and to the point so that all can share.
- **Be discreet.** In some cases, you need not share more than absolutely necessary. Some things are between you and the Lord.
- **Be kind.** Reply to the comments of others lovingly and courteously.
- **Be mindful.** Remember your group members in prayer throughout the week.

SMALL-GROUP LEADER CHECKLIST

- **Be prayerful.** Pray that the Holy Spirit will "guide you into truth" so that your leadership will guide others.
- **Be faithful.** Prepare by reading the Bible passage and studying the lesson ahead of time, highlighting truths and applying them personally.
- **Be prompt.** Begin and end the study on time.
- **Be thorough.** For optimum benefit, allot one hour for small-group discussion. This should allow plenty of time to cover all of the questions and exercises for each lesson.
- **Be selective.** If you have less than an hour, you should carefully choose which questions you will address and summarize the edited information for your group. In this way, you can focus on the more thought-provoking questions. Be sure to grant enough time to address pertinent "Live Out" exercises, as this is where you and the women will clearly see God at work in your lives.
- **Be sensitive.** Some of the "Live Out" exercises are very personal and may not be appropriate to discuss in a small group. If you sense that this is the case, feel free to move to another question.

- **Be flexible.** If the questions in the study seem unclear, reword them for your group. Feel free to add your own questions to bring out the meaning of a verse.

- **Be inclusive.** Encourage each member to participate in the discussion. You may have to draw some out or tone some down so that all have the opportunity to participate.

- **Be honest.** Don't be afraid to admit that you don't have all the answers. When in doubt, encourage ladies to take difficult questions to their church leadership for clarification.

- **Be focused.** Keep the discussion on tempo and on target. Learn to pace your small group so that you complete a lesson on time. When participants get sidetracked, redirect the discussion to the passage at hand.

- **Be patient.** Realize that not all people are at the same place spiritually or socially. Wait for the members of your group to answer the questions rather than jumping in and answering them yourself.

The Best Is Yet to Come
John 2:1–12

"The Best Is Yet to Come," sung by Frank Sinatra, was written with newlyweds in mind. It expresses the joyous anticipation of beginning their lives together:

> The best is yet to come,
> Come the day you're mine....
> We've only tasted the wine,
> We're gonna drain that cup dry.[1]

The biblical story of the wedding in Cana also conveys anticipation and the desire to honor the newlyweds and their guests. However, halfway through the celebration, the host and father of the bride ran out of wine. One commentator wrote, "Had the wine actually failed, the occurrence would have been regarded as an insult to those present, and would have banished the host and hostess to practical isolation."[2] But Jesus was in attendance—and when the Messiah is present, the best is yet to come.

As believers, we know that even when we're grounded by grief, sidelined by sorrow, or diminished by distress, "the sufferings of this present time are not worthy to be compared with the glory which shall be revealed in us" (Rom. 8:18). Earthly sorrows simply can't be compared to heavenly joys.

There was a time when Skip and I were slammed by waves of suffering and felt that one more ripple might take us under. A card arrived from Pastor Greg Laurie that helped us shift our focus from a painful present to a hopeful future. His message? "The best is yet to come!"

Day 1: John 2:1–2   **Wedding Guests**

Day 2: John 2:3–5   **Catering Chaos**

Day 3: John 2:6–8   **Preparing for the Toast**

Day 4: John 2:9–10   **The Best for Last**

Day 5: John 2:11–12   **First Time for Everything**

DAY 1
Wedding Guests

LIFT UP ...

Lord, I want to live with an understanding of Your power in my life today, and in anticipation of the wonderful things that are yet to come. In Jesus' name. Amen.

LOOK AT ...

This week, we journey to Cana to enjoy our first dining experience with Jesus. The miracles of Moses are often regarded as meeting basic needs for food and water. Similarly, when Jesus turned water into wine, this also provided a necessity. According to the Jewish custom, wine represented enjoyment and sacred blessing. Moses changed the water of the Nile into blood, pointing to the curse of the law; Jesus changed water into wine, illuminating the grace of the new covenant.

Are you wandering in the wilderness of guilt and shame, thirsting for forgiveness? Today you can drink the wine of the new covenant: "[Jesus] took a cup of wine and gave thanks to God for it ... and said, 'Each of you drink from it, for this is my blood, which confirms the covenant between God and his people. It is poured out as a sacrifice to forgive the sins of many'" (Matt. 26:27–28 NLT).

READ JOHN 2:1–2.

On the third day there was a wedding in Cana of Galilee, and the mother of Jesus was there. Now both Jesus and His disciples were invited to the wedding. John 2:1–2

1. When did these events occur? Why do you think John included time frames in his gospel?

Learn About ...

3 Remote

Cana of Galilee was in an obscure corner of Israel, about seven and a half miles from Nazareth. Jerusalem held the country's greatest population and was home to prideful politicians and rabbis. With His first miracle, Jesus honored the simple country folk of Galilee over the big-city sophisticates.

---

4 Reflects

Scripture elevates marriage and teaches wives to submit to their husbands as unto the Lord and husbands to love their wives as Christ loves the church. Paul wrote, "The two shall become one flesh. This is a great mystery, but I speak concerning Christ and the church" (Eph. 5:31–32).

---

6 Reinforce

Until now, the disciples had not witnessed a miracle. They followed Christ based on His teachings and charisma. From this point on, they would see the dead raised, the lame walk, the blind see, and the deaf hear. They, too, would perform miracles in Jesus' name.

2.   Review John 1:43–51, then describe the circumstances that occurred before this event.

3.   Where did this incident take place?

4.   Why did Jesus make this journey? What spiritual significance do you think this holds?

5.   Who arrived before Jesus, and how did her attendance differ from the Lord's? (Look up John 2:1–2 in the KJV and the NLT. Referring to other Bible translations often provides further insight.)

6.   Who else was invited to this wedding, and why were they included?

Live Out ...

7.   Describe your hometown. Was it bustling or quiet? Describe how Jesus would be received if He visited your hometown for a celebration.

8.   Mary, the mother of Jesus, knew that Jesus had supernatural abilities. Read the following passages, and explain how Mary understood the divine nature of Jesus.

a. Luke 1:28–35

b. Luke 2:15–20

c. Luke 2:43–51

9. We've learned that every marriage is meant to reveal the mystery of Jesus and His bride, the church. Is Jesus intertwined in your marriage? If you are not married, how does it feel to know that Jesus is your Bridegroom? Rewrite the following passage into a personal prayer:

> Though one may be overpowered by another, two can withstand him. And a threefold cord is not quickly broken. (Eccl. 4:12)

LEARN ABOUT ...

7 Reserved

Jesus miraculously turned water into superior wine through unwitting accomplices while taking no credit. "Do not let your left hand know what your right hand is doing, that your charitable deed may be in secret; and your Father who sees in secret will Himself reward you openly" (Matt. 6:3–4).

8 Revered

Mary was the only family member who "held fast" to her belief that Jesus was the Messiah—even when His life appeared to be ending in tragedy. From the cross, Jesus gave Mary into the care of the beloved disciple, John. According to *Nelson's Illustrated Bible Dictionary,* "The last mention of Mary is in the upper room in Jerusalem, awaiting the coming of the Holy Spirit (Acts 1:14)."

When we were planning our son Nathan's wedding, we submitted a list of desired guests. We knew we were in trouble when we realized we had a large guest list—but only a modest budget. We determined to invite only those people whose presence would be missed. eHow suggested:

1. Invite all those people who have been in your life from day one. Your parents, grandparents, aunts and uncles, these people all qualify. Chances are they'll have heard about the wedding long before they receive the invitation....

2. Talk to your parents about a few close friends they want to invite. Even though it is your day, your parents are proud of you and want to share your big day with their closest friends too.

3. Think about where your wedding and reception will be held. If each venue only holds two hundred people comfortably ... increase or decrease your numbers accordingly.[3]

The couple in Cana had no such dilemma. Although Mary may have been related to the bride or groom, ancient Jewish weddings included the whole community.

The wedding began at the bridegroom's parents' house with a procession of friends, musicians, and singers. The bridal party was waiting at the bride's home. Upon arrival, the groom was welcomed with blessings, and then the whole gathering returned to the groom's home for the nuptials—seven to fourteen days of festivities!

Running out of wine halfway through this prolonged celebration would be disastrous. Jesus' miracle rescued the host from embarrassment and grumbling guests.

Listen To ...

Knit your hearts with an unslipping knot.

—*William Shakespeare*

Catering Chaos

For many English couples, a "destination wedding" provides a sunny escape from Britain's legendary gloom. Yet Paul and Tracy Swannick's plans for an exotic wedding turned into a nightmare. The First Choice Holiday Village Hotel in Sarigerme, Turkey, commanded a price tag of ten thousand pounds (almost sixteen thousand dollars), but during the wedding celebration, an outbreak of food poisoning swept through the entire wedding party. The couple realized something was terribly wrong when one by one their guests gagged back nausea or bolted to the restroom. The groom said, "Tracy had on a lovely dress but instead of enjoying the day she had to concentrate on keeping the contents of her stomach down." The couple is now among four hundred other tourists who are suing the hotel in hopes of recouping damages caused by the toxic trip.[4]

No one wants a wedding celebration to turn into litigation, and the host of the wedding in Cana was no exception. Wine was as essential to ancient Hebrews as the expression and symbol of joy. If a host failed to provide adequately, he could be sued. It's true! The rabbis had a saying: "Without wine there is no joy." Running out of wine was the equivalent of saying the bride and groom were not happy. The psalmist extolled, "Wine that makes glad the heart of man" (Ps. 104:15).

Today we'll see who wanted to be certain the joy wasn't drained from the wedding in Cana.

Lift Up ...

Heavenly Father, even my best efforts often fall short of my own expectations. Give me understanding of Your desire to be part of the great and small things that make up my life. In Jesus' name. Amen.

LEARN ABOUT ...

1 Wine

The Old Testament regards wine as a necessary and integral part of the simplest meals (Gen. 14:18; Judg. 19:19; 1 Sam. 16:20). According to the *International Standard Bible Encyclopedia*, wine was consumed by men and women of all classes and ages—"even the very young. An abundance of wine was a special token of God's blessing."

---

5 Woman

Calling Mary "woman" wasn't a sign of disrespect from Jesus (John 19:26), but established a division between His earthly and heavenly ties. Mary may have wanted Jesus to show off for their family, but this slight rebuke made it clear that she must not interfere with His purposes.

LOOK AT ...

Previously we discovered that Mary, Jesus, and some of His disciples were invited to the wedding in Cana. Mary may have been related to someone in the bridal party, as she seemed to hold a place of honor. The disciple Nathaniel was from Cana, so the invitation may have also come through him. Regardless, Jesus was welcomed at the joyous celebration. James Montgomery Boice writes, "This is the first of many stories suggesting that Jesus was always welcome among those who were having a good time."[5]

In your view, does God laugh, play, or make jokes? Some Christians think that being spiritual means you must be staunchly serious. But Jesus came to make life joyous: "These things I have spoken to you, that My joy may remain in you, and that your joy may be full" (John 15:11). The word *joy* means being cheerful, glad, or delighted. If you want to be like Jesus—smile!

READ JOHN 2:3–5.

And when they ran out of wine, the mother of Jesus said to Him, "They have no wine." Jesus said to her, "Woman, what does your concern have to do with Me? My hour has not yet come." His mother said to the servants, "Whatever He says to you, do it." John 2:3–5

1. Describe the catering chaos in Cana. Why do you think this was a problem?

2. Who noticed the problem?

3. What did this person do about the problem? Explain why.

4. List the two reasons Jesus gave for not intervening:

(1)

(2)

5. How did Jesus address His mother? Describe how she might have felt.

6. In your own words, explain how Jesus' mother responded and why.

Live Out ...

7. Running out of wine could have resulted in the celebration losing its joy, thereby shaming the host.

   a. Describe some of the resources that have run dry in your life.

   b. Did these losses result in a lack of joy? Explain how your joy was restored.

8. Fill in the following chart to discover some of the uses of wine in Scripture.

Scripture	Wine's Uses
2 Samuel 16:2	
Proverbs 31:6	
Luke 10:34	
1 Timothy 5:23	

9. While wine was a staple and a source of joy in biblical times, it also had many misuses. Drunkenness is never encouraged in Scripture. Look up Proverbs 23:29–35, and answer the following questions.

   a. Make a list of the conditions of those who "linger long at the wine" (vv. 29–30).

Learn About ...

6 Willing

Mary was not offended by this remark; instead, she showed her belief and confidence that her son was the Savior. She could not command Him, but she could instruct the servants to obey His instructions.

7 Wonder

According to *The New Unger's Bible Dictionary*, "Joy is a delight of the mind arising from the consideration of a present or assured possession of a future good ... called gladness; raised suddenly to the highest degree it is exultation; when the desires are limited by our possessions it is contentment; vanquished opposition we call triumph."

9 Warning

In the Old Testament, the first mention of wine finds Noah in his vineyard, drunk and naked. Paul warned, "Don't be drunk with wine, because that will ruin your life" (Eph. 5:18 NLT).

b. Describe the allurement of wine (v. 31).

c. What two creatures does wine mimic? Explain why (v. 32).

d. What physical repercussions will a drunkard incur (vv. 33–35)?

○ ○ ● ○ ○

Celebration, not drunkenness, was the goal at this wedding. Perhaps Mary was concerned that the wine shortage was due to the presence of Jesus' disciples. Although the text tells us the Lord and His companions were invited to this event, some commentators suggest that the invitation came at the last minute, just as the men arrived in town. Or they were included in the invitation for the entire community. Either way the host appeared unprepared for extra out-of-towners. Maybe the mother of Jesus prompted Him to help because she knew He was the Messiah. He seemed to be gathering men to His cause, and she might have thought this was a good time to have a "coming out" event. Like many Jewish mothers, she was nudging her son, the rabbi, forward.

At this site of the Savior's first miracle, we see both His divinity and humanity manifested. Jesus knew He was on a heavenly timetable when He told Mary, "My hour has not yet come." This rich term speaks of the series of miracles preceding the ultimate death and resurrection of our Lord. It was important for Mary to know that Jesus' heavenly Father—not His earthly mother—would initiate the timetable. In spite of this, Jesus did not want the host to be humiliated or the wedding feast to be robbed of its joy. So we see Him move quietly yet miraculously to remedy the situation.

LISTEN TO ...

If you have no joy in your religion, there's a leak in your Christianity somewhere.

—*Billy Sunday*

DAY 3
Preparing for the Toast

Most wedding receptions include a toast offered by a close acquaintance to honor the newly-weds. Over the years, attending countless weddings, I have heard some wonderful toasts. Some of them were so touching they brought me to tears, and some of them were pretty funny:

> Marriages are made in heaven. But, again, so are thunder, lightning, tornados, and hail.

> Marriage is when a man and woman become as one; the trouble starts when they try to decide which one.

> Adam and Eve had an ideal marriage. He didn't have to hear about all the men she could have married, and she didn't have to hear about how well his mother cooked.

Not all wedding toasts are meant to be humorous. In fact, including a joke can often be a big mistake. Here are a few dos and don'ts for toast preparation:

Do	**Don't**
Do introduce yourself	Don't ever give a toast while drunk
Do prepare something in advance	Don't ad-lib or go impromptu
Do include anecdotes about the couple	Don't mention past partners or embarrassing stories
Do end on a warm, uplifting note	Don't ramble on forever

No toast would be possible without the requisite beverage. Because Skip and I are not wine drinkers, our wedding had champagne glasses filled with sparkling apple cider. With glasses held high, Skip's best man gave a nervous but endearing blessing. We smiled as the room chimed their glasses with crystal notes of joy. Today we'll see that before a toast could be made at the wedding in Cana, it was essential that the appropriate beverage was provided.

LIFT UP ...

Lord, open my heart to understand this first of Your great miracles. Let me be moved to raise my glass to the compassion and love that spill from Your every action. In Jesus' name. Amen.

LOOK AT ...

We've learned that wedding feasts were considered the supreme events in ancient Hebrew life. Instead of going on a honeymoon, the bride and groom were the king and queen of a weeklong celebration. For those few days, they wore crowns and robes, and their word was the law. These occasions were greatly anticipated, especially by the peasants.

The wedding in Cana points to the grandest wedding of all! Jesus will be in attendance, but this time He will be the Bridegroom who has come to gather His bride—the church—for a nuptial feast in heaven. Angels will rejoice, "Blessed are those who are called to the marriage supper of the Lamb!" (Rev. 19:9).

Have you received your invitation to this blessed event? If not, decide to invite Jesus into your life as your Savior. Those who follow the Son will rule and reign with Him forever.

READ JOHN 2:6–8.

Now there were set there six waterpots of stone, according to the manner of purification of the Jews, containing twenty or thirty gallons apiece. Jesus said to them, "Fill the waterpots with water." And they filled them up to the brim. And He said to them, "Draw some out now, and take it to the master of the feast." And they took it. John 2:6–8

1. Describe the composition of the waterpots. Why do you think this is important?

2. Explain the intended purpose for these containers.

3. How much liquid could the pots contain? What does this tell you about the Lord's provision?

4. What did Jesus ask the servants to do?

5. What phrase describes their complete obedience?

6. What did Jesus ask to be done next? How did the servants respond?

7. Describe how those who obeyed Jesus may have felt as they waited for the host to sample the wine.

LIVE OUT ...

8. a. That the waterpots were made of stone ensured that the vessels would be untainted by contaminates. What worldly pollutants have contaminated your life?

❑ Foul language ❑ Worldly philosophy ❑ Anger
❑ Pornography ❑ Drug use ❑ Jealousy
❑ Drunkenness ❑ False religion ❑ Family history
❑ Greed ❑ Ungodly friendships ❑ Other_____

b. Rewrite the following passage into a personal prayer for purification:

> [Jesus] gave Himself for us, that He might redeem us from every lawless deed and purify for Himself His own special people, zealous for good works. (Titus 2:14)

LEARN ABOUT ...

2 Purification

Waterpots were used during ceremonial cleansing for violating God's law: "All the Jews do not eat unless they wash their hands in a special way, holding the tradition of the elders" (Mark 7:3). Stone vessels were believed to prevent contamination from the previous contents and contained only ceremonial water.

3 Multiplication

The total capacity of these six waterpots is estimated to be 150 gallons. The average cup held about a half pint of liquid. Therefore, Jesus would have provided enough wine for 2,400 servings—more than enough for a large number of people to be satiated for several days.

7 Fascination

Consider the servants' faith. First, they filled the waterpots "to the brim"—no half measures; the pots were filled to the tippy top. Second, they served the host immediately. They didn't wait for an "Alacazam!" The Savior's command was sufficient for them to act in faith. Imagine their anticipation for the results.

Learn About ...

8 Purification

Purification means to make a person clean or pure before God and men. According to *Nelson's Illustrated Dictionary*, "The Mosaic Law detailed purification rituals for: leprosy (Lev. 13–14), sexual discharges (Lev. 15), and contact with a dead body (Num. 19:11–19)." The priests added burdensome and taxing purification laws that Jesus denounced.

---

10 Motivation

Jesus said that love is the motivation for obedience: "If you love Me, keep My commandments" (John 14:15). According to *Nelson's Illustrated Dictionary*, obedience means "to carry out the word and will of another person, especially the will of God. It is a positive, active response ... God summons people to active obedience to His revelation."

9. Read 1 Peter 2:4–8, and answer the following questions.

a. How did Peter describe Christians (v. 4)?

b. What was God's purpose for these "living stones" (v. 5)?

c. Who do you think is the chief cornerstone (v. 6)? Compare and contrast the differences between believers and unbelievers in their response to Jesus (vv. 7–8).

10. The servants obeyed Jesus completely and unquestioningly. Using OBEY as an acrostic, describe some of the ways you have been obedient to the Lord.

O

B

E

Y

∘ ∘ ● ∘ ∘

Muslims, like the New Testament Pharisees, have rigorous cleansing rituals. Here's a sample of typical ritual cleansing:

1. Perform every action with intention; cleanse thoroughly before prayer to honor Allah.

2. Say silently, "In the name of Allah, Most Gracious, Most Merciful."

3. Wash hands three times. Water must reach between each finger and the whole hand.

4. Bring a handful of water to the mouth and rinse three times, thoroughly.

5. Sniff water in the nose three times, using the right hand to sniff and left hand to expel.[6]

In the Bible, purification rituals began with the law of Moses. The most frequent cleansing agent was water, but sometimes priests employed blood or oil (Lev. 8:10). *Purification* "is especially applied to the ritual observances whereby an Israelite was formally absolved from the taint of uncleanness."[7]

By the New Testament era, the religious leaders added encumbrances to the purification process. The Lord condemned these rituals, teaching that uncleanness comes from the heart or mind. He declared that true purification comes only through His redemptive power: "You are already clean because of the word I have spoken to you" (John 15:3 NIV). We don't need rituals—we need a Redeemer!

LISTEN TO ...

If you pore over God's Word, his cleansing power will pour over you.

—*Anonymous*

DAY 4

The Best for Last

Are you a dessert-first kind of person, or do you save the best for last? I fall into the second category, enduring vegetables because I know a sweet treat awaits. I also devise reward systems to motivate me to clean the windows or organize closets. Incentives vary from lunch with a friend to reading a good book. In keeping with this best-for-last philosophy, on Christmas morning we save the best gift for last. One holiday, an envelope tucked in the Christmas tree branches contained clues that sent my son on a treasure hunt leading to his special gift.

Jesus elevated the position of last place to preeminence: "If anyone desires to be first, he shall be last of all and servant of all" (Mark 9:35). On the sixth and final day of creation, God made man from the dust of the earth and then fashioned Eve from Adam's rib. Humans are the culmination of creation, reflecting the very "image of God."

Our new bodies will not compare to these weak, fragile tents: "The body is sown in corruption, it is raised in incorruption. It is sown in dishonor, it is raised in glory. It is sown in weakness, it is raised in power" (1 Cor. 15:42–43). Revelation tells us that the new heaven, the new earth, and the New Jerusalem will far exceed the beauty of the firsts. The Lord cries out, "Behold, I make all things new" (Rev. 21:5). As Christians, our "ending" will far exceed our beginning.

LIFT UP ...

Holy God, help me find Your balance in a world that values the rich, the first, and the beautiful and disregards the humble and ordinary. Let me be a humble vessel You can use for Your glory and purpose. In Jesus' name. Amen.

LEARN ABOUT ...

1 Master

"Master" is better translated "the governor" and may refer to the best man or master of ceremonies. As chief servant, he made certain that guests had enough to eat and drink. He may have been a priest who monitored the festivities to ensure no one behaved indecently or was disorderly.

LOOK AT ...

We have seen Jesus miraculously transform six stone pots of water into wine that far exceeded the needs for this feast. The surplus was a gift that kept on giving to the newlyweds.

Abundance is characteristic of God's miracles. In the New Testament, Jesus turned a few loaves and fishes into a meal for five thousand. In the Old Testament, we read of the poor widow who had only a little jar of oil and many debts. The prophet Elisha told her to borrow many jars and to fill all the vessels from her one small jar. She could then sell the excess to pay her creditors (2 Kings 4:1–7).

God has resources beyond imagination. Paul promised, "My God shall supply all your need according to His riches in glory by Christ Jesus" (Phil. 4:19). Not sure God can meet your needs? Perhaps it's time you put Him to the test.

READ JOHN 2:9–10.

When the master of the feast had tasted the water that was made wine, and did not know where it came from (but the servants who had drawn the water knew), the master of the feast called the bridegroom. And he said to him, "Every man at the beginning sets out the good wine, and when the guests have well drunk, then the inferior. You have kept the good wine until now!" John 2:9–10

1. What did the "master of the feast" do?

2. What knowledge was withheld from the master, and why?

3. Who understood the origin of the wine, and what do you think they thought and felt after witnessing this miracle?

4. How did the master respond to the wine sampling?

5. Describe the expected sequence and quality of wines served from the beginning to the end of a feast.

6. How would the guests feel about the best wine being served at this point in the feast?

Live Out ...

7. The master of the feast tasted a miracle but did not know of its origin. Many blessings in our lives come through the prayers of others.

   a. Name a person you know who is unsaved:

   _____

   b. Spend some time praying that God would orchestrate miraculous events in that person's life. Pray that he or she will "taste and see that the LORD is good; blessed is the man who trusts in Him!" (Ps. 34:8).

8. Psalm 45 is a Messianic psalm that speaks of the marriage of Jesus and His bride, the church. Read the psalm, and answer the following questions.

   a. List some of the many attributes of our Bridegroom.

   b. Describe how He is dressed and prepared for the wedding.

   c. In your own words, describe His bride and the advice given to her.

Learn About ...

4 Mister

The master of the feast called mister bridegroom aside after sampling the extraordinary wine. What makes superior wine superior? Aging. Jesus did not create new wine from the water. Instead, the miracle possessed a signature of excellence, producing aged, fine wine. The master of the feast looked at the bridegroom with greater admiration as a result.

6 Magnify

This was the best wine with the fullest body. Matthew Henry wrote, "Christ's works commend themselves even to those that know not their author. The products of miracles were always the best in their kind." "Every good gift and every perfect gift is from above, and comes down from the Father" (James 1:17).

8 Messianic

Christ reminds His disciples, "All things must be fulfilled which were written in the Law of Moses and the Prophets and the Psalms concerning Me" (Luke 24:44). In the Old Testament, the Messiah was called the Seed of David, the Prince of Peace, and the Bridegroom.

9. Journal about a time when God saved the best for last in your life. How did this make you feel?

· · ● · ·

God often uses unwitting people to accomplish His provision. During the 1830s cholera epidemic in Bristol, England, a huge number of orphans roamed the streets, searching for food and shelter. When George Müller became aware of this, he brought thirty orphans to live in his home. Soon he prepared three more houses to accommodate 130 more children. By May 1870, 1,722 children were living in five additional homes. Müller never requested financial support from his friends, family, or congregation, nor did he go into debt. He simply prayed and asked God to provide.[8]

The needs were often basic. One morning three hundred children sat at the dining room table, waiting for breakfast, but the cupboards were bare. The workers came to George and asked what they should do. Müller went to the head of the table and prayed, "God, we thank You for what You are going to give us to eat. Amen."

Immediately, a knock came at the door. A local baker stood there with a delivery of warm bread. He explained that he had awakened at 3:00 a.m. with the impression that the orphans needed food. Soon after that, a milk truck broke down outside the orphanage. The truck could not be fixed unless the milk was first removed. Because the milk would sour before the repairs could be completed, the driver donated the milk to the orphans.[9]

George Müller didn't grind the flour, bake the bread, or milk the cow. He simply prayed.

LISTEN TO …

Man's poverty is no strain on God's provision.

—*Anonymous*

DAY 5

First Time for Everything

First times are often awkward. I still remember my son's first wobbly steps. While pushing a toy lawn mower, he accidentally let go. With outstretched arms, he toddled sideways four or five steps before landing on his bottom.

Remember your first kiss? If it was at all like mine, you probably wondered whether you did it right *or* if you even liked it. The first time I spoke publicly, butterflies erupted in my stomach, and my voice quivered.

In His human life, Jesus' firsts probably appeared awkward. Imagine our Savior learning to talk, walk, or learn to eat with utensils. When He started work in Joseph's carpentry shop, did He hit His thumb learning the tools of the trade? It's mind-boggling to imagine the God of the universe humbling Himself to come to us through such small beginnings on earth—from embryo to Emmanuel.

However, on the divine side of things, there's no scriptural indication that Jesus needed to practice before performing a miracle. When did it dawn on the Christ child that He was God? How long had He been yearning to show the world heavenly signs?

This week we learned that God had a timeline for Jesus' life and ministry that even His mother could not rush. The Lord's first miracle seemed effortless and was flawless. He didn't lift a finger. He simply ordered servants and willed the water to turn into wine. His first miracle was right on time and magnified His Father.

Lift Up ...

Heavenly Father, remind me that You understand that my steps to be a godly woman take practice and patience. I want my ordinary life to be a sign of Your extraordinary love. In Jesus' name. Amen.

LEARN ABOUT ...

1 Sign

Sign is often translated "miracle" and is used to describe a supernatural wonder. John often used this word rather than *miracle* to point to an event that was greater than reality. Sadly, the religious leaders could not read the signs: "But although He had done so many signs before them, they did not believe in Him" (John 12:37).

LOOK AT ...

Yesterday's lesson ended with the thought that man's poverty makes way for God's provision. In New Testament times, most wealthy individuals lived in Jerusalem and had occupations related to the temple, while those living in the Galilee region made their livelihood as fishermen, herdsmen, or farmers. Galileans were derided for their country dialect just as city people today sometimes mock the vernacular of country folks. Yet the majority of the Lord's ministry took place in this province.

Jesus identified with the lower class:

> The Spirit of the LORD is upon Me,
> Because He has anointed Me to preach the gospel to the
>   poor;
> He has sent Me to heal the brokenhearted,
> To proclaim liberty to the captives
> And recovery of sight to the blind,
> To set at liberty those who are oppressed. (Luke 4:18)

If you are weak, weary, or lacking in wealth, you are just the kind of person Jesus most enjoys.

READ JOHN 2:11–12.

This beginning of signs Jesus did in Cana of Galilee, and manifested His glory; and His disciples believed in Him. After this He went down to Capernaum, He, His mother, His brothers, and His disciples; and they did not stay there many days. John 2:11–12

1. Reread the entirety of this week's text. Record the phrases that indicated this was among the Lord's first miracles.

2. Underline the phrases that begin and end our text to define location. Record your findings in the space provided.

3. What was the first reason Jesus performed this sign? Explain how it was accomplished.

4. Explain the second outcome of this miracle and why this was so.

5. Where did Jesus go next? What was the length of His stay?

6. List the individuals who accompanied Jesus.

LIVE OUT ...

7. The miracles Jesus performed were meant to be signs that pointed to His divinity. Fill in the following chart to discover who else understood the signs.

SCRIPTURE	WHO SAW THE SIGN?
Luke 2:8–14	
Luke 11:30	
John 3:1–3	
John 9:11–16	
John 20:30–31	

8. Jesus' signs were meant to glorify His Father in heaven. We are called to shine forth good works for the same reason.

   a. List some of the good works you have witnessed. How did they make you feel?

LEARN ABOUT ...

3 Shine

The miracles Jesus performed were done to glorify the Lord. *Glorify* means "to exalt God through praising His name or obeying His commandments." We, too, can glorify God: "Let your light so shine before men, that they may see your good works and glorify your Father in heaven" (Matt. 5:16).

5 Stay

Capernaum became the headquarters and hometown of Jesus during His three and a half years of ministry. Many of His miracles and monologues occurred there. Simon Peter and Andrew were residents of the city. Matthew and Levi were there when they were chosen to be apostles as well. Capernaum sat on the western shores of the Sea of Galilee.

7 Seeing

The disciples witnessed Jesus' miracles, which strengthened their faith. But we Christians must learn to walk by faith and not by sight: "Then Jesus told him, 'Because you have seen me, you have believed; blessed are those who have not seen and yet have believed'" (John 20:29 NIV).

LEARN ABOUT ...

9 Servants

The disciples followed the Lord from country to city and on the hills and in the valleys. Whether they were feasting at a wedding or gleaning grain from the fields of harvest, Jesus said, "Whoever serves me must follow me; and where I am, my servant also will be" (John 12:26 NIV).

b. List some of the good works you have done. How did others respond?

c. Describe a good work you could act upon this week. Ask the Lord to shine His glory through your life.

9. Disciples follow Jesus no matter where He goes. With this in mind, write the following Scripture into a personal prayer:

> If anyone desires to come after Me, let him deny himself, and take up his cross, and follow Me. For whoever desires to save his life will lose it, but whoever loses his life for My sake will find it. For what profit is it to a man if he gains the whole world, and loses his own soul? … For the Son of Man will come in the glory of His Father with His angels, and then He will reward each according to his works. (Matt. 16:24–27)

∘ ∘ ● ∘ ∘

For decades, suffering Christians have drawn comfort from the poem entitled "Footprints in the Sand." The author, Mary Stevenson, was born shortly before the Great Depression. She lost her mother at the age of six, leaving her father to raise eight children alone. Mary wrote the poem as a young teenager, and at sixteen she entered into a marriage so abusive she ran for her life and ended up on an Indian reservation in Oklahoma. She did not return home until her husband left to fight in WWII.

> One night I dreamed I was walking along the beach with the Lord.
> Many scenes from my life flashed across the sky.
> In each scene I noticed footprints in the sand.

Sometimes there were two sets of footprints,
    other times there were one set of footprints.

    This bothered me because I noticed
    that during the low periods of my life,
    when I was suffering from
  anguish, sorrow or defeat,
I could see only one set of footprints.

So I said to the Lord,
  "You promised me, Lord,
    that if I followed you,
      you would walk with me always.
      But I have noticed that during
        the most trying periods of my life
        there have only been one
          set of footprints in the sand.
          Why, when I needed you most,
            you have not been there for me?"

    The Lord replied,
  "The times when you have
  seen only one set of footprints,
is when I carried you."[10]

LISTEN TO ...

Follow Me: I am the way, the truth, and the life. Without the way there is no going; without the truth there is no knowing; without the life there is no living.

—Thomas à Kempis

Dolmades

Remember the movie *My Big Fat Greek Wedding?* The father of the bride insisted that *every-thing* could be traced to Greek origins. According to Greek mythology, *dolmades*—grape leaves stuffed with rice and lamb—were served on Mount Olympus by the gods. Later, the Byzantines were credited for stuffing other types of leaves and adding a larger variety of ingredients including hazelnuts, figs, and spices. Appropriately, the word *dolma* is Turkish for "to be stuffed." We know they existed during the Ottoman Empire of the Turks and the siege of Thebes by Alexander the Great.[11]

Grapevines held importance both for their fruit and their foliage. Farmers ate the fruit fresh or dried it into raisin cakes for later. Of course, many vineyards produced wine. They wasted nothing—even the leaves provided nourishment when they were stuffed with minced lamb, rice, and spices. A vegetarian version was filled with rice and fresh herbs. Both are garnished with olive oil and lemon and can be served hot or cold. Either way, biting into dolmades is a divine experience.

Preparation Time: 15 minutes
Cook Time: 15 minutes

Ingredients:

    36 to 40 fresh or brine-packed grape leaves

    1 1/2 cups cooked long-grain rice

    1 tablespoon fresh parsley leaves

    5 fresh mint leaves, chopped

    1 teaspoon cumin, ground and heated slightly in a dry pan to release its aroma

    A generous amount of freshly ground black pepper

    A pinch of salt if needed

    1 onion, finely chopped

    Juice of 2 lemons, divided

    1 teaspoon of lemon zest

    1/4 cup of Greek olive oil

Instructions:

1. In a bowl, mix together the rice, parsley leaves, mint leaves, cumin, pepper, salt, lemon zest, and onions, and set aside.

2. If you are using fresh vine leaves, immerse them in boiling water for a few minutes and then immediately into ice-cold water. If you are using the canned leaves, rinse completely in cold water. Drain on paper towels.

3. Place the dull side of the leaf up with the stem facing you. Place a small amount of the filling (about a teaspoonful or so) in the center of the leaf and fold over, first on one side, then the other; then roll to make a roll. The glossy side of the leaf should be on the outside.

4. Repeat this process with the remaining leaves and mixture. Line a pan with a layer of grape leaves (to prevent burning) and place all of the dolmades in the pan side by side.

5. Take three-fourths of the lemon juice and pour into pan. Pour enough water to come halfway up the stuffed leaves, and drizzle the entire pan with olive oil. Using a plate on top of the dolmades to keep them flat, simmer them gently for ten to fifteen minutes. Remove from heat, and transfer the dolmades to a serving platter. Squeeze the remaining lemon juice, and drizzle more olive oil over the top. Dolmades can be served hot or cold.

GRACE NOTE

Lord,

This recipe reminds us of the importance of being filled with substance. What is seen on the outside is but a thin covering for the content of our hearts and minds. Like the Greek father of the bride who insisted the wedding be everything Greek, we want everything in our lives to originate in You. In Jesus' name. Amen.

Happy Hour
John 4:1–40

The term *happy hour* originated in the US Navy during the 1920s. It was slang for a period of entertainment aboard ship that often featured boxing or wrestling matches. After being at sea for extended periods of time, the sailors needed ways to cope with the pressures and close quarters of their seafaring lives. These sessions provided them with an opportunity to regularly blow off a little steam. Drinking establishments later adopted the term, promising patrons discounted prices on alcohol and a happy, relaxing atmosphere after the workday pressures. Unfortunately, this alcohol-soaked decompression often resulted in a pressure cooker of barroom brawls and impaired drivers. During the height of this trend, my family experienced tragedy up close when my young cousin was killed by a drunk driver. She was buried in my prom dress. In the wake of a noticeable increase in civil disturbances, car injuries, and deaths, people demanded an end to the so-called "happy hour." During the 1980s, bars made a slight concession to the outcry by offering free appetizers in hopes of reducing alcohol absorption in the bloodstream. Then, in 1984, the US military abolished the happy-hour tradition at all military bases. Clearly much grief has come from the thirst to find happiness and meaning at the bottom of a bottle.[1]

This week we'll study an unusual interaction between Jesus and a spiritually dehydrated woman. We'll discover a way to quench our thirst for satisfaction and truth that lasts much longer than 5:00 p.m. to 7:00 p.m.

Day 1: John 4:1–8	PIT STOP
Day 2: John 4:9–19	WONDROUS WATER
Day 3: John 4:20–26	MEN OR THE MESSIAH?
Day 4: John 4:27–33	SOUL FOOD
Day 5: John 4:34–40	HARVEST TIME

DAY 1
Pit Stop

LIFT UP ...

Lord Jesus, I don't want to waste my life pursuing destructive activities or meaningless pastimes. Teach me to use my time in a way that honors the life You have entrusted to me. In Jesus' name. Amen.

LOOK AT ...

This week we find the Lord ousted from Judea. He chose the unlikely route through Samaria to reach safety in Galilee. Water was scarce along this route. After their long walk, Jesus and the disciples stopped at Jacob's well for refreshment. This break in Jesus' journey was memorable not because He *received* water, but because He *gave* living water to a Samaritan woman. Like the Samaritan woman, we sometimes try to find satisfaction in worldly pursuits such as shopping, movies, food, or something else that never quite delivers. Without the Lord, these activities are like drinking salt water from the ocean—they will never satisfy our true thirst. God warned His people, "For My people have committed two evils: They have forsaken Me, the fountain of living waters, and hewn themselves cisterns—broken cisterns that can hold no water" (Jer. 2:13). Quench your true thirst: dive into the satisfying water of God's Word.

READ JOHN 4:1–8.

Therefore, when the Lord knew that the Pharisees had heard that Jesus made and baptized more disciples than John (though Jesus Himself did not baptize, but His disciples), He left Judea and departed again to Galilee. But He needed to go through Samaria.

So He came to a city of Samaria which is called Sychar, near the plot of ground that Jacob gave to his son Joseph. Now Jacob's well was there. Jesus therefore, being wearied from

His journey, sat thus by the well. It was about the sixth hour. A woman of Samaria came to draw water. Jesus said to her, "Give Me a drink." For His disciples had gone away into the city to buy food. John 4:1–8

Learn About ...

3 Samaria

During New Testament times, according to Nelson's *Illustrated Bible Dictionary,* "Palestine west of the Jordan River was divided into the three provinces of Galilee, Samaria, and Judea. Because of their intermarriage with foreigners, the people of Samaria were shunned by Orthodox Jews. Situated between Galilee and Judea, Samaria was the natural route for traveling between those two provinces."

4 Jacob's Well

Jacob placed this well in the parcel of ground he bought from the sons of Hamor (Gen. 33:19). Wells were essential to survival in Palestine. They were dug with difficulty from solid limestone rock, often reaching depths of 150 feet. Today, Jacob's well is an often-visited site called Bir Ya'qub.

5 Sixth Hour

In ancient times an hour was defined as a twelfth part of the period from sunrise to sunset. If sunrise were at 6 a.m., the sixth hour would be between 12 noon and 1:00 p.m. In Acts 10:9, the sixth hour is mentioned as the regular hour to pray.

1. What was Jesus' purpose in leaving Judea?

2. Why did He want to return to Galilee?

3. Compared to Judea and the region around the Sea of Galilee, what was different about Samaria?

4. What was significant about the well near Sychar?

5. What time was it?

6. Who came to the well? What did Jesus ask of her?

7. What was significant about Jesus being alone with this person at the well?

Live Out ...

8. Jesus departed again for Galilee because the Pharisees had intentions that could thwart His purposes. Scripture tells us how to respond to threats and weakness in our own lives. Read Ephesians 6:10–18.

a. Describe what threatens your spiritual life.

b. With spiritual armor in mind, explain where you need protection. Which piece of armor is essential to you right now?

c. Rewrite Ephesians 6:10–18 into a personal prayer. Consider your resources in Christ Jesus, and thank Him for His provision.

9. After a long walk, our Lord was thirsting for a cool drink of water. What are you thirsting for right now? Check those answers that apply.

    I thirst for:
    ❏ More time in God's Word
    ❏ Financial security
    ❏ Freedom from health problems
    ❏ Confidence in my salvation
    ❏ A loving husband
    ❏ The return of a prodigal child
    ❏ Something else: _____

10. a. Journal about what has threatened you or created an unquenched thirst.

    b. Describe a time when God brought help to you in a time of need. How does this alter your feelings about facing your future?

LEARN ABOUT ...

8 Tranquility

We women live demanding lives. We can feel overwhelmed by our responsibilities to and for others. Threats to our equanimity arise daily and can lead to feelings of vulnerability and fear. God is with you, so relax—but don't zone out. Put on your spiritual armor daily.

10 Aid

Do you sometimes feel overwhelmed and wonder who will help? Rely on God: He promised He will never leave you or forsake you. You can "trust in the LORD with all your heart ... In all your ways acknowledge Him, and He shall direct your paths" (Prov. 3:5–6).

o o ● o o

Today we learned that Jesus followed the path that kept Him out of harm's way, while never deviating from His purposes. Neither threats nor thirst could alter His ordained route. Whether His journey crossed the border into the rival territory of the Samaritans or through the religious turf in Jerusalem, Jesus looked to fulfill the ultimate will of His Father.

In the summer of 1982, Larry Walters set out on an adventure that later inspired the children's movie *Up.* Larry used forty-two helium-filled weather balloons hooked to a lawn chair and embarked on a forty-five–minute flight from San Pedro to Long Beach California. When asked why, he simply said, "It was something I had to do ... I couldn't just sit there."[2]

Are you just sitting there? You don't have to do something silly to gain attention from the world. What could be more discouraging than regarding life as a meaningless path from conception to grave? God has a preordained journey for your life—one that has eternal significance and one that no one else can make: "Ponder the path of your feet, and let all your ways be established" (Prov. 4:26). God offers us an abundant, exciting life filled with opportunity and adventure.

LISTEN TO ...

Happy is the hour when Jesus calls one from tears to joy of spirit.

—Thomas à Kempis

Wondrous Water

Water is essential to life. Without it our bodies are incapable of properly functioning. A person can live for about a month without food, but only a week or so without water. Water carries nutrients to the cells and does double duty by carrying away bacteria and waste. Seventy percent of the adult body is water. Bone cells are made up of around 20 percent water, while brain cells are 70 percent and blood cells are about 80 percent water.[3] Water simply *is* life.

When we are not tuned in to the water needs of our bodies, we can quickly find ourselves in trouble. If we wait until we are experiencing thirst or a dry mouth, we're already on our way to dehydration. Doctors, nutritionists, and those who have suffered the consequences of dehydration give the same advice: pay attention to your body's need for water, and stay well hydrated.

Physical dehydration brings obvious signals: dizziness, headache, and dry mucous membranes. Spiritual dehydration also has its symptoms: fearfulness, worry, and compliance to the world and its futile ways. To keep our souls well hydrated, we need the living water of the Lord.

In Psalm 63:1 the psalmist said, "My soul thirsts for You; my flesh longs for You in a dry and thirsty land where there is no water." Are you thirsting for the living water only Jesus can provide?

LIFT UP ...

Psalm 42:1–2 says, "As the deer pants for the water brooks, so pants my soul for You, O God. My soul thirsts for God, for the living God." Lord, I know I must first have thirst before I seek water. Create in me a thirsty soul that can only be quenched by You. In Jesus' name. Amen.

LOOK AT ...

In the previous text, we read that Jesus stopped at an unpopular destination to get a drink of water. Because He was a human being, His thirst was real. But because He is also God, His deeper purpose was to seek and save a woman whose sins had separated her from God. Their interaction was interesting, complex, and as much about what was *not* spoken as what *was* spoken.

READ JOHN 4:9–19.

Then the woman of Samaria said to Him, "How is it that You, being a Jew, ask a drink from me, a Samaritan woman?" For Jews have no dealings with Samaritans. Jesus answered and said to her, "If you knew the gift of God, and who it is who says to you, 'Give Me a drink,' you would have asked Him, and He would have given you living water."

The woman said to Him, "Sir, You have nothing to draw with, and the well is deep. Where then do You get that living water? Are You greater than our father Jacob, who gave us the well, and drank from it himself, as well as his sons and his livestock?"

Jesus answered and said to her, "Whoever drinks of this water will thirst again, but whoever drinks of the water that I shall give him will never thirst. But the water that I shall give him will become in him a fountain of water springing up into everlasting life."

The woman said to Him, "Sir, give me this water, that I may not thirst, nor come here to draw."

Jesus said to her, "Go, call your husband, and come here."

The woman answered and said, "I have no husband."

Jesus said to her, "You have well said, 'I have no husband,' for you have had five husbands, and the one whom you now have is not your husband; in that you spoke truly."

The woman said to Him, "Sir, I perceive that You are a prophet." John 4:9–19

1. How did the Samaritan woman know that Jesus was a Jew?

2. Jesus referred to the "gift of God." What is that gift?

3. Why did the Samaritan woman think Jesus was unable to get water from the well without her help?

4. What did Jesus see in this woman that prompted Him to tell her how to have eternal life?

5. How did the Samaritan woman respond to His offer?

6. What did Jesus hope to expose in the Samaritan woman's life when He asked her to call her husband?

7. What did Jesus say that convinced the Samaritan woman He was a prophet?

LIVE OUT ...

8. Are there people to whom you will not reach out? Do you separate yourself from outsiders in the same way the Jews separated themselves from Samaritans? Do you avoid non-Christians? Look up the following Scriptures to see what the Bible says about reaching out to others and being hospitable.

SCRIPTURE	WHAT IS SAID ABOUT HOSPITALITY?
Genesis 18:1–8	
Matthew 25:35, 40	
Luke 14:13–14	
Acts 2:45–46	
1 Peter 4:9	

LEARN ABOUT ...

2 Living Water

Living water brings spiritual and abundant life. As water satisfies thirst and produces energy and strength, so also the Spirit of God satisfies the inner person and enables him to bear spiritual fruit: "Therefore with joy you will draw water from the wells of salvation" (Isa. 12:3).

4 I Know You

Jesus knew this woman's sins, yet He also knew the ready thirst of her soul. The Holy Spirit had prepared her to eagerly ask for the gift of living water when Jesus described it to her. She asked in faith, without knowing He was God, who knew all about her sinful life.

6 Honesty Is the Best Policy

Although this woman lived immorally (the other women would not even draw water with her because she was of such poor reputation), she did not lie to Christ. Her heart was open to Him: "Examine me, O LORD, and prove me; try my mind and my heart" (Ps. 26:2).

8 Fluid Hospitality

In the ancient Middle East, the giving and receiving of water was a covenant of hospitality. For these purposes, a brief truce was called between even the fiercest enemies.

10 Saved by Water

"Water, water, everywhere, nor any drop to drink" was the cry of the ancient mariner. Imagine the torture of dying of thirst while surrounded by water. For those with spiritual thirst, there is a promise: "For the Lamb who is in the midst of the throne will ... lead them to living fountains of waters" (Rev. 7:17).

9. Think about modern outcasts from the Christian culture: those in lifestyles contrary to biblical teaching, women who have had abortions, or individuals who are outright hostile toward God. Have you written them off, or are you willing to offer them the opportunity to receive living water? Answer the following questions:

a. Do you know someone who might fall into the category of a "modern outcast"? If so, who?

b. List the concrete steps you can take to establish a dialogue of trust and acceptance with this person. Pray that God will guide you and prepare that person's heart.

c. Write about a subject that might serve as a segue into a conversation about faith.

10. Are you ready to dive in? Using the word THIRST as an acrostic, think of some ways you might relieve the thirst of the unsaved.

T

H

I

R

S

T

∘ ∘ ● ∘ ∘

"The Rime of the Ancient Mariner," a poem by Samuel Taylor Coleridge, was published in 1798. A macabre tale, it describes difficulties encountered during a long sea voyage. The story tells of a ship cutting through the Antarctic Ocean and becoming hemmed in by icebergs.

When an albatross appears, the sailors kindly feed it. Miraculously, the icebergs melt! However, once the ship is freed, the mariner inexplicably kills the bird. The sailors are furious and, fearing bad luck, make the mariner wear the bird around his neck as punishment.

Perhaps as a result of the senseless killing of the bird, the wind stalls, the drinking water is depleted, and one by one the sailors die. Only the mariner remains. Although in agonizing thirst, he can't die.

He survives to tell his tale to a person at a wedding, concluding: "O Wedding Guest! This soul hath been alone on a wide sea: So lonely 'twas, that God himself scarce seemed there to be…. He prayeth best, who loveth best all things both great and small; for the dear God who loveth us, He made and loveth all."[4]

This man's actions affect both the "great and small" around him. He concludes that loving God and others is what matters most. In His greatness, Jesus reached out to the "small" Samaritan woman and offered His living water. What can you offer to a world thirsting for meaning and love?

LISTEN TO …

He who sees a need and waits to be asked for help is as unkind as if he had refused it.

—*Dante Alighieri*

DAY 3

Men or the Messiah?

Worship is part of our spiritual DNA. Whether or not we acknowledge it, we all worship something. Some people may resist such an admission, but when worship is defined as admiration, fixation, fascination, preoccupation, or adulation, it is clear that we are creatures made for worship.

In spite of this, the idea of worshipping one true God is offensive to some people. These same individuals might not have any problem with the worship of work, physical fitness, a sports team, education, or even family. Man-made things or activities that center on human beings are easily accepted as being worship-worthy.

This is not a twenty-first-century phenomenon. The ancient Egyptians erected a temple to the goddess Bast, who was portrayed as a wise and regal cat. Because rats, mice, and snakes carried disease into the Egyptians' homes and crops, cats were valuable and became objects of worship.[5] Similarly, modern Hindus worship many gods and even offer prayers to the tools of their trade, often including their vehicles. They honor their cars by decorating them with flowers and pictures and even offering prayers to them.[6]

The absence of God as the object of our worship often is evident in the presence of frantic activity and the acquisition of material goods. Blaise Pascal, a seventeenth-century philosopher, introduced the idea that every person possesses a God-shaped vacuum in his or her heart that no created thing can fill. Only God, made known through Jesus Christ, can fill that void.

LIFT UP ...

Holy Father, it is Your will that I honor You with my worship. Help me become sensitive to the subtle and overt competitors for my heart. In Jesus' name. Amen.

Look At ...

Previously we studied the first half of the dialogue between Jesus and the Samaritan woman. We found that the Lord's physical thirst was quite different from the spiritual thirst of the Samaritan woman. The conversation between Jesus and this woman exposed her unspoken longing to be deeply understood and accepted.

Meaningful conversations and connections are also a means of reducing our stress and bringing deep satisfaction. Studies show that a simple phone call to a friend can increase the production of the hormone oxycotin. Through conversation, we can convert stressful experiences into opportunities for bonding with another person. In turn, this lowers the levels of the stress hormone, cortisol, in the blood. One-to-one contact is vital to our ability to cope with our demanding lives.

Today, we'll see how both Jesus and the woman defined worship. Jesus then claims His right to receive worship by affirming that He is the Messiah.

READ JOHN 4:20–26.

"Our fathers worshiped on this mountain, and you Jews say that in Jerusalem is the place where one ought to worship."

Jesus said to her, "Woman, believe Me, the hour is coming when you will neither on this mountain, nor in Jerusalem, worship the Father. You worship what you do not know; we know what we worship, for salvation is of the Jews. But the hour is coming, and now is, when the true worshipers will worship the Father in spirit and truth; for the Father is seeking such to worship Him. God is Spirit, and those who worship Him must worship in spirit and truth."

The woman said to Him, "I know that Messiah is coming" (who is called Christ). "When He comes, He will tell us all things."

Jesus said to her, "I who speak to you am He." John 4:20–26

1. To what did the Samaritan woman refer when she spoke of her forefathers' worship on the mountain?

2. What did Jesus mean when He said that an hour would come when the Samaritan woman would not worship the Father on either of the mountains?

3. What vital piece of information was the Samaritan woman missing?

4. Thoughtless worship doesn't please God. What two qualities is He looking for in our worship?

5. How does worshipping God in "spirit" affect our understanding of Him? How does it affect our practice of worship?

6. List three facts the Samaritan woman correctly understood about the Messiah.

   a.

   b.

   c.

7. Who did Jesus say He was?

LIVE OUT ...

8. What does worship mean to you? Is it singing hymns in church or maybe in the shower? Is it communal prayer or individual pleas? Is it falling on your face before God or standing upright with arms

LEARN ABOUT ...

1 Where to Worship?

The Samaritans had altered history and religion to suit them. They built their temple atop Mount Gerizim, a holy site that was their equivalent to Judaism's Jerusalem. They claimed this was the site where Abraham sacrificed Isaac. Their beliefs were a mixture of paganism and the Torah (2 Kings 17).

2 The Hour Is Come

The time to worship in a temple or atop a mountain has come to an end. Worship no longer needs to be ritualistic and ceremonial. Worshippers recognize that God's Spirit indwells them, and therefore, they can worship Him anywhere at any time. A believer's heart is His temple.

5 Spirit

Matthew Henry said, "God is a spirit ... an infinite and eternal mind, an intelligent being, incorporeal, immaterial, invisible, and incorruptible.... If God were not a spirit, He could not be perfect, nor infinite, nor eternal, nor independent, nor the Father of spirit."

LEARN ABOUT ...

9 Truth

Jesus tells us plainly, "I am the way, the truth, and the life" (John 14:6). Jesus is the personification of truth, and He detests dishonesty in our worship. Outward worship can be faked before men but not before God. Worship worthy of God *must* be truthful—it must be real.

10 Meeting Messiah

This simple and sinful Samaritan woman knew Messiah was coming. She also knew He would be identified by the fact that He would tell all things, and therefore, would know all things. The Holy Spirit stirred her heart and allowed her to recognize the Savior.

opened wide? Read the Scriptures cited below to learn more about worship.

SCRIPTURE	WHAT DID YOU LEARN ABOUT WORSHIP?
Exodus 4:31	
Acts 7:42	
Acts 24:14–15	
Philippians 3:3–4	
1 Timothy 2:8	

9. In your private relationship with the Lord, how do you worship Him in spirit and in truth?

10. When discussing the coming Messiah, Jesus tells the woman, "I who speak to you am He." If a stranger said this to you, how would you determine if He was telling the truth?

o o ● o o

Human beings are wired to worship. When left to our own devices, we will worship something—anything—*everything!* Paul saw this demonstrated in a spectacular way when he was in Athens. There, in the middle of the Areopagus, he regarded the courtyard filled with idols to every imaginable god. Paul seized the opportunity to strike at the core of the people's striving for a worship-worthy God: "Men of Athens, I perceive that in all things you are very religious; for as I was passing through and considering the objects of your worship, I even found an altar with this inscription: TO THE UNKNOWN GOD. Therefore, the One whom you worship without knowing, Him I proclaim to you" (Acts 17:22–23).

The world has changed very little since Paul made this proclamation—it is still starving for the one true God while filled to the point of nausea with the junk food of man-made gods. Whether in ancient Athens or modern America, worship is only as meaningful as the object of that worship.

How very blessed we are. No longer is it necessary to be on just the right mountaintop, or in just the right temple, or in just the right city in order to worship. We have the incomprehensible gift of worshipping God right here, right now—in spirit and in truth.

LISTEN TO ...

Is not dread of thirst when your well is full, thirst that is unquenchable?

—*Kahlil Gibran*

DAY 4
Soul Food

"Soul food" was a term popularized in the 1960s that referenced southern-style cooking or "comfort foods." Although we associate this kind of cooking with the southern United States, in reality its origin was in West Africa. The sad truth is that the African captives brought to America were often poorly fed by those who enslaved them. They were forced to be creative with what little they were given or could grow or hunt. Common vegetables like okra, turnip greens, corn, sweet potatoes, and beets were given soul flavoring with onions, garlic, thyme, and bay leaves. Protein sources reflected what was available by hunting or fishing and included pork, squirrel, opossum, turtle, rabbit, and chicken.

Recipes were passed down orally from person to person since it was illegal for enslaved Africans to learn to read or write. It's interesting that this food, coming out of such deprivation and oppression, came to be known as "soul food," implying that this food satisfied a need deeper than mere hunger.

As human beings, we possess a profound longing in our souls for a relationship with God. St. Augustine prayed with understanding when he said, "Our hearts are restless until they find their rest in You." Jesus never ignored the physical hunger common to men, but He longed to give us food that would impart knowledge and understanding—leaving our souls eternally satisfied.

LIFT UP ...

Lord God, I hunger for You. I don't want to be one who cries out, "My soul is bereft of peace, I have forgotten what happiness is" (Lam. 3:17 RSV). In Jesus' name. Amen.

LOOK AT ...

Our previous lesson focused on the experience of worshipping in spirit and in truth. Have you changed your thinking about worship?

LEARN ABOUT ...

2 Regard

Jewish piety demanded that men limit public conversation with women. In doing so, men avoided temptation as well as any behavior that might suggest impropriety or moral weakness. The disciples demonstrated their trust and respect for Jesus by not questioning Him about His conversation with the woman.

3 Return

Leaving behind her water jar suggested that her excitement about the living water Jesus offered had eclipsed the need for mere well water. It also implied that she planned to return.

We can worship God in various ways. We can worship by giving ourselves as instruments to fulfill His purposes. And we can sing praises to Him, rejoice in Him, pray to Him, and be continually aware of Him. Because God is Spirit, He is everywhere—around us at every single moment. We are blessed.

Today we will examine the Samaritan woman's reaction to her encounter with Jesus, as well as the disciples' behavior upon their return to Jacob's well.

READ JOHN 4:27–33.

And at this point His disciples came, and they marveled that He talked with a woman; yet no one said, "What do You seek?" or, "Why are You talking with her?" The woman then left her waterpot, went her way into the city, and said to the men, "Come, see a Man who told me all things that I ever did. Could this be the Christ?" Then they went out of the city and came to Him.

In the meantime His disciples urged Him, saying, "Rabbi, eat."

But He said to them, "I have food to eat of which you do not know."

Therefore the disciples said to one another, "Has anyone brought Him anything to eat?" John 4:27–33

1. Look back at yesterday's lesson, and record the moment the Samaritan woman recognized that Jesus was the Messiah. Who arrived to spoil the moment?

2. Why did the disciples marvel when they realized that Jesus had spoken to a woman? What two questions did they not ask Him?

3. The Samaritan woman came to the well to fill her water jar. When she went to the city, she left it behind. What did that demonstrate about her changed priorities?

4. What was the demeanor of the Samaritan woman when she returned to Sychar?

5. When the woman told the people of the city that she believed she had met the Christ, how did they respond?

6. Explain what Jesus meant when He told the disciples He had food of which they were not aware. What was the difference between the food they brought and the food Jesus already had?

7. The disciples suspected that someone brought food to Jesus while they were away. Why was this a matter of interest?

LIVE OUT ...

8. a. Jesus tells His disciples in John 4:32, "I have food to eat of which you do not know." We might call this soul food. Fill in the following chart to discover what satisfies your soul.

SCRIPTURE	MY SOUL
Psalm 16:2	
Psalm 23:3	
Psalm 35:9	
Lamentations 3:20–22	
Luke 1:46–47	

   b. Journal about the condition of your soul today.

9. If you met Messiah as the Samaritan woman did, to whom would you run to tell? What would you say? Place a check in the box of

LEARN ABOUT ...

5 Come

The people of Sychar did not tarry; they went from the city and came to Jesus. We are called to do the same: "If anyone desires to come after Me, let him deny himself, and take up his cross, and follow Me" (Matt. 16:24).

9 Messiah

The Samaritan expectation of the Messiah, called *Taheb*, or "restorer," was that He would be a prophet like Moses: "The LORD your God will raise up for you a Prophet like me from your midst.... Him you shall hear, according to all you desired of the LORD" (Deut. 18:15–16).

LEARN ABOUT ...

10 Nourishment

Our spiritual nutrients come from God's Word. Just as we must feed our bodies daily, we also need to regularly feed our souls. Reading Scripture and praying come from thoughtful planning and making priorities, as they do for all disciplines. Thomas à Kempis said, "As our intention is, so will be our practice." [7]

those to whom you'd run, then write your message in the space provided.

- ❑ My family: _____
- ❑ My friends: _____
- ❑ A neighbor: _____
- ❑ My pastor: _____
- ❑ Random strangers: _____
- ❑ Other believers: _____

10. Journal about some of the activities you pursue that sustain your faith.

○ ○ ● ○ ○

Horatio G. Spafford was a successful lawyer and man of faith who lived in Chicago. Horatio had an affluent upbringing, a successful career, a wife he loved, and five children.

In early 1871, Horatio's four-year-old son died from scarlet fever. Shortly thereafter, his fortune, heavily invested in real estate in downtown Chicago, burned in the Great Chicago Fire of 1871. Horatio turned his efforts to his work, helping to rebuild the city and giving aid to the homeless.[8]

By 1873, life had stabilized. Mr. Spafford planned to travel to Europe with his family. As they boarded the SS *Ville du Havre,* Spafford was called back to work on urgent business. He sent his family ahead, saying he would follow as soon as possible.

In the early morning of November 22, 1873, their ship collided with another vessel, the *Loch Earn,* and sank in twelve minutes. All four of Spafford's daughters drowned. From Europe, his wife sent him a chilling telegram: "Saved alone."

Devastated, he left for Europe to join his grieving wife. On that voyage, the ship's captain pointed out the area where the ship had likely sunk. Horatio retreated to his cabin. Unable to sleep, he wrote the famous hymn "It Is Well with My Soul," which would comfort generations of suffering people:

> When peace, like a river, attendeth my way,
> When sorrows like sea billows roll;
> Whatever my lot, Thou hast taught me to say,
> It is well, it is well with my soul.[9]

Listen To ...

The soul, like the body, lives by what it feeds on.

—*Josiah Gilbert Holland*

Harvest Time

In our culture, we generally have little familiarity with harvesting crops. Our closest experience might be an annual fall trip to the pumpkin patch with our children. However, for the Hebrew people, who were involved with agriculture daily, harvest time was the culmination of months of work and a time of celebration.

The primary feasts of the Jews corresponded with the three harvest seasons: the Feast of the Passover at the barley harvest, the Feast of Pentecost at the wheat harvest, and the Feast of Tabernacles during the fruit harvest.

During the lean years of World War II, many people in our country experienced the process of sowing and harvesting as they were called upon to plant a "Victory Garden." Transportation shortages made it difficult to get fresh produce, and rationing of dairy products, sugar, coffee, and meat further squeezed the diet.

Americans embraced the opportunity to help the war effort in any way they could. People used empty lots, backyards, and even rooftops to plant their gardens. For many, this necessity brought great joy and satisfaction as they enjoyed the harvest of fresh fruits and vegetables they had nurtured from seed.[10]

Jesus said, "The harvest truly is plentiful, but the laborers are few" (Matt. 9:37). As His followers, we are privileged to work in this field of souls. Ask God to entrust you with a small part in the victorious harvest of men and women who seek to put their faith in Christ.

Lift Up ...

Lord Jesus, You are the ultimate Harvester of souls. Help me cultivate the heart of a farmer when I meet people hungering for Your Word. In Jesus' name. Amen.

LOOK AT ...

We now move toward the end of the story of the Samaritan woman and Jesus. In today's lesson, Jesus described what is needed to complete the work of the Lord's harvest. As we've discussed, the concept of harvesting is not typically part of our day-to-day realities. Unlike the time-consuming process of sowing and reaping, our harvesting usually comes down to choosing between fresh or processed foods. Processed foods are quicker and easier to prepare, but fresh foods provide more nutrients.

Most of us probably buy some of both. But if we are only of the quick-and-easy mind-set when it comes to gleaning the Word of God, we are likely to miss some vital spiritual nutrients. We might be fed for the moment by hearing what someone else has learned, but nothing replaces the deep satisfaction of discovering God's spiritual truths for ourselves.

In our fast-food culture, there's no substitute for a lifelong occupation, fascination, concentration, and incorporation of God's Word in our lives. You can't purchase this precious harvest, for there is no currency valuable enough to buy spiritual food. Salvation is free (Rom. 6:23) and the fruits of the Holy Spirit are gifts (Gal. 5:22).

READ JOHN 4:34–40.

Jesus said to them, "My food is to do the will of Him who sent Me, and to finish His work. Do you not say, 'There are still four months and then comes the harvest'? Behold, I say to you, lift up your eyes and look at the fields, for they are already white for harvest! And he who reaps receives wages, and gathers fruit for eternal life, that both he who sows and he who reaps may rejoice together. For in this the saying is true: 'One sows and another reaps.' I sent you to reap that for which you have not labored; others have labored, and you have entered into their labors."

And many of the Samaritans of that city believed in Him because of the word of the woman who testified, "He told me all that I ever did." So when the Samaritans had come to Him, they urged Him to stay with them; and He stayed there two days. John 4:34–40

1. What did Jesus tell the disciples about the signs of the impending harvest? What does this mean to you?

2. At this time, there were technically still four months until the harvest. What did Jesus mean when He said the fields are already "white" for harvest?

3. What do you envision when you think of sowing God's Word in the world? How does that differ from reaping?

4. Why is it unusual for the same person to both sow and reap where God's Word is concerned?

5. To whom was Jesus referring as the "others" who have labored?

6. How did the woman convince her community of Samaritans to believe that she had been with the Christ?

7. Why do you think Jesus subsequently gave two days of His life to the Samaritans?

LIVE OUT ...

8. a. Place a check in the box that best describes your relationship with food.

   ❑ It has become my focus.
   ❑ It has increased my faith.
   ❑ It has led me to be over/under weight.
   ❑ It has given me something to share.

   b. Journal about the ways you can incorporate spiritual nutrition into your daily diet.

LEARN ABOUT ...

2 Ripe

By the time the tassels are visible, the wheat is absolutely ripe and must be harvested. If not, ripe will soon turn to ruin. There is a window of opportunity when the field is "white."

---

4 Reaping

Sowing is the planting or scattering of seed in order to grow crops. Reaping is the process of collecting the product after it matures. Sowers may not see the harvest result, and harvesters may not have dropped the seed into the soil—yet both are vital to yield the crop.

---

5 Others

Moses, the prophets, and John the Baptist sowed the seed, and the disciples reaped the crop. If this Samaritan woman had not been familiar with the writings of the Old Testament, she would neither have anticipated the coming of the Messiah nor have recognized or received Him.

LEARN ABOUT ...

9 Work

Your works are your deeds or your actions. As a child of God, your accomplishments are His accomplishments as He works in you, with you, and through you: "For it is God who works in you both to will and to do for His good pleasure" (Phil. 2:13).

___

10 Service versus Sin

In whatever task we have before us, we have a choice: we can do it to serve and glorify God or to magnify ourselves. "That you also aspire to lead a quiet life ... and to work with your own hands" (1 Thess. 4:11).

9. Christ stated that His food was to do the will of God and accomplish His work. Is this also your food? What are you doing to bring in God's harvest? What *could* you do?

10. a. The Samaritan woman said Jesus "told me all that I ever did" (John 4:39). Fill in the comparison chart below with what you would like Him to tell you about yourself as compared to what He might actually say.

    WHAT I WANT TO HEAR   **WHAT HE MIGHT TELL ME**

    b. Journal a prayer to the Lord, asking Him to guide you toward the work He wants you to do for Him. "For God is not unjust to forget your work and labor of love which you have shown toward His name" (Heb. 6:10).

○ ○ ● ○ ○

I'm so grateful this story was included in the Bible. In this record of the Samaritan woman, we have learned about a strong yet fallen individual who met and verbally jousted with none other than the Messiah. Despite her initial bravado and flippant attitude, she was a soul absolutely ripe for harvest.

When she understood the incredible gift the Savior offered, she dropped all pretense and pleaded, "Sir, give me this water" (John 4:15). She was desperate in her thirst. No well water could quench the dehydration of her soul.

What qualified her to receive the living water? Questionable reputation? Absolutely. Living in sin? Obviously. Shunned by respectable men and women? Constantly.

Ripe for harvest? Totally.

This woman was no dummy. She knew a good thing when she heard it—and she recognized God when she met Him.

What about you? Before you can be a part of harvesting the ripe souls of others, you must take stock of your own condition. The Samaritan woman received her living water before abandoning her waterpot to run to the city and tell others.

"'Come!' And let him who hears say, 'Come!' And let him who thirsts come. Whoever desires, let him take the water of life freely" (Rev. 22:17). Share your water.

LISTEN TO ...

Downcast and troubled Christian, come and glean today in the broad field of promise. Here are abundance of precious promises, which exactly meet thy wants.... Grasp these sweet promises, thresh them out by meditation and feed on them with joy.

—Charles Spurgeon

Feta–Stuffed Dates

Date palms grew abundantly throughout the Promised Land from Jericho down toward En Gedi and the Dead Sea region. I own an ancient Israeli coin with the image of palms imprinted on it that proves their symbolic importance. Growing in clusters and shaped like an acorn, dates provide fruit to be eaten raw or dried. Honey is made by boiling the dates into sweet syrup. The Hebrew word for *date* can also be translated "honey." Some believe the term *land flowing with milk and honey* came from the abundance of dates found in Israel.

Almonds held a special place in the hearts of the Hebrew people. The Hebrew word for *almond* means "early awakening," most likely describing the beautiful pink blossoms that preceded the nut. This tree blossoms before most, usually in late January to early February. The almond blossom was the motif for the golden lamp stand that provided the only light in the Holy of Holies. Aaron's rod was an almond branch, and Jacob sent almonds to Joseph in Egypt to gain his favor.

Feta cheese comes from curdled milk squeezed into molds. Middle Easterners drank sheep and goat milk, carrying it in skin bladders. Although cheese is only mentioned three times in Scripture, historians believe it was very common. In fact, the Tyropoeon Valley in Jerusalem is literally translated "the cheese-makers valley." Ancient Jews refused to consume milk or cheese made by Gentiles in case it had been previously offered to idols.

Preparation Time: 15 minutes
Cook Time: 12 minutes

Ingredients:

12 Medjool dates
1 cup feta cheese
1 1/2 tablespoons extra virgin olive oil
1 teaspoon lemon juice
1/2 teaspoon finely grated lemon zest
12 whole almonds
Honey for drizzling

Instructions:

1. Preheat oven to 375 degrees. Spray a cookie sheet with nonstick spray or lay a piece of parchment paper on it.

2. Place almonds on cookie sheet and roast until golden.

3. Slice the dates along the top, carefully pop them open, and remove the pit.

4. Using a food processor, mix together the feta, olive oil, lemon zest, and lemon juice until it is creamy with no lumps. Spoon about one teaspoon of the cheese mixture into each date.

5. Insert toasted almonds into the middle of cheese mixture. Bake at 375 degrees for ten to twelve minutes.

6. Remove from oven and drizzle each warmed date lightly with honey.

GRACE NOTE

Heavenly Father,

It's wonderful to learn how Your bounty was appreciated and honored. The land You provided for the children of Israel was described as a "land flowing with milk and honey." Lampstands that lit the Holy of Holies were carved with images of almond blossoms. There was reverence for Your provision and creativity in the preparations. Thank You, Lord, for these wonderful foods. In Jesus' name. Amen.

In Knead of Bread

John 6:1-58

Nearly nine thousand years ago, nomads inhabiting Palestine harvested grains such as einkorn, emmer wheat, and barley. Wild einkorn wheat still grows in the Middle East today and contains more protein than other indigenous grains. In Jesus' time, before wheat became flour, it was first threshed by large animals that trampled the kernels or by humans who beat the grain with sticks. Rock millstones powered by a mule resulted in larger quantities and a finer quality of grain. Next the grain was milled by hand, requiring a pestle and mortar to grind it into flour. Ancients believed that bread making was woman's work. Therefore, the virtuous woman "rises while it is yet night, and provides food for her household" (Prov. 31:15).

The simplest form of bread was made by mixing the flour with oil and/or water to create batter. The flour was then formed into a flat, round loaf and placed directly onto the fire's hot ashes. Jesus used this method to make breakfast: "They saw a fire of coals there, and fish laid on it, and bread" (John 21:9). Another baking method consisted of placing bread dough on a porous stone heated in the midst of the fire. This bread resembled a pita or tortilla and had a smoky taste.

Our text finds Jesus, the disciples, and a multitude far from grain fields—and very hungry. Modern bakeries were nonexistent. They were nowhere near a town large enough to bake the quantity needed. They were in "knead of bread." Let's examine their predicament.

Day 1: John 6:1–9	CAN THE BREAD RISE?
Day 2: John 6:10–15	SLICED BREAD
Day 3: John 6:16–27	BREAD LINE
Day 4: John 6:28–40	BREAD OF LIFE
Day 5: John 6:41–58	BREAKING BREAD

Can the Bread Rise?

LIFT UP ...

Heavenly Father, there is so much to learn from Your Word. Please give me an appetite for truth and wisdom that can be satisfied only through You. In Jesus' name. Amen.

LOOK AT ...

So far we've seen Jesus provide wine at a wedding and water at a well. Both of these miraculous encounters happened out of public view. The source of the extravagant wine was unknown, and the woman at the well had one-on-one time with Jesus while the disciples were away on an errand. Today we'll see Jesus going public with a miraculous meal. His disciples and a little boy will be in on the act, with a crowd as their witnesses.

We meet Philip, one of the twelve disciples. Philip was from Bethsaida of Galilee, as were Andrew and Peter. We know little of Philip's family; however, his first act as a disciple was to invite Nathanael to "come and see" the Messiah (John 1:46). He longed to know God and asked Jesus, "Show us the Father" (John 14:8). Like Philip, encourage your friends to seek Jesus.

READ JOHN 6:1–9.

After these things Jesus went over the Sea of Galilee, which is the Sea of Tiberias. Then a great multitude followed Him, because they saw His signs which He performed on those who were diseased. And Jesus went up on the mountain, and there He sat with His disciples.

Now the Passover, a feast of the Jews, was near. Then Jesus lifted up His eyes, and seeing a great multitude coming toward Him, He said to Philip, "Where shall we buy bread, that these may eat?" But this He said to test him, for He Himself knew what He would do.

Learn About ...

3 Healing

Sadly, most people followed Jesus for the signs and wonders He performed rather than to hear and know the Savior. Our text shows the crowd following in hopes of seeing others healed, or to be healed themselves. Healings were miraculous signs meant to point to the power and person of God.

4 Hosting

Passover, or the Feast of Unleavened Bread, commemorated the hasty exodus from Egypt. Hebrews lacked time to prepare bread with yeast and instead made ash bread thrown quickly on the fire. Jesus realized the multitude needed unleavened bread to celebrate. He included His disciples in hosting and providing the bread.

6 Hoping

Jesus knew exactly how to provide bread for the crowd. But the disciples did not. Jesus asked a question to examine the level of their faith. The word *test* means to prove, examine, or scrutinize. God tests us to (1) expose the depth of our faith and (2) develop faith through the testing.

Philip answered Him, "Two hundred denarii worth of bread is not sufficient for them, that every one of them may have a little."

One of His disciples, Andrew, Simon Peter's brother, said to Him, "There is a lad here who has five barley loaves and two small fish, but what are they among so many?" John 6:1–9

1. Read John 5:1–18, then record what "after these things" includes.

2. List the two names for the body of water Jesus crossed.

3. Who followed Jesus, and why?

4. Where did the Lord go next? Who joined Him?

5. What time reference is given? Explain its importance.

6. In your own words, describe Jesus' question to Philip. What was the purpose of His question?

7. How did Philip answer? How do you think this expressed his faith?

8. Describe Andrew's suggestion. What did this reveal about Andrew's faith?

Live Out ...

9. The crowd followed Jesus for a variety of reasons. Place a check next to the reasons that best describe your pursuit of God.

❑ Financial gain   ❑ Escape from hell
❑ Peace of mind   ❑ Entrance to heaven

❏ Forgiveness of sin   ❏ To join a church
❏ Witness wonders   ❏ Embrace the Savior
❏ Receive His Word   ❏ Other_____

10. Fill in the following chart to discover what ingredients were included in the Passover Feast.

SCRIPTURE	PASSOVER INGREDIENT
Exodus 12:5–9	
Numbers 9:11	
Deuteronomy 16:3	
Joshua 5:11	
Matthew 26:27–29	

11. Jesus tested His disciples by requesting great provision for the multitude. Using the word TEST as an acrostic, describe some of the ways God has tested you:

T

E

S

T

∘ ∘ ● ∘ ∘

Many people called Jesus "teacher," sometimes out of respect and sometimes out of rivalry. The Herodians devised a quiz to trap Jesus: "Teacher, we know that You are true, and teach the way of God in truth.… Tell us, therefore, what do You think? Is it lawful to pay taxes to Caesar, or not?" (Matt. 22:16–17). The rich young ruler sought the teacher to find the path to salvation: "Good Teacher, what good thing shall I do that I may have eternal life?" (Matt. 19:16).

LEARN ABOUT …

9 Hearing

God can use our ulterior motives to reach hearts and capture attention. Fearing hell can be transformed into fearing God. Seeking friendships at church may lead to fellowship with the Lord. Exposure to Scripture can change cynics to seekers: "The word of God is living and powerful" (Heb. 4:12).

10 Holding

The word *Passover* means "to spring over" or "to spare." The celebration recalls the time in Egypt when the Hebrews sacrificed lambs in order to paint their doorposts with blood. God passed over these blood-marked homes, sparing their firstborn males while the Egyptian firstborns perished. Passover was observed on the fourteenth day of the first month, Abib.

Jesus used various teaching methods: (1) He taught in parables that identified true from false believers (Matt. 13:1–13); (2) He taught by reading Scripture in synagogues and the temple (Matt. 4:23; 26:55–56); and (3) He taught through practical illustrations such as shepherding and farming (Luke 15:3–7; Matt. 13:1–9).

He also used a tool we might call a "pop quiz." A pop quiz is a test given without advance warning. If you've ever had a pop quiz, you remember the groans from your class-mates who were unprepared—just like you. Today we see that Jesus sprang a pop quiz on His disciples. He did so for various reasons: (1) to show the disciples that they didn't know everything; (2) to help them examine their faith; (3) to reveal that He knew everything; and (4) to show them they must fully trust Jesus to increase their faith.

God's commandments come with His enablement. Though a task may appear humanly impossible, "with God all things are possible" (Matt. 19:26).

LISTEN TO ...

We never test the resources of God until we attempt the impossible.

—*F. B. Meyer*

DAY 2

Sliced Bread

Remember the old saying, "That's the best thing since sliced bread"? In 1928, housewives were still appreciating the new convenience of wrapped bread when bakeries improved it further by pre-slicing it. Before this, bread was kept in a breadbox, where it could dry out or become moldy. Packaging helped preserve freshness, and factory slicing meant sandwich prep was a breeze.

In 1943 a temporary ban on sliced bread was enacted to economize and aid the war effort, as heavier wrappers were needed to keep sliced bread from drying out. On January 26, 1943, a letter appeared in the *New York Times* from a distraught housewife:

> Sliced bread is [important] to the morale and saneness of a household.
> Without ready-sliced bread I must do the slicing for toast—two pieces for
> each [person]. For their lunches I must cut by hand at least twenty slices, for
> two sandwiches apiece … to be cut in a hurry![1]

The folks of Jesus' day simply tore off a piece and passed it on. The burly men probably ripped off a large portion while those more slightly built tore off a smaller piece. But at the end of the meal, every individual, from the largest to the smallest, was satisfied.

LIFT UP ...

Lord, needing Your provision is still an ongoing part of everyday life. Sometimes fear robs me of the faith to remember that You are still a miracle-working God. Thank You for Your faithful provision. In Jesus' name. Amen.

LOOK AT ...

Yesterday we began to study the feeding of the five thousand. Interestingly, all four Gospels repeat this narrative. This miracle stands apart as the one sign Jesus performed that appears in all

LEARN ABOUT ...

3 Filled

The meager lunch of one small lad, just five loaves and two fish, fed five thousand. Little becomes much when given to the Lord. The people went from fasting to feasting, for each had "as much as they wanted." Jesus gave thanks before the food was distributed. Perhaps praise precedes plenty.

four Gospels from four different perspectives. For instance, John underscored that Jesus intended His questions to provide a test for the disciples. Philip showed himself to be a pessimist when he calculated the financial enormity of feeding so many. In contrast, Andrew's response carried a hopeful note when he observed a child with a small amount of food.

Which disciple best describes your outlook? Are you an optimist or pessimist? Do you see the problem as overwhelming, rather than as an opportunity to volunteer your help or look for a creative solution? The next time you face a problem that seems overwhelming, set your focus on God's provision more than your poverty. With God, small offerings bring great outcomes.

READ JOHN 6:10–15.

Then Jesus said, "Make the people sit down." Now there was much grass in the place. So the men sat down, in number about five thousand. And Jesus took the loaves, and when He had given thanks He distributed them to the disciples, and the disciples to those sitting down; and likewise of the fish, as much as they wanted. So when they were filled, He said to His disciples, "Gather up the fragments that remain, so that nothing is lost." Therefore they gathered them up, and filled twelve baskets with the fragments of the five barley loaves which were left over by those who had eaten. Then those men, when they had seen the sign that Jesus did, said, "This is truly the Prophet who is to come into the world."

Therefore when Jesus perceived that they were about to come and take Him by force to make Him king, He departed again to the mountain by Himself alone. John 6:10–15

1. What did Jesus command? Describe the setting and the crowd's response.

2. Explain the method for distributing the food.

3. What two phrases demonstrate to you that everyone was satisfied?

a.

b.

4. In your own words, describe the leftovers and what was done with them.

5. For those who witnessed this miracle, what conclusion did they draw about Jesus?

6. Describe their plan for Jesus in view of the miracle He had just performed. Why did Jesus resist their plan?

7. Where did Jesus go when He left the crowd? What leads you to believe He frequented this place?

LIVE OUT ...

8. Although Jesus is God, He thanked His heavenly Father for the loaves and fishes. Do you thank God for things both big and small? Make a list of things for which you are thankful.

9. a. Jesus wanted the leftovers to be gathered so "nothing is lost." Check off the leftovers that you have available to share, and describe them in the corresponding space.

❏ Time _____

❏ Clothing _____

❏ Finances _____

LEARN ABOUT ...

4 Frugal

Nothing is wasted in God's economy. The leftovers collected were even more precious because of their miraculous source. We Christians know that our provision comes from the hand of God. Therefore, we mustn't waste a minute or a meal: "God shall supply all your need according to His riches in glory" (Phil. 4:19).

6 Force

The men plotted to force Jesus to become king. Jesus was born King, but His kingdom was not yet to come. Jesus said, "My kingdom is not of this world" (John 18:36). Thirty-two times, His reign is described as the "kingdom of heaven." Seventy-two times, it's called the "kingdom of God."

8 Faithful

Are you faithful to be thankful? Paul wrote, "In everything give thanks; for this is the will of God in Christ Jesus for you" (1 Thess. 5:18). Ingratitude mimics unbelievers who "although they knew God, they did not glorify Him as God, nor were thankful" (Rom. 1:21).

LEARN ABOUT ...

10 Follow

Many follow the Lord's example by practicing an incredible work ethic. However, some take this trait a bit too far and become workaholics, with no time for God or family. They work worship right out of their lives. Thankfully, Jesus showed us how to work and play, rally and rest.

❑ Toys _____

❑ Books _____

❑ Household goods _____

❑ Food _____

❑ Tools _____

❑ Other _____

b. Journal about how you will share your leftovers. Will you volunteer your time at church? Will you donate food to a shelter? Will you take your clothes to Goodwill?

10. Jesus displayed a proper balance between work and rest. After feeding the five thousand, He went on a mountain retreat.

a. Where do you go to be alone with God?

b. When was the last time you visited this place?

c. Write down a plan, time, and place when you can return to your retreat.

d. What conversation do you need to have with the Lord in private?

· · ● · ·

Like his grandpa, Nathan hates leftovers. No matter how I fancy them up, they're rejected. On the other hand, Skip and I seriously compete for them. I make some meals just so I can enjoy them as seconds. Meatloaf sandwiches are better than the original loaf fresh out of the oven.

Chicken potpie made with the scraps from a roasted chicken: divine. And ham and bean soup prepared from the leftover Christmas ham leaves Campbell's in the can.

I guess Jesus enjoyed leftovers too. When He multiplied the loaves and fishes, not only did it adequately provide for five thousand, there was enough left over for the next day, too. Jesus provided "exceedingly, abundantly more" than the situation required.

Twelve baskets of bread fragments were gathered. Perhaps Jesus intended one for each apostle to reward their willingness to share the loaves and fishes with the public. Matthew Henry reminds us of a Jewish custom: "The Jews lay it as a law upon themselves, when they have eaten a meal, to be sure to leave a piece of bread upon the table, upon which the blessing after meat may rest; for it is a curse upon the wicked man (Job 20:21) that there shall none of his meat be left."[2] God not only fills up my empty cup, He ensures that "my cup runs over" (Ps. 23:5).

LISTEN TO ...

Take rest; a field that has rested gives a bountiful crop.

—Ovid

DAY 3

Bread Line

During the Great Depression, bread lines were an all-too-common sight. Long lines snaked around buildings as hungry people waited for free food from public agencies or charitable soup kitchens. As Roosevelt took office in 1933, the unemployment rate was around 25 percent.[3] New York City's unemployed jammed the city's sidewalks, with men standing four abreast waiting for food. Although humbling, these handouts meant survival for thousands of families.

The needs were felt in other American cities and towns as well. In downtown Chicago, thousands of men protested on the streets, shouting for food. In Washington DC in 1932, unemployed veterans demanded their pay from serving in World War I.[4]

Ancient Palestine had its own equivalent of bread lines. God provided for the poor through the law of gleaning (Lev. 19:9–10), where farmers were commanded to leave the corners and edges of their fields untouched by the harvesters so the impoverished could gather freely. Similarly, fallen fruit from vineyards and orchards was left for the needy.

In John 6, after Jesus provided food for five thousand, a bread line formed around the Lord as people viewed Him as the means to a full stomach rather than the way to a full life free from the consequences from sin. You can have a full belly and still wind up in hell. Today we'll see how Jesus offered them salvation—not just supper.

LIFT UP ...

Lord God, I realize there is more than one kind of depression. Please guide me toward a life filled with meaning and usefulness to Your purposes. In Jesus' name. Amen.

LOOK AT ...

Imagine the disciples' delight as the bread multiplied right in their hands. They began with only five loaves, yet the supply didn't diminish. What miraculous proof that Jesus was the Christ! Even the multitude concluded that Jesus was the long-awaited Messiah, saying, "This is truly the Prophet who is to come" (John 6:14). Sadly, the disciples and the multitude responded differently to this miracle. The disciples honored the Lord by gathering the fragments while the crowd ganged up on Jesus, determined to take Him by force.

Today we'll see reactions widen between these two groups. The disciples continued to follow the Lord by faith, but the multitude pursued Jesus for mere food. One group was looking for a hand up, the other a handout. Which group best represents you? Think about your devotional time. Do you spend more time asking for stuff or asking for spiritual strength? Rather than treating God like a Santa Claus, worship Him as the Savior.

READ JOHN 6:16–27.

Now when evening came, His disciples went down to the sea, got into the boat, and went over the sea toward Capernaum. And it was already dark, and Jesus had not come to them. Then the sea arose because a great wind was blowing. So when they had rowed about three or four miles, they saw Jesus walking on the sea and drawing near the boat; and they were afraid. But He said to them, "It is I; do not be afraid." Then they willingly received Him into the boat, and immediately the boat was at the land where they were going.

On the following day, when the people who were standing on the other side of the sea saw that there was no other boat there, except that one which His disciples had entered, and that Jesus had not entered the boat with His disciples, but His disciples had gone away alone—however, other boats came from Tiberias, near the place where they ate bread after the Lord had given thanks—when the people therefore saw that Jesus was not there, nor His disciples, they also got into boats and came to Capernaum, seeking Jesus. And when they found Him on the other side of the sea, they said to Him, "Rabbi, when did You come here?"

Jesus answered them and said, "Most assuredly, I say to you, you seek Me, not because you saw the signs, but because you ate of the loaves and were filled. Do not labor for the food which perishes, but for the food which endures to everlasting life, which the Son of Man will give you, because God the Father has set His seal on Him." John 6:16–27

1. Where did the disciples go that evening? How did they travel?

2. Describe the conditions of the disciples' journey. How far did they travel?

3. Whom did the disciples encounter? What was their response?

4. What was Jesus' demeanor?

5. Describe what the people investigated and how they responded to their findings.

6. Paraphrase the question the people asked Jesus.

7. What did the following crowd really want from Him?

8. Jesus knew that their physical needs were their driving force in seeking Him. What did He tell them should be their highest priority?

Live Out ...

9. The disciples discovered that it was slow going without Jesus in their boat. Describe a trip that you attempted to take without Jesus in your boat.

Learn About ...

1 Slow Going

The disciples got into the boat "when evening came," which corresponds with dusk. Matthew and Mark commented that Jesus came walking on the water during the "fourth watch." That means that the disciples had rowed only three or four miles in nine hours. Surely, they were exhausted from rowing all night after working all day.

4 Fast Track

The disciples went from sweating at the oars to being docked at the shore. Jesus revealed His deity and power over the natural realm by walking on the water, calming an angry sea, and guiding the ship to their destination. These feats served to bolster the disciples' faith and foster their confessions later in John 6.

8 Long Lasting

Jesus chastised the crowd for having earthly, rather than heavenly, cravings. Worldly pursuits perish, but the words of Christ are eternal. Jesus said, "Man shall not live by bread alone, but by every word that proceeds from the mouth of God" (Matt. 4:4).

Place of departure and reason

Description of the journey

Place of arrival and how

10. a. The people were following Jesus for the wrong reasons. Describe someone you know who is following Jesus for the wrong reason.

b. Rewrite the following Scripture into a prayer for that person:

> If any of you wants to be my follower, you must turn from your selfish ways, take up your cross, and follow me. If you try to hang on to your life, you will lose it. But if you give up your life for my sake, you will save it. And what do you benefit if you gain the whole world but lose your own soul? Is anything worth more than your soul? (Matt. 16:24–26 NLT)

11. The people had the wrong priorities. Make a list of your priorities, and number them in order of their importance to you.

∘ ∘ ● ∘ ∘

In Joppa, Dorcas was a woman known for her good works and kind deeds. When she died, her friends begged Peter to resurrect their dear friend: "All the widows stood by him weeping, showing the tunics and garments which Dorcas had made while she was with them" (Acts 9:39). This simple woman kept her priorities straight: honoring God first, loving her neighbors second, and putting everything else after that.

Another person with proper perspective is Alvin Cavin. When his wife became a resident at the Cedar Crest Manor nursing home, Alvin, a retired dairy farmer in Kansas, milked a dozen cows each morning before arriving at the nursing home for breakfast with his wife. Throughout the day he kept his wife's water pitcher filled and made sure her needs were met. Before long, Alvin could be found in his Stetson hat, filling all the residents' pitchers as well. After two years his wife went to be with the Lord, yet eight years later the diminutive farmer was still at the nursing home, setting tables, helping with wheelchairs, and filling water pitchers.

Connie Moore, activity director at Cedar Crest Manor, said, "I'd estimate Alvin Cavin weighs 90 pounds, but 89 of those pounds make up his big heart. He keeps busy by giving to others."

"Life's so much better when you get your priorities straight," Alvin explained. "It begins when you make the Lord your first priority."[5]

LISTEN TO ...

Whenever we place a higher priority on solving our problems than on pursuing God, we are immoral.

—*Larry Crabb*

DAY 4

Bread of Life

Bread is synonymous with life—and for good reason. For thousands of years, bread has been made with living microorganisms that fall into the fungi category. We know this substance as the yeast. A writer for NASA noted, "Yeast microbes are probably one of the earliest domesticated organisms.... Archaeologists digging in Egyptian ruins found early grinding stones and baking chambers for yeasted bread, as well as drawings of 4,000-year-old bakeries."[6] Baking yeast converts fermentable sugars already present in the dough into gas pockets or bubbles. The extreme heat of baking kills the yeast, leaving air pockets that create a springy, airy texture. Interestingly, most yeast used in baking is also the acting agent for fermentation to create alcohol.

To make bread, yeast is added to a mixture of flour, salt, and warm liquids such as water or milk. The result is dough, which is then kneaded and left to rise in a warm place. Some bread dough is knocked back after rising and left to rise again. Great cooks know that the longer the dough is left to rise, the better the taste.

In today's text, Jesus states that He is the Bread of Life. And just like yeast dough, He must be knocked down to rise again. Jesus told His followers that after His persecution and death, the Father would raise Him up in the last days. Those who follow the Lord will also rise again with Him.

LIFT UP ...

Lord, please guide me into a deep understanding of knowing You as the Bread of Life rather than seeking only the temporary, transitory, or transient. In Jesus' name. Amen.

LOOK AT ...

Previously, Jesus admonished the people not to labor for perishable food, but rather for eternal nourishment. Today we'll see that the word *work* appears several times in the first sentences of this text. Rather than freely receiving salvation, the people preferred to work their way to heaven.

Others asked this same question in the Bible. The rich young ruler asked, "Good Teacher, what good thing shall I do that I may have eternal life?" (Matt. 19:16). On another occasion a lawyer queried, "Teacher, what shall I do to inherit eternal life?" (Luke 10:25). Upon witnessing the release of Paul and Silas from bondage, the Philippian jailer asked, "Sirs, what must I do to be saved?" (Acts 16:30). The same answer applies to all of them: "Believe on the Lord Jesus Christ, and you will be saved" (v. 31). The only work a Christian must do to be saved is to simply believe.

READ JOHN 6:28–40.

Then they said to Him, "What shall we do, that we may work the works of God?"

Jesus answered and said to them, "This is the work of God, that you believe in Him whom He sent."

Therefore they said to Him, "What sign will You perform then, that we may see it and believe You? What work will You do? Our fathers ate the manna in the desert; as it is written, 'He gave them bread from heaven to eat.'"

Then Jesus said to them, "Most assuredly, I say to you, Moses did not give you the bread from heaven, but My Father gives you the true bread from heaven. For the bread of God is He who comes down from heaven and gives life to the world."

Then they said to Him, "Lord, give us this bread always."

And Jesus said to them, "I am the bread of life. He who comes to Me shall never hunger, and he who believes in Me shall never thirst. But I said to you that you have seen Me and yet do not believe. All that the Father gives Me will come to Me, and the one who comes to Me I will by no means cast out. For I have come down from heaven, not to do My own will, but the will of Him who sent Me. This is the will of the Father who sent Me, that of all He has given Me I should lose nothing, but should raise it up at the last day. And this is the will of Him who sent Me, that everyone who sees the Son and believes in Him may have everlasting life; and I will raise him up at the last day." John 6:28–40

1. Describe the first question the crowd asked. Explain how Jesus responded.

2. What follow-up questions did the crowd pose? What example did they provide?

3. Explain how Jesus corrected their false assumption. Who was the true provider of manna in the desert and bread at the seashore?

4. Explain the request the crowd made and what it revealed about their motives.

5. What revelation did Jesus make regarding Himself? What two human necessities would He fulfill?

6. What two phrases describe the difference between believers and nonbelievers? Describe the differences in your own words.

7. Explain the reason that Jesus came to earth.

8. Underline the phrase *this is the will* and circle the phrase *raise him up*. What is the Father's will?

LIVE OUT ...

9. The multitude was confused about the difference between laboring in the flesh and leaning on Jesus to gain entrance to heaven. Fill in

LEARN ABOUT ...

I Believe

The word *believe* means "to have faith in something or someone." Christians place their trust in Christ: "I am not ashamed of the gospel, because it is the power of God for the salvation of everyone who believes" (Rom. 1:16 NIV).

3 Bread

Bread played an important role in Jewish worship. The Passover bread revealed the quickness of God's deliverance. At Pentecost, two loaves of leavened bread and an animal were sacrificed as a sacred offering. Each week, the Levites placed twelve loaves of showbread in the tabernacle to symbolize God's presence.

7 Behest

Jesus said He came at the Father's command: "Not to do My own will, but the will of Him who sent Me" (John 6:38). Christians are also called to live according to their heavenly Father's will: "Your kingdom come. Your will be done on earth as it is in heaven" (Matt. 6:10).

LEARN ABOUT ...

9 Behave

These men were looking for actions that would take the place of relying on faith in God. Contrary to the beliefs of their religion, good works did not guarantee salvation. Just the day before, they watched the Lord feed the masses with a few loaves and fishes—and still they asked for a sign.

---

10 Boast

If you climbed Mt. Everest, wrote a best-selling novel, or gave away half your income, you might have earned some bragging rights. But if you were pronounced dead and miraculously brought to life, it's doubtful you would take credit. We are spiritually dead until receiving the free gift of eternal life.

the following columns with some of the ways people either labor or lean to be saved.

LABORING	LEANING

10. Salvation can never be earned. Read Ephesians 2:4–10, and answer the following questions.

    a. Describe God's heart toward you (v. 4).

    b. List the things God did for you and why (vv. 5–7).

    c. In your own words, describe how you are saved (vv. 8–9).

    d. Explain the origin of any good works that you perform (v. 10).

11. Jesus taught His disciples how to trust in God through prayer. Rewrite this passage into a personal prayer:

    Our Father in heaven,
    Hallowed be Your name.
    Your kingdom come.
    Your will be done
    On earth as it is in heaven.
    Give us this day our daily bread.
    And forgive us our debts,
    As we forgive our debtors.
    And do not lead us into temptation,
    But deliver us from the evil one.

For Yours is the kingdom and the power and the glory forever. Amen.
(Matt. 6:9–13)

o o ● o o

Have you wondered why God didn't just blow the Pharisees out of the water with a tsunami of His wondrous power? They wanted a sign. Why was God reluctant to show them miracles that would demand belief?

In 1 Kings 19 we find the prophet Elijah on the run from Jezebel. He was depressed, isolated, hungry, and tired. God came to him and cared for him. Twice He instructed the exhausted prophet to sleep; twice He provided food: "a cake baked on coals, and a jar of water" (v. 6). Clearly, Elijah was off course, out of fellowship with God, and smarting from defeat. After he was rested and fed, the Lord asked him a soul-searching question: "What are you doing here, Elijah?" (v. 9).

After Elijah answered, the Lord summoned an earthquake, awakened the wind, and stirred a fire, but God was not found in these overt acts of power. Then, in the hush following this drama, came a whisper—a small voice—a gentle word. Now Elijah finally recognized God's voice—and immediately responded (vv. 11–13).

The Word is the voice of God that asks us to believe rather than see—the living voice that tells us to "be still, and know that I am God" (Ps. 46:10). Miracles may excite the mind, but faith engages the heart. God wants our hearts.

Is God asking you, "What are *you* doing here?" Are you tired? Depressed? Out of fellowship with Him? Open your Bible. Listen with your heart, and hear the voice of God.

LISTEN TO ...

He does not believe that does not live according to his belief.

—*Thomas Fuller*

DAY 5

Breaking Bread

The days of the American family routinely sitting down at the dinner table together may have gone the way of the 1950s TV show *Leave It to Beaver*. The June Cleavers of today are more likely to walk through the front door at six o' clock, bearing a bucket of chicken or a pizza rather than presenting a homemade dinner at the dining-room table. But even without a homemade meal, breaking bread (or pizza) together still has great value. Studies have shown that regular meals together lessen the likelihood of substance abuse and eating disorders in teenagers and keep communication active and updated between parents and their kids.

The obstacles to family meals and togetherness we experience today were simply unimaginable in the 1950s. How many times have you seen a family out to dinner and someone at the table is on a cell phone, or a teenager is surreptitiously texting someone with his phone in his lap? Certainly times have changed, but the need for an uninterrupted time with our families has not.

Can you imagine having a meal with Jesus? As with the five thousand, He would probably want to serve you. He would bless the food, and as He offered you the bread that He had torn into pieces, could anything draw your attention away from that moment? Jesus is present! You are eating the bread that is passing from His hand to yours. Let the phone ring. Let the texts wait. What could be more important?

LIFT UP ...

Heavenly Father, times may change, but Your Word does not. The world begs, cajoles, entices, flatters, and flat-out steals my attention. Please focus my mind, Lord Jesus, and focus my heart on You. In Jesus' name. Amen.

LOOK AT ...

Today we see the Jews caught in a quagmire between seeing and believing. On the one hand, they had *seen* Jesus and knew Him in the context of daily life—the son of Joseph and Mary. How could He be more than they had observed? On the other hand, they refused to *believe* Jesus' claim to be the Bread of Life without seeing a sign on par with their ancestors' experience of receiving manna from heaven. The Jews wanted to see before they would believe—but Jesus required belief before they could see.

In calling Himself the Bread of Life (John 6:48), Jesus made a strong statement about the necessity for us to be partakers of Him. Without the sustenance of bread, man would die physically. Without the sustenance of Jesus, man would die eternally. The people who ate the manna from heaven still died. Jesus offered abiding life through Him—the Bread of Life. The very literal Jews were outraged at this claim.

READ JOHN 6:41–58.

The Jews then complained about Him, because He said, "I am the bread which came down from heaven." And they said, "Is not this Jesus, the son of Joseph, whose father and mother we know? How is it then that He says, 'I have come down from heaven'?" Jesus therefore answered and said to them, "Do not murmur among yourselves. No one can come to Me unless the Father who sent Me draws him; and I will raise him up at the last day. It is written in the prophets, 'And they shall all be taught by God.' Therefore everyone who has heard and learned from the Father comes to Me. Not that anyone has seen the Father, except He who is from God; He has seen the Father. Most assuredly, I say to you, he who believes in Me has everlasting life. I am the bread of life. Your fathers ate the manna in the wilderness, and are dead. This is the bread which comes down from heaven, that one may eat of it and not die. I am the living bread which came down from heaven. If anyone eats of this bread, he will live forever; and the bread that I shall give is My flesh, which I shall give for the life of the world."

The Jews therefore quarreled among themselves, saying, "How can this Man give us His flesh to eat?"

Then Jesus said to them, "Most assuredly, I say to you, unless you eat the flesh of the Son of Man and drink His blood, you have no life in you. Whoever eats My flesh and drinks My blood has eternal life, and I will raise him up at the last day. For My flesh is food indeed, and My blood is drink indeed. He who eats My flesh and drinks My blood abides in Me, and I in him. As the living Father sent Me, and I live because of the Father, so he who feeds on Me will live because of Me. This is the bread which came down from heaven—not as your fathers ate the manna, and are dead. He who eats this bread will live forever." John 6:41–58

1. What two complaints did the Jews have against Jesus?

   a.

   b.

2. Jesus was continually explaining His purpose on earth and His desire to draw people into the family of God. He used analogies to accomplish understanding. Draw a line from the physical reference to its true and spiritual meaning.

PHYSICAL REFERENCE	ETERNAL MEANING
Bread of Life	Have faith in Him
Eat His flesh	Disbelieve
Drink His blood	Jesus
"See" the Son	Honor His death
Murmur and complain	Make Him our own

3. What is the difference between the manna consumed in the wilderness and the bread that Jesus offers?

4. How does God the Father draw us to Him? How are we to respond?

5. Why do you think it angered the Jews when Jesus called Himself the Bread of Life?

LEARN ABOUT ...

3 Death vs. Life
The Jews found validation in the story of Moses and the manna provided for their ancestors in the wilderness. While the Jews revered Moses as the source of the manna, Jesus reminded them that it was heaven-sent. Those who ate miraculous manna eventually died. Jesus is the bread that leads to eternal life.

4 Draw vs. Drag
We are drawn to the Lord through the teachings in the Bible. Without the Holy Spirit, we are unable to properly sense our need and depravity apart from Him. Our awareness develops as we listen to the Father and learn from His teachings. God draws us, but we must respond.

Learn About ...

6 Do vs. Be

For the Jews, doing works that proved their worth were prideful actions meant to draw attention to them, not God. Abiding in Christ is a way of living patiently, enduring humbly, and remaining stable—in other words, *being*. As roots abide invisibly but inseparably with the tree, so we are to be in Christ.

7 Deity vs. Man

Three times in this passage, Jesus said, "I am." He never conveyed doubt about His deity or His purpose. He may have looked like Jesus the son of Joseph and Mary, but the Jews certainly understood the reference to the "I AM," or Yahweh, who proclaimed Himself to Moses (Ex. 3:14).

9 Diligence vs. Neglect

Paul looked at his life in Christ as that of a marathon runner. He trained every day in every moment: "I press toward the goal for the prize of the upward call of God in Christ Jesus. Therefore let us, as many as are mature, have this mind" (Phil. 3:14–15).

6. The Jews were repulsed at the notion of eating Jesus' flesh and drinking His blood. Why did Jesus use these examples?

Live Out ...

7. You have a spiritual identity in Jesus Christ. Until you know who you are, you will stumble through your life. What do the following passages say about your spiritual identity?

Scripture	Your Spiritual Identity
1 Thessalonians 1:4	
John 1:12	
Philippians 3:20	

8. a. Name someone in your life who has difficulty reconciling the changes in you since you began following Jesus Christ.

   b. Journal a prayer asking God to use this discomfort to draw him or her to Christ.

9. Journal about how you are living your physical life in view of your eternal life in Christ.

10. Using the word FEED as an acrostic, list some of the ways you can feed on Jesus and His Word.

   F

   E

   E

   D

o o • o o

We live in a commitment-phobic world. Gone are the days of a verbal contract or a firm handshake between men who know and trust each other. Business contracts designed to bind, blind, and baffle are drawn up with the expectation that one day a judge will have to translate the legalese and make a judgment that often has little to do with justice.

This trend of noncommitment has taken its toll on our relationships. Couples are more inclined to share a lease than a till-death-do-us-part promise of a life together. Children are often the unacknowledged collateral damage of such decisions, growing up in unstable homes where the foundation of the family has never been properly laid. Ironically, if these commitment-shy couples eventually decide to wed, they are over 50 percent more likely to divorce than couples who marry before they cohabit.

Jesus wants committed followers. He made His terms clear: We must first be drawn by the Father, believe and feed upon God's Word, follow Him wholeheartedly, love no one or nothing more than Him. And He, in turn, gives us nothing less than unconditional love, guidance for each step, an opportunity to share in His will on earth, and His promise of eternal life with Him.

There is no lease option here, no pre-nup, and no escape clause. He wants us to abide with Him forever—starting now! The contract is drawn up and witnessed by the Father and the Holy Spirit, and signed by the Son—in His own blood.

Listen To ...

For God to reveal His Son in us is not the result of research or searching; it is entirely a matter of mercy and revelation. It is an inward seeing, an inner knowing.

—Watchman Nee

Lebanese (Syrian) Bread

This flatbread, similar to tortillas, extends far into antiquity and appears in most ancient societies. Some historians believe that pita was one of earth's first recipes since it required no oven or utensils. It originally bore the name "ash bread," as the dough was cooked on porous stones placed atop hot coals and ashes. Pita bakes at high temperatures (about 450 °F), forcing the flat discs of dough to puff up dramatically. Immediately after removal from the oven, the bread deflates, leaving a pocket to stuff with most anything. In Israeli and Palestinian cuisine, almost everything, from falafel to hummus to tabouli to lamb or chicken kebabs to various salads are eaten inside a pita.[7]

Bread's portability and sustainability made it the favorite of ancient travelers. Hebrews made their bread round and flat. Bedouins transported their bread in leather pouches that served as both carriers and tables. They did not cut bread with a knife, but broke it by hand. Therefore, the Bible describes breaking bread as eating, sitting down to a table, taking a repast. By New Testament times, the term referred to the Lord's Supper, reminding us of Christ's broken body for our sin.

Preparation Time: 60 minutes
Cook Time: 10 minutes

Ingredients:

> 2 packages of active dry yeast
> 1/3 cup of water
> 1 tablespoon of flour
> 2 tablespoons of sugar
> 3 cups of flour
> 1 cup of water
> 1 teaspoon of salt

Instructions:

1. Sprinkle the yeast over 1/3 cup of water and add one tablespoon of flour and sugar. Stir and set aside to rise for about ten minutes.

2. Sift the three cups of flour with the salt. Add the yeast mixture. Knead, adding one cup of water gradually, to make a stiff but not dry dough.

3. Set in a warm place to rise until doubled in bulk. Punch the dough down.

4. Divide into six to eight round balls. Place on lightly floured surface. With a rolling pin, flatten into quarter-inch–thick circles.

5. Cover with a kitchen towel and let it rise again for fifteen to twenty-five minutes. Brush with milk.

6. Preheat oven and baking sheets to 500 degrees. Place the bread on baking sheets or a baking stone in the oven until puffed up and golden brown, about five minutes. Then turn over so the other side browns also.

When the bread is a little cool, place the pieces in plastic bags to soften.

GRACE NOTE

Father in Heaven,

Like this delicious bread, Your Word is the bread of life. Scripture is the substance, the basis, the very heart of being spiritually satisfied. Create a hunger in us for the bread of the Word, just as we hunger for the comfort of bread. In Jesus' name. Amen.

Good Company Corrects Bad Morals

Mark 2:13–28

Remember in grade school when teams were being chosen for PE or recess? Waiting to be picked was excruciating. While the captains made their selections, sideline advisors shouted out the names of the best and the strongest to make up their team. Nothing was worse than being the last one chosen and hearing the sighs and moans from the team who got stuck with the weakest link.

It may have happened long ago, but those feelings of rejection can quickly rise to the surface in situations today. Perhaps we weren't included on a guest list or were passed over for a promotion. We may even bring it on ourselves when we compare ourselves to others and decide we've come up short.

These situations are challenging, and—just as on the playground—we often have no control over them. How wonderful to know there is a Person who enthusiastically chooses us just as we are. On Jesus' team, the weak are often considered the strongest, and the outcasts are drawn into the inner circle. Our Captain welcomes us regardless of our hot tempers, cool commitments, good intentions, or bad morals. His good company can correct our flaws, heal the wrongs we've endured, and soothe our hurting hearts.

Life can be lonely and people mean, but Jesus asks us to join Him on a glorious adventure that will make our rejections pale in comparison.

Day 1: Mark 2:13–15   **Mixed Company**
Day 2: Mark 2:16–17   **Bitter Conversation**
Day 3: Mark 2:18–20   **Feast or Fast?**
Day 4: Mark 2:21–22   **The Problem with Wineskins**
Day 5: Mark 2:23–28   **Hard to Swallow**

DAY 1
Mixed Company

LIFT UP ...

Father, I am amazed that You love me despite my flaws and weaknesses. Grow me into the woman You want me to be. Open my heart and my ears that I may hear Your voice and obediently follow after You. In Jesus' name. Amen.

LOOK AT ...

So far in our study, we've seen Jesus perform a miracle at a wedding, share living water at a well, and walk on water. Now we find Him choosing a very diverse and unlikely team of disciples. Some in this group of twelve men had checkered pasts and shady family backgrounds, but Jesus chose them "that they might be with Him and that He might send them out to preach" (Mark 3:14). Jesus called Simon Peter and his brother Andrew to leave their work as fishermen. James and John, the sons of Zebedee, left both their boat and their father.

When Levi, the tax collector, received his call, not only did he follow Jesus without hesitation, he opened his home to the Lord and invited many other people who needed what Jesus offered. The disciples responded immediately to the compelling call of Jesus.

READ MARK 2:13–15.

Then He went out again by the sea; and all the multitude came to Him, and He taught them. As He passed by, He saw Levi the son of Alphaeus sitting at the tax office. And He said to him, "Follow Me." So he arose and followed Him.

Now it happened, as He was dining in Levi's house, that many tax collectors and sinners also sat together with Jesus and His disciples; for there were many, and they followed Him. Mark 2:13–15

Learn About ...

4 Tax Collectors

When Judea became a Roman province, Rome's tax laws were levied on the Jews. Tax collectors set up shop at ports and city entrances and often extorted money from fellow Jews in order to increase their own wealth. They were thoroughly despised and considered traitors who were in league with Rome.

---

5 Levi

Levi is another name for Matthew. Matthew lived in Capernaum, a thriving business community where he collected dues and customs from those who crossed the Sea of Galilee or major highways. He was a wealthy man who became Jesus' disciple and later wrote the gospel of Matthew.

---

6 Dinner at Levi's

Luke recorded, "Levi gave Him a great feast in his own house" (Luke 5:29). Hospitality was considered a chief virtue in the ancient world. Being a man of wealth, Levi spared no expense in hosting Jesus, His disciples, and many acquaintances who were deemed "sinners."

1. Where did this event occur?

2. Review Mark 1:16–20. What was Jesus doing the last time He was by the sea?

3. Who continued to pursue Jesus? What was His response?

4. What was Levi doing when Jesus spoke to him?

5. What command did Jesus give Levi? How did he respond?

6. What invitation can we assume Levi extended to Jesus? Describe the others included on the guest list.

7. Summarize what you know about the people surrounding Jesus.

Live Out ...

8. In Levi's profession as a tax collector, literacy, detail orientation, and people skills were important. After his conversion, these skills were transformed and used to write the gospel of Matthew.

   a. List some of the skills you acquired as an unbeliever.

   b. How can these skills be redeemed for God's glory?

   c. Name one of these skills you will put into practice this week.

   d. Journal a prayer echoing Paul's: "God causes everything to work together for the good of those who love God and are called according to His purpose for them" (Rom. 8:28 NLT).

9. Levi gave up great wealth to follow Jesus; it was a life to which he could never return. Is there something about your lifestyle God has asked you to give up in order to follow Him completely? Make a list of those things in the space provided.

10. Levi was accustomed to being hated, but when he chose to follow Jesus, the Savior Himself immediately accepted him into His family. Levi finally "belonged." Are you certain that you are part of God's family?

❏ Yes!

Journal a note of thanksgiving to God, and thank Him for His acceptance of you.

❏ No!

Journal a prayer asking the Lord to receive you into His family.

· · • · ·

LEARN ABOUT ...

9 "Follow Me"

Jesus calls us to follow Him just as He called each disciple: "If anyone desires to come after Me, let him deny himself, and take up his cross daily, and follow Me" (Luke 9:23). Like Levi, we each must make our own decision to follow Christ.

10 Accepted

"Behold what manner of love the Father has bestowed on us, that we should be called children of God!" (1 John 3:1). God has lavished us with the gift of acceptance. However, a gift must be received in order to be enjoyed.

Can you recall a time when you experienced the thrill of embarking on a new adventure? Maybe it was the elation of receiving an acceptance into your first-choice college, the giddy happiness of getting married, or the honor of being offered a promotion. It's exciting to consider new possibilities, and there is special pleasure and fulfillment when you know you are wanted. Add to that the deep satisfaction of being part of something honorable and meaningful. Although the initial warm feelings may be followed by hard work, challenge, and even disappointment, each opportunity has the potential of bringing new opportunities.

When Levi accepted Jesus' call to follow Him, his life was forever changed. Jesus said, "If anyone serves Me, let him follow Me.… If anyone serves Me, him My Father will honor" (John 12:26). The disciples instinctively knew that the call to follow Jesus was no ordinary summons. Their decisions held life-changing potential, and while difficult times would come as a result, they came to love Jesus and were devoted to Him.

Following Jesus still requires service and sacrifice, but the Father has promised He will honor our efforts. What is your response to Jesus' call to follow Him? Levi responded immediately. Will you?

LISTEN TO ...

The golden rule for understanding in spiritual matters is not intellect, but obedience.

—*Oswald Chambers*

DAY 2

Bitter Conversation

Sometimes an ailment calls for a specialist. A podiatrist would be of little help in dealing with a migraine headache, a cardiologist is not equipped to cast a broken arm, and even the most respected psychologist can't bind a broken spirit or fill a longing heart. In matters of the heart and soul, there is only one qualified to offer healing: Jesus, the Great Physician.

For centuries people have sought remedies for spiritual sickness. Sometimes they found relief for a season, but permanent change was illusive. The Pharisees sought righteousness through complex and lengthy rituals that made a relationship with God virtually unattainable—even for themselves!

Jesus said, "But woe to you, scribes and Pharisees, hypocrites! For you shut up the kingdom of heaven against men; for you neither go in yourselves, nor do you allow those who are entering to go in" (Matt. 23:13). This is like barring the door of an emergency room to keep out the sick! So it comes as no surprise that the Pharisees hated Jesus. They tried to discredit Him and when that failed, they plotted His death. Jesus didn't mince words when dealing with them. In Matthew 23, the Great Physician diagnosed the condition of their souls, referring to them as "blind guides" (v. 24), "whitewashed tombs" (v. 27), and "serpents, brood of vipers" (v. 33)!

LIFT UP ...

Father, I need You. Only You can cure me of sin and spare me from its consequences. Sometimes, understanding my need is a bitter pill to swallow. I pray for the humility to seek You as my personal Great Physician. In Jesus' name. Amen.

LOOK AT ...

Today we focus on the reaction of the scribes and Pharisees to Jesus enjoying a meal at Levi's house. Imagine the scene: these religious leaders were so curious and threatened by

1 Pharisees

A powerful religious party in Jesus' day, the Pharisees' name was rooted in the Hebrew word for "separated." Ironically, in their quest to maintain the law, they added trifling and insignificant rituals and works that burdened their lives and obscured a genuine relationship with God.

---

2 Eating

For the Jews, the act of eating with someone had serious cultural implications. Sharing a meal was more than casual association; it was an act of assimilating their character and those with whom they dined. Eating a meal with sinners was to be avoided because it meant you were either a sinner already or would soon become one.

---

5 Jesus Listens

Jesus always listens to the heart. The Pharisees slyly took their complaint to the disciples, but Jesus heard them and knew their true intent. They rejected the Messiah because He abhorred their traditions and He associated with "wicked" people. The Pharisees valued legal compliance; Jesus valued loving obedience.

Jesus that they actually followed Him to Levi's house! They must have lingered outside, whispering to one another, peering into the house, straining to catch a few words of what was being said. They had one objective: to find evidence to discredit Jesus and secure their superiority.

And they found what they needed. Jesus engaged in the intimate sharing of a meal with tax collectors and sinners. The scribes and Pharisees were probably as delighted as they were appalled. Yet rather than confront Jesus directly, they chose to complain to His disciples.

There would be more conflict with these pious leaders and more instances when Jesus directly and indirectly confronted their arrogance, hardened hearts, and self-righteous ways.

READ MARK 2:16–17.

And when the scribes and Pharisees saw Him eating with the tax collectors and sinners, they said to His disciples, "How is it that He eats and drinks with tax collectors and sinners?"

When Jesus heard it, He said to them, "Those who are well have no need of a physician, but those who are sick. I did not come to call the righteous, but sinners, to repentance." Mark 2:16–17

1. In addition to those who were invited, who else showed up at Levi's house? What do you know about them?

2. Describe what they observed Jesus doing.

3. Explain the Pharisees' criticism. What was their unspoken motive?

4. To whom did they bring their grievance? Why didn't they go to the source of their complaint?

5. Who overheard this interchange?

6. Compare and contrast the Lord's view of the sick and sinful with the Pharisees' view.

7. Whom did Jesus say He came to call?

Live Out ...

8. a. Jesus dined with saints and sinners. His loving purpose was to draw sinners to repentance and saints to greater faith. Repentance reveals our need for a Savior. In the columns below, list the names of your acquaintances who are either repentant or rebellious.

REPENTANT   **REBELLIOUS**

b. Journal a prayer to God, asking Him to bring the rebellious to repentance.

9. Matthew records this same event and notes that Jesus also said, "But go and learn what this means: 'I desire mercy and not sacrifice'" (Matt. 9:13). Read Hosea 6:6. What do you think Jesus implied?

10. a. In every society, there have been those who are shunned or avoided because of their scandalous behaviors or associations. List some of these people groups that society has shunned:

b. Journal about a time you reached out to such a person or group. If you have not, then pray for an opportunity to demonstrate mercy to someone in need.

Learn About ...

7 Righteous—Not

The Pharisees felt superior and righteous because they followed their laws with painful precision. Jesus told them He had not come to call the righteous but rather the sinners. Did they detect His sarcasm? The righteous don't need a savior—but no one is righteous, not even a Pharisee.

8 Repentance

The Pharisees made righteousness so rigorous and unattainable that people were separated from God. *Repentance* means "to be sorry for your sin and turn from wrong behavior." Through repentance, Jesus drew sinners close and gave them an opportunity to be in right standing with God.

9 Mercy vs. Sacrifice

The religious ritual of sacrifices was a strict equation originally meant to nourish one's relationship with God. The Pharisees and scribes performed endless rituals with neither love for God nor mercy for God's people. Without humility and obedience, the equation backfired: sacrifice minus love equals pride.

○ ○ ● ○ ○

Not all Pharisees encountered in the New Testament were hardened toward Jesus. Several were notable in their desire to learn and their hunger for truth. Nicodemus, a ruler of the Jews, recognized Jesus was "a teacher come from God" (John 3:2). He met Jesus at night to ask earnest questions about being "born again." Later, he protested the unfairness of Jesus' trial (John 7:50–52) and brought gifts to anoint His body following the crucifixion (John 19:39–40).

Joseph of Arimathea, a prominent Pharisee, courageously asked Pilate for Jesus' body and saw to His proper burial in his own personal tomb (Mark 15:42–46). Saul (later renamed Paul) was a prominent Pharisee who viciously hated Christ and His followers. He was dramatically converted on the road to Damascus (Acts 9:3–19) and was instrumental in spreading the gospel around the world. He acknowledged his transformation when he said, "This is a faithful saying and worthy of all acceptance, that Christ Jesus came into the world to save sinners, of whom I am chief" (1 Tim. 1:15).

Like the Pharisees, we are all sinners when we meet the Lord. Jesus is less concerned with our past behaviors than with our decisions after salvation. He asked His disciples, "But who do you say that I am?" Peter answered without hesitation, "You are the Christ" (Mark 8:29). The question still applies to each one of us: Who do you say Jesus is?

LISTEN TO ...

Mercy is compassion in action.

—*Anonymous*

DAY 3
Feast or Fast?

I love to throw elaborate parties. For example, my husband's thirtieth birthday party was themed around a Victorian murder mystery. Dressed in period costumes, we followed clues to solve a dastardly crime. Then, for my dad's sixtieth birthday, we honored his Scottish heritage by dressing in plaid and greeting him at the airport while dancing the jig to a live bagpipe. One of my favorite parties was for my son's fifth birthday. He loved dinosaurs, so we turned a dirt lot into an archaeological dig by hiding bones, eggs, and dinosaur remains everywhere. Finally, we treated the kids to a scary jeep ride and then fed them gummy-worm cake.

Across time and cultures, celebrations are a consistent part of life. We are social creatures wired to enjoy fellowship with one another. In fact, we are admonished in Hebrews 10:25 not to forsake "the assembling of ourselves together." We need one another.

The disciples had the rare privilege of enjoying Jesus face-to-face. They shared celebrations that included both simple and elaborate meals. No doubt they laughed with Him and marveled at His ways. Yet I suspect they didn't realize how special these times were until He was gone.

Resolve to take time now to enjoy fellowship with friends and family—and with God. "That which we have seen and heard we declare to you, that you also may have fellowship with us; and truly our fellowship is with the Father and with His Son Jesus Christ" (1 John 1:3).

LIFT UP ...

Heavenly Father, thank You for sending Your Son, Jesus. Make me aware that even in lonely times, I am the treasured bride of the perfect Bridegroom. I want to savor my time with You here on earth until the day I celebrate with You in heaven. In Jesus' name. Amen.

LEARN ABOUT ...

1. Disciples of John

John the Baptist's ministry paved the way for Jesus' coming. John, who was ordained from birth to be separated for service to God, had attracted a large following and had disciples of his own. He would have taught his disciples to fast and pray.

---

2 Fasting

In Matthew 6:16–18, Jesus described the guidelines for fasting. He warned that fasting was a private matter between an individual and God. Hypocrites wanted to impress others, so they wore a "sad countenance" and tended to "disfigure their faces." Jesus taught His disciples to look their best outwardly so God would reward them secretly.

LOOK AT ...

In yesterday's lesson, we learned that the Pharisees and scribes criticized Jesus for socializing with sinners. Today we see their continued accusations when they observed that Jesus' disciples were not fasting.

As always, Jesus stood in stark contrast to the religious leaders of the day. He refused to partake in rituals devoid of meaning. While fasting and sacrifice had their place, that place was not at this time for the disciples. For the short interval while Jesus accompanied them, they needed to feast rather than fast. How could mourning coexist with celebration?

Jesus vibrantly embraced children, the sick, and the poor. He enjoyed close friendships with Lazarus, Mary, and Martha. He attended social gatherings, weddings, and even dinner at a tax collector's house. Sometimes He served as host, and sometimes He sat as a guest. Jesus came both to speak to the people and to be *with* them. He mixed. He mingled. He cared.

READ MARK 2:18–20.

The disciples of John and of the Pharisees were fasting. Then they came and said to Him, "Why do the disciples of John and of the Pharisees fast, but Your disciples do not fast?"

And Jesus said to them, "Can the friends of the bridegroom fast while the bridegroom is with them? As long as they have the bridegroom with them they cannot fast. But the days will come when the bridegroom will be taken away from them, and then they will fast in those days." Mark 2:18–20

1. List the two groups of people who fasted.

2. Rephrase the questions asked by the scribes and Pharisees in your own words.

3. How did Jesus handle the scrutiny and criticism of this departure from custom?

4. Why do you think He referred to Himself as a bridegroom? Who were the "friends of the bridegroom"?

5. Under what conditions did the bridegroom's friends refrain from fasting?

6. What was expected to happen in the days to come?

7. How would the friends of the bridegroom behave after this event?

Live Out ...

8. Contrast the usual mood at a wedding to the typical mood of the Pharisees. Which group best describes your attitude? Are you observing religious rites at the expense of enjoying fellowship with Jesus? Ask God if He wants you to make any changes in your attitude.

9. Fasting has a place in our lives today. Is God calling you to fast and pray about a situation in your life? Using the word FAST as an acrostic, list reasons you might fast.

F

A

S

T

10. John the Baptist recognized the deity of Jesus: "He who has the bride is the bridegroom; but the friend of the bridegroom, who stands and hears him, rejoices greatly because of the bridegroom's voice" (John 3:29). Have you committed to become Jesus' bride? Recite these vows to your heavenly Bridegroom:

Learn About ...

4 Bridegroom and Bride

The Old Testament portrayed the spiritual relationship between God and His people as that of a bridegroom with his bride. Isaiah 62:5 says, "And as the bridegroom rejoices over the bride, so shall your God rejoice over you." As Messiah, Jesus used this analogy to depict His relationship with believers.

8 Celebrations

In the Old Testament, fasts were reserved for repentance, grieving, or asking for divine favor. God didn't require regular fasting except on the Day of Atonement. Instead He instituted seven different feasts, indicating that He wanted joy and celebration to be part of His people's lives.

10 Confusion

Initially, John's disciples were confused about Jesus. They came to him saying, "Rabbi, He ... to whom you have testified—behold, He is baptizing, and all are coming to Him!" (John 3:26). John's disciples were threatened by Jesus' popularity, but John insisted, "He must increase, but I must decrease" (John 3:30).

I, _____, take You, Jesus, to be my heavenly Husband, to have and to hold from this day forward, for better or for worse, for richer, for poorer, in sickness and in health, to love and to cherish, from this day forward and for all of eternity. In Your name, amen.

∘ ∘ ● ∘ ∘

First John 1:3 says, "That which we have seen and heard we declare to you, that you also may have fellowship with us; and truly our fellowship is with the Father and with His Son Jesus Christ." John described the critical link between our fellowship with believers and fellowship with the Father and Son. In order to grow in our relationship with God, we need like-minded people. We need friends. Edgar Albert Guest wrote a poem about friendship:

> Be a friend. You don't need glory.
> Friendship is a simple story.
> Pass by trifling errors blindly,
> Gaze on honest effort kindly,
> Cheer the youth who's bravely trying,
> Pity him who's sadly sighing;
> Just a little labor spend
> On the duties of a friend.[1]

In the best sense of the word, a friend can provide strength when we are weak and bring light and encouragement when we are under a cloud of troubles. Without even realizing it, a friend brings us the love of God to remind us that God is near. By sharing the anticipation of waiting for our Bridegroom to return, we encourage each other to focus on the coming eternal joy and keep the trials of the present in perspective.

LISTEN TO ...

The enjoyment of [God] is the only happiness with which our souls can be satisfied.

—Jonathan Edwards

The Problem with Wineskins

Do you keep a journal? Or, as a child, did you keep a diary? If so, you understand the comfort and attachment of picking up that familiar book to record your thoughts or prayers. It's like an old friend. It contains pages that reflect your baby steps of understanding, your fears, and your milestones of faith and hope. You poured yourself into it. Even with a new and pristine journal waiting, when you've filled that familiar book, it can be painful to close it and place it on the shelf. Yet if you refused to let go of it and tried to write your new thoughts over the old, both the old and new journals would be ruined.

The Pharisees fought the idea of abandoning the Jewish legalism they had added to the old covenant. When God gave Moses the law, it was a new and exciting way to live. It wasn't meant to oppress the people but to keep them safe and separated for God's purposes. However, over time, man turned these laws into oppressive rules and empty rituals.

The old covenant had served its purposes; but with the advent of Christ, it was time for something new. The Jews didn't want to leave the comfort and safety of the law even though they could never fully keep it. In today's text, Jesus helped them understand that His new covenant must stand alone—rather than fit over the old.

LIFT UP ...

Lord, help me see Your Word and Your truth clearly, the way You meant it to be seen and understood. Check me when I attempt to impose my beliefs over Your pure truth. In Jesus' name. Amen.

LOOK AT ...

Recall yesterday's lesson, when Jesus taught His disciples the principle of thoughtful observance of custom rather than blind ritual. While He was in their presence, fasting and

LEARN ABOUT ...

2 New Cloth

The new cloth eventually shrank over time or when it was washed. The shrinking ruined the old cloth and made it worse than the original tear. In addition, Luke 5:36 states that the new cloth wouldn't match the old. Jesus illustrated how His message would not fit in with the old religious ways.

---

3 Wineskins

These were goatskins sewn to form a watertight bag. New wine was poured into the skins, and as it fermented, gasses formed that caused expansion. A new wineskin enlarged with the new vintage, but old wineskins lacked the same flexibility and would likely burst.

mourning had no place. But when the day came, they would appropriately fast in His absence.

In today's passage Jesus elaborates on the reasons why fasting in His presence is both inappropriate and ineffective. He uses two illustrations: one of a worn-out garment being repaired with a new piece of cloth, and the second of new wine being put into old wineskins. His explanation is matter-of-fact: The old cloth and the old wineskin have served their purposes—they no longer meet the present needs.

The Old Testament served as preparation for the coming of the Messiah, and when He came, it was time to view a relationship with God with new eyes. In this passage, Jesus prepared to establish a new covenant with His people.

READ MARK 2:21–22.

No one sews a piece of unshrunk cloth on an old garment; or else the new piece pulls away from the old, and the tear is made worse. And no one puts new wine into old wineskins; or else the new wine bursts the wineskins, the wine is spilled, and the wineskins are ruined. But new wine must be put into new wineskins. Mark 2:21–22

1. Describe what happens when an old garment is repaired with a new piece of cloth.

2. What happens when the new cloth pulls away from the old?

3. Where was wine traditionally stored?

4. Explain what happened when old wineskins were used to hold new wine.

5. What was the proper way of storing new wine?

6. Read Luke 5:36–39. How did people regard old wine as compared with new wine?

LIVE OUT ...

7. Yesterday we spoke about the importance of fellowship. Old friendships can either help or hinder a new life in Christ. Journal about an old relationship that has either helped and hindered your growth as a believer.

8. Read Hebrews 8:13. Jesus came to lead us into a new covenant, not to put patches on the old one. Are there ill-fitting parts of your old life that you are clinging to? How might God replace these with new garments?

OLD PATCHES   **NEW GARMENT**

9. Jesus doesn't offer to mend our old garment but to give us a garment as grand as a wedding dress: "For He has clothed me with the garments of salvation, He has covered me with the robe of righteousness" (Isa. 61:10). Draw, describe, or paste a picture of what you imagine your heavenly wedding dress to look like. Be extravagant!

o o ● o o

There are two ways for something to come to an end: either it is destroyed, or it lives out its natural and intended purpose. For example,

LEARN ABOUT ...

6 Old Wine

Having acquired a taste for old wine, Jesus knew it would take time to desire the new. The religious leaders of the day were accustomed to their old ways and rejected Jesus as Messiah. They could not conceive of the new message exceeding their old rituals.

8 New Covenant

The old covenant was a contract of works. God promised to bless men as a by-product of perfect obedience. The new covenant is a promise of grace. God promises salvation for those who believe Jesus is the Christ and receive Him as Savior.

9 Righteousness

For Jesus, the cost of clothing us in righteousness was unfathomable: "For He made Him who knew no sin to be sin for us, that we might become the righteousness of God in Him" (2 Cor. 5:21). If we attempt to adorn ourselves with self-righteousness, the garments appear as "filthy rags" (Isa. 64:6).

a seed can be thrown away or planted. When allowed to grow, the seed produces fruit. In fulfilling its highest purpose, the seed comes to its natural end.

The seed of the old covenant came to an end through the fruition of Jesus' perfect fulfillment of the law. The Pharisees struggled with this, perhaps hoping for a compromise that allowed them to maintain their comfortable yet useless rules. Jesus exposed the futility of this approach with His illustrations of the garments and wineskins.

Although it's not a popular mind-set in today's culture, the salvation Jesus offers is without compromise: "Nor is there salvation in any other, for there is no other name under heaven given among men by which we must be saved" (Acts 4:12).

LISTEN TO ...

Just as I am, Thou wilt receive,
Wilt welcome, pardon, cleanse, relieve;
Because Thy promise I believe,
O Lamb of God, I come.

—*Charlotte Elliott*

DAY 5

Hard to Swallow

Food, water, shelter, and clothing are basic human needs. According to Feeding America, the nation's leading domestic hunger-relief charity, in "2009, 48.8 million Americans lived in food insecure households of these 32.6 million were adults while 16.2 million represented children."[2] Just one year later, during "2010, 4.8 percent of all U.S. households (5.6 million households) accessed emergency food from a food pantry one or more times."[3] While the Unites States provides food across the globe, Americans at home rely on one of the three major federal food assistance programs: Food Stamps, National School Lunch Program, or Special Supplemental Nutrition Program for Women, Infants, and Children. Tragically, the "Land of Plenty" can't keep up with the impoverished.

The sad truth is that the poor and hungry will always be among us. God was not unsympathetic to this fact and made provisions in the Old Testament law to meet their needs. As we learned earlier, farmers did not harvest the outside perimeter of their fields so that the poor and hungry could come gather food. The Pharisees went along with this practice, as long as it was done on a weekday. The hardness of the Pharisees' hearts put the religious ritual of observing the Sabbath above human need. This is what happens when compassion and mercy are sacrificed in the name of tradition. For the Pharisees, this painfully obvious truth was hard to swallow.

LIFT UP ...

Lord, am I hardened to the needs of others? Give me eyes to see what You have to teach me. Open my heart to Your truth, and help me change my behavior to please You. In Jesus' name. Amen.

2 Plucking Grain

Travelers were allowed to satisfy their immediate hunger, but they could not reap the harvest the farmer had labored to produce: "When you come into your neighbor's standing grain, you may pluck the heads with your hand, but you shall not use a sickle on your neighbor's standing grain" (Deut. 23:25).

3 Work on the Sabbath

The law was very clear about the serious consequences for those who performed work on the Sabbath: "Work shall be done for six days, but the seventh is the Sabbath of rest, holy to the LORD. Whoever does any work on the Sabbath day, he shall surely be put to death" (Ex. 31:15).

LOOK AT ...

We have seen how the religious leaders of the day hounded Jesus and His disciples, criticizing their everyday activities such as eating. In yesterday's lesson Jesus pointed out the rigidity that made the Pharisees incapable of accepting a new message.

Jesus was—and still is—controversial. Even today, there is a continued quest to expose Him as a rebel and instigator. The Pharisees used their wide power and narrow interpretation of the law to accuse Jesus and His disciples of violating tradition by simply satisfying their hunger.

Once again, Jesus drew them back to Scripture and, in the process of defending His disciples, clued them in to who He really is.

As we've seen this week, the religious leaders' hearts were closed to His message. This would not be the last of their confrontations.

READ MARK 2:23–28.

Now it happened that He went through the grainfields on the Sabbath; and as they went His disciples began to pluck the heads of grain. And the Pharisees said to Him, "Look, why do they do what is not lawful on the Sabbath?"

But He said to them, "Have you never read what David did when he was in need and hungry, he and those with him: how he went into the house of God in the days of Abiathar the high priest, and ate the showbread, which is not lawful to eat except for the priests, and also gave some to those who were with him?"

And He said to them, "The Sabbath was made for man, and not man for the Sabbath. Therefore the Son of Man is also Lord of the Sabbath."
Mark 2:23–28

1. Where were Jesus and His disciples on this Sabbath?

2. Describe how the disciples satisfied their hunger.

3. What infraction were they accusing the disciples of committing?

4. To what story of David did Jesus refer?

5. Explain what made David's meal more shocking than the Lord's.

6. Why did God create the Sabbath?

7. Who bears the title "Lord of the Sabbath"? How would the Pharisees respond to this declaration?

LIVE OUT ...

8. The Pharisees followed Jesus in hopes of catching Him violating the law. Have you ever watched for flaws in others rather than following the Savior yourself? Using the word FOLLOW as an acrostic, describe how you will keep your eyes on Jesus instead of on others.

   F

   O

   L

   L

   O

   W

9. God created the Sabbath for man's benefit, to allow for vital physical rest and spiritual refreshment. Is this a priority in your own life? Journal about how you will set aside a day this week to rest and renew.

LEARN ABOUT ...

5 Showbread

Showbread was unleavened bread that was placed on a table in the tabernacle in the presence of the Lord. Twelve fresh loaves were presented every Sabbath, representing the twelve tribes of Israel. They remained there until the following Sabbath, when the priests ate them and replaced them with new loaves.

8 Observing the Law

The Pharisees took the observance of the law seriously. In their view, Jesus' willingness to permit the desecration of the Sabbath indicated He was capable of greater violations. Successfully branding Him as a lawbreaker made their goal to discredit Him easier.

9 The Sabbath

The word *Sabbath* means "a day of rest" or "to cease to do." It was established after the Israelites left Egypt. Moses commanded them to remember how God had delivered them with a mighty hand and an outstretched arm (Deut. 5:15). This day of rest was extended to all, including slaves and animals.

10. Jesus asked the Pharisees, "Have you never read …?" How often would we have avoided a mistake in judgment or speech if we could have readily recalled Scripture? Write down a verse from this week's passages and commit it to memory.

· · • ○ ○

Charles Francis Adams, the nineteenth-century political figure and diplomat, kept a diary. One day he entered, "Went fishing with my son today—a day wasted." His son, Brooks Adams, also kept a diary. On that same day, Brooks Adams made this entry: "Went fishing with my father—the most wonderful day of my life!" What the father saw as waste, his son saw as the best thing that could happen—a day with his dad.[4]

Both the Pharisees and the disciples spent time with Jesus. The former found it offensive and aggravating, while the latter recognized the privilege of being with God's only Son. It's sad to think of a life dedicated to the idea of God but lacking any meaningful relationship with Him.

Jesus came to replace ritual with a personal relationship. Whether speaking to a tender or hardened heart, He wanted a rapport with mankind—His creation. The Pharisees would have fainted at such a radical notion: Who could ever have a personal relationship with God? We have learned and benefitted from these misguided religious leaders. In your estimation, is time in prayer and in the Word a waste or an investment in a relationship that will last throughout eternity?

LISTEN TO …

The trouble oftentimes with religious people is that they try to be more spiritual than God himself.

—*Frederick Buechner*

Tabouli Salad

Tabouli (also spelled tabbouleh) comes from fabled beginnings. It is said that on a hot summer day, Cleopatra commanded her slaves to bring her a refreshing salad. Tradition holds that her cook created a salad with soaked cracked wheat grains, chopped green parsley, ripe red tomato, chopped mint from the garden, and onion. For the dressing, he combined fresh lemon juice and virgin olive oil. The thrilled queen named the salad "Cleopatra Salad."

Emperor Caesar, who had also recently named a salad after himself, became furious when he heard of Cleopatra's salad. Not wanting to share the spotlight, he ordered her to change the salad's name. And so, instead, the salad became known as "Tabouli."[5] Formal Arabic translates the word *tabouli* as "much sacred."

Today, tabouli accompanies several other salads in a Middle Eastern first course known as *mezze*. This Turkish word (pronounced "mez-ay") means snack, taste, or relish. This course includes hummus, baba ghanoush, olives, toasted almonds, and more. The Spanish call this style of eating *tapas*. We recognize this course as appetizers.

Preparation Time: 15 minutes
Cook Time: 15 minutes

Ingredients:
  1 cup fine bulgur
  1 1/2 cups boiling water
  10 sprigs parsley, chopped
  1/2 bundle mint, chopped
  1 medium-sized onion, chopped
  1 cucumber, seeded and chopped
  2 fresh and firm tomatoes, chopped
  1/2 cup extra virgin olive oil
  Juice of one freshly squeezed lemon
  Pinch of sea salt to taste

Instructions:

1. Add the bulgur to the bowl, and pour in boiling water. Water level should be half an inch above the bulgur.

2. Put the plate on top of the bowl, and soak the bulgur in water for fifteen minutes, until it swells in size.

3. Mix the bulgur in a bowl together with other ingredients—your tabouli salad is ready to serve.

GRACE NOTE

Lord Jesus,

Like a cool, delicious salad, Your Word brings refreshment and flavor to our lives. As we appreciate the variety and creativity of these foods, help us ponder Your inexhaustible and diverse elements. You are so much more than a meat-and-potatoes God. In Jesus' name. Amen.

Busy or Blessed?

Luke 10:38–42; John 12:1–8

"Let me catch my breath before it's taken away again," a woman wrote on her blog. I feel her pain. We live in a multitasking, microwaveable, high-speed-Internet world. Recently, I saw a young mother pushing a stroller, munching a breakfast bar, and talking on her cell. I could tell she suffered from the same pressures I felt earlier in my life. I thought I had to get everything done in a day.

My need to please trapped me in the game of great expectations. As I transitioned from single student to pastor's wife and mother, I fell prey to the "You Should" syndrome: "You should homeschool." "You should attend every church function." "You should recycle." A voice of sanity finally broke through: "Don't let others 'should' you to death."

My friend Penny never told me what I *should* do; in fact, she encouraged me *not* to do some things. After a week of entertaining guests, I still felt obligated to prepare a home-cooked meal and attend a women's meeting. I called Penny to vent.

"Lenya, just order takeout and stay home," she said.

"You mean I have permission to play hooky?!"

She replied, "You need a break. Everyone will understand."

At home that night, the Lord spoke to me: "Not only are you out of breath physically; you've lost your spiritual wind." I was too busy for God.

Can you relate? Martha could. We'll see that she struggled with the same "You Should" syndrome. Jesus encouraged her to catch her spiritual breath too.

Day 1: Luke 10:38–40   **HAND AND FOOT**

Day 2: Luke 10:41–42   **ONE THING**

Day 3: John 12:1–3   **FAMILY DINNER**

Day 4: John 12:4–6   **FRIEND OR FOE?**

Day 5: John 12:7–8   **OIL AND VINEGAR**

DAY 1
Hand and Foot

LIFT UP ...

Lord, I want to find Your balance for my life. The world pushes and pulls for my attention. Help me learn to sit at Your feet before I put my hands to work. In Jesus' name. Amen.

LOOK AT ...

Previously, we saw Jesus eat dinner with tax collectors and sinners—much to the annoyance of the religious leaders. Next, a friendly family invited Jesus into their home. John wrote, "Now Jesus loved Martha and her sister and Lazarus" (John 11:5). The Lord felt welcome at their home in Bethany. Inns were rare in the Middle East, so it wasn't uncommon for Jesus and His disciples to drop in for dinner or a night's rest.

Paul wrote to Philemon, "Prepare a guest room for me, because I hope to be restored to you in answer to your prayers" (Philem. 1:22 NIV).

Do your friends feel free to invite themselves for dinner or an overnight stay on their way through town? Perhaps developing the habit of making an extra serving at mealtime or purchasing an inflatable mattress would help you feel prepared. You never know who might stop in.

READ LUKE 10:38–40.

Now it happened as they went that He entered a certain village; and a certain woman named Martha welcomed Him into her house. And she had a sister called Mary, who also sat at Jesus' feet and heard His word. But Martha was distracted with much serving, and she approached Him and said, "Lord, do You not care that my sister has left me to serve alone? Therefore tell her to help me." Luke 10:38–40

Learn About ...

1 Entourage

In Luke 10:1 and 17 we discover that seventy disciples followed Jesus at this time. These men were given instructions similar to those given to the twelve apostles. Perhaps God's selection of twelve tribes influenced Jesus to choose twelve apostles. Similarly, Jesus chose seventy leaders just as Moses recruited seventy national leaders.

3 Enthusiastic

The Bible encourages God's people to be filled with hospitality and to enthusiastically invite people into their homes. Peter commanded, "Be hospitable to one another without grumbling" (1 Peter 4:9). In addition to Mary and Martha, Lydia (Acts 16:14–15) and Priscilla (Acts 18:2-3) offered hospitality to the saints.

6 Envy

Envy reveals feelings of resentment or jealousy toward others because of their possessions, personalities, or practices. Usually the emotion results from comparing ourselves to others or coveting something they possess. "For since there is jealousy and quarreling among you, are you not worldly?" (1 Cor. 3:3 NIV).

1. Review Luke 10. Describe those included in the phrase *they went*.

2. Who lived in this village and home?

3. Describe each sister's demeanor as the entourage arrived.

4. Think about how the sisters felt when a large group arrived unexpectedly. How would you respond in this situation?

5. Once the guests were settled, describe how the role of each sister differed.

   Mary:

   Martha:

6. What question did Martha ask Jesus? What was her reason?

Live Out ...

7. Martha exhibited the gift of hospitality by welcoming the guests into her home. Read Romans 12:4–13.

   a. How did Paul describe the church? In your own words, explain our diversity (vv. 4–5).

   b. How should each individual express her gifts (vv. 6–8)?

c. Which of the exhortations in verses 9–13 best describe each sister? Place the attributes in the appropriate column.

MARY   **MARTHA**

d. Make a list of the gifts or attributes from our text that best describe you.

8. Although each sister began the visit with devotion, earthly demands eventually distracted Martha from serving with a heavenly heart. Journal about a situation where work eclipsed your worship. How did you feel? What helped you regain balance?

9. Martha took her eyes off Jesus and placed her focus on Mary. Using ENVY as an acrostic, describe the ways you have judged others harshly.

E

N

V

Y

· · ● · ·

LEARN ABOUT ...

7 Encouragement

Paul compared spiritual gifting to facets of the body. The mouth and the eyes are evident—but the unseen lungs sustain life. Gifts are given to encourage others: "A spiritual gift is given to each of us so we can help each other" (1 Cor. 12:7 NLT).

───────────

8 Eclipsed

Sometimes we are so earthly minded, we're no heavenly good. We need to be reminded that this earth is not our home; we're just passing through. Paul wrote, "Set your mind on things above, not on things on the earth. For ... your life is hidden with Christ in God" (Col. 3:2–3).

In the blink of an eye, distractions have the power to pull us off center. One summer our family took a road trip to Colorado. Colorado's landscape of majestic mountains and natural beauty distracted my husband's attention. Appreciating God's creation is a good thing—unless you're driving the car. As he appreciated the green trees and sloping hills, the car swerved peril-ously along the highway. No one was hurt, but it gave us quite a scare.

Consider other possible spiritual distractions. For Samson, it was a beautiful woman. For Lot's wife, it was a backward glance. For Martha, it was comparing herself to Mary. Comparisons are like cataracts: although painless, cataracts form a cloudy area on the lens of the eye, which blocks light to the retina and results in blurry vision. When we compare ourselves to others, we block God's light. And we can't see the motives of others clearly. Paul warned, "For we dare not class ourselves or compare ourselves with those who com-mend themselves. But they, measuring themselves by themselves, and comparing themselves among themselves, are not wise" (2 Cor. 10:12).

As when we drive a car, we must have a focal point in the Christian life—or better yet, a focal Person. Hebrews exhorts us to run, "looking unto Jesus, the author and finisher of our faith" (Heb. 12:2). Our gaze is to be squarely set on Jesus! He is the light of the world. We must not dim our sight with anything or anyone else.

Listen To ...

We must picture hell as a state where everyone is perpetually concerned about his own dig-nity and advancement, where everyone has a grievance, and where everyone lives the deadly serious passions of envy, self-importance, and resentment.

—*C. S. Lewis*

One Thing

"Focus, focus, focus!" My piano teacher's words from my adolescence still echo in my memory. Sadly, I never did. *Outliers,* a book by Malcolm Gladwell, states that while success includes opportunities provided by providence or chance, it depends largely on practice.[1] He observes that those who enjoy wild success spend a minimum of ten thousand hours practicing a specific discipline. For instance, before the Beatles became a screaming success in the mid-1960s, they practiced intensely and performed over a thousand times in obscure nightclubs throughout Europe.

No doubt, God agrees with Gladwell. Although many saints experienced the blessing of God's providence, they also sought God wholeheartedly. Through no effort of his own, David, the shepherd boy, was anointed by Samuel and became king of Israel. However, the psalmist had the reputation of being a man after God's own heart (1 Sam. 13:14). No denying that God's anointing fell upon him with obvious gifting. But the king also spent hours in prayer and worship. He understood the value of seeking one thing above all others. And that one thing was the one true God.

As Christians, we are the recipients of amazing grace. But we must also passionately pursue our Savior. Success wears different faces. Financially, it wears Gucci. Famously, it hides behind Foster Grants. But spiritually, it's unwavering devotion to God.

Lift Up ...

Heavenly Father, it's so difficult to concentrate my energies on one single thing. Yet, like the hub of a wheel, You must be at the center before my activities have meaning. Thank You, Lord. In Jesus' name. Amen.

LEARN ABOUT ...

2 Repetition

The great Teacher, Jesus, employed repetition for a variety of reasons. The King James Version records one of the Lord's reoccurring phrases as "verily, verily." The New King James Version translates this into "most assuredly." The idea is that when Jesus said something important, He highlighted it through repetition.

---

4 Redirection

The Bible often uses the term *one thing* to help redirect distracted human beings from multitasking. Those who become experts in their fields place attention on one subject in which to excel. You can fiddle around with many things, but to become first fiddle, you must have a single focus.

LOOK AT ...

Yesterday we discovered both the human and heavenly sides of Martha. She loved to serve others through hospitality. But at times she struggled with stress. Worry prevented her work from being an act of worship. Faith and works are two sides of the same coin. In faith, we relax in the finished work of Christ. Through works, we provide evidence of our salvation. The trick is not to turn our works into a means to make ourselves worthy. God's grace is a gift that can never be repaid with religious activity: "For by grace you have been saved through faith, and that not of yourselves; it is the gift of God, not of works, lest anyone should boast" (Eph. 2:8–9).

Now we'll see how Jesus helped Martha regain her eternal perspective. He didn't demean her—instead He patiently pointed her back to worship.

READ LUKE 10:41–42.

And Jesus answered and said to her, "Martha, Martha, you are worried and troubled about many things. But one thing is needed, and Mary has chosen that good part, which will not be taken away from her." Luke 10:41–42

1. Reflect on yesterday's lesson. What question and circumstance prompted the Lord's response?

2. Why do you think Jesus repeated Martha's name?

3. Describe the state of Martha's heart. How did that influence her attitude?

4. Underline the phrase intended to redirect Martha's focus. Explain how this advice was helpful.

5. How did Jesus describe Mary's choice? Explain why.

6. How did Jesus honor Mary's choice? Describe the difference between worship and works.

LIVE OUT ...

7. Jesus repeated Martha's name on purpose. Fill in the chart to discover others who received a double salutation.

SCRIPTURE	SALUTATION
Genesis 46:1–3	
Exodus 3:2–4	
1 Samuel 3:4–10	
Acts 9:3–6	

8. a. The Bible is full of exhortations to focus on "one thing." Place a check in the box of the "one thing" you sense God is asking you to do.

   ❏ "One thing I have desired of the LORD, that will I seek: that I may dwell in the house of the LORD all the days of my life" (Ps. 27:4).

   ❏ "One thing I know: that though I was blind, now I see" (John 9:25).

   ❏ "One thing I do, forgetting those things which are behind and reaching forward to those things which are ahead" (Phil. 3:13).

   ❏ "Do not forget this one thing, that with the Lord one day is as a thousand years, and a thousand years as one day" (2 Peter 3:8).

   b. Journal a prayer asking God to give you singular focus. Describe how you will do this "one thing."

LEARN ABOUT ...

6 Reflection

Jesus did not want Mary's devotion to be diluted with unimportant details. He guarded her worship jealously. As a husband is toward his wife, God is jealous for our affection: "I am jealous for you with a godly jealousy. For I have betrothed you to one husband ... to Christ" (2 Cor. 11:2).

7 Redistribution

"Double portion" was a biblical practice of offering extra honor to someone. The firstborn received twice the inheritance to maintain the family name. Elkanah married two wives but "to Hannah he would give a double portion" (1 Sam. 1:5). Elisha asked for a double portion of Elijah's anointing (2 Kings 2:9).

8 Reinforce

The Bible warns about the double-minded individual. Double mindedness leads to a divided heart. Jesus said it is impossible to love God and money. James warned that "a double-minded man [is] unstable in all his ways" (James 1:8). We must choose to love the Savior over success and worship over work.

9. a. God longs for your worship more than your works. Name one activity you will forego and replace with a time for worship.

    b. Journal about your choice.

○ ○ ● ○ ○

Thanks to Lewis Carroll, most of us have heard of the church mouse. But have you ever heard of a church cat? In the small town of Fairford in Gloucestershire, England, stands St. Mary's. In the surrounding churchyard is the beloved sculpture of "Tibbles" the cat.[2] Church members erected the monument because the cat often wandered into the building during worship services and made himself at home. Villagers chided that the cat likely spent more time worshipping than any other parishioner. It doesn't take much imagination to picture the feline curled up in the sunlight streaming through a stained glass window.

Mary curled up in the light of the Son at every opportunity. Once He was in the door, she was at His feet. Martha thought she was lazy, and the disciples may have begrudged her intrusion. But Mary's desire for God's touch outstripped the hand of others.

David understood the privilege of being in God's house and in His presence: "A single day in your courts is better than a thousand anywhere else! I would rather be a gatekeeper in the house of my God than live the good life in the homes of the wicked" (Ps. 84:10 NLT).

I think I'd like being a church cat too. What a privilege to roam freely in the presence of God and His people! It would be purr-fect to soak in the worship and the Word both day and night.

LISTEN TO ...

The highest Christian love is not devotion to a certain work or cause of God, but to Him.

—*Oswald Chambers*

Family Dinner

It may sound old-fashioned, but I love preparing the family dinner. The tradition runs deep in my family's history. Both my mother and grandmother taught me the time-honored custom. Meals varied from chicken divan to lasagna to grilled cheese sandwiches, and all were homemade. We set the table with place mats, napkins, dishes, and utensils. No labeled bottles were allowed on the table. Instead they were served in separate dishes and enjoyed by candlelight. No one dared to take the first bite until everyone was seated. And nobody left the table until each person finished. My fondest memories surround dining tables—both past and present.

The Israelites ate a modest breakfast and two additional daily meals. Midway through the day, they enjoyed a small repast. The main meal was eaten between six and seven in the evening.

Some of their dinner customs included washing their hands before dining and sitting around a table. In fact, the Palestinian evening meal was called "sitting at the table."[3] The Romans introduced the *triclinium,* a dining room that contained a three-sided, u-shaped couch: "The couches were provided with cushions, on which the left elbow rested in support of the upper part of the body, while the right arm remained free."[4] Such was the case in the upper room (John 13). While modern Christians offer grace before a meal, Jews recited prayers at the meal's end.

Mary, Martha, and Lazarus practiced the habit of a proper evening meal too. They sat around the table with one another and enjoyed the food and fellowship of others.

LIFT UP ...

Heavenly Father, I sometimes feel that I'm living at the speed of light rather than in the grace of life. Help me to live my life as a beautiful reflection of You. In Jesus' name. Amen.

LEARN ABOUT ...

2 A Place

Tucked into the southern slope of the Mount of Olives is Bethany. Scholars believe the town derived its name from the indigenous palm trees. This meal took place in Bethany, at Simon the leper's home (Matt. 26:6). The triumphal entry started in Bethany and went to Jerusalem, which was a journey of less than two miles.

LOOK AT ...

Yesterday we focused on focus. Jesus implored the multitasking Martha to choose the better thing: time with Him. We must practice devotion because we are prone to wander and become distracted by the pressing things that come during the course of any day. There are so many things that beg for our attention—perhaps more in our generation than in any other. As in Martha's case, distraction with many things can indicate restlessness and an unsettled spirit. It's much easier to do (like Martha) than to be (like Mary). Jesus reminds us to keep the main thing the main thing.

Today, the lesson turns to the manifestation of devotion: worship. We will look at an evening in the presence of the Savior. Common things take on a beautiful fragrance when we are mindful of the Lord.

READ JOHN 12:1–3.

Then, six days before the Passover, Jesus came to Bethany, where Lazarus was who had been dead, whom He had raised from the dead. There they made Him a supper; and Martha served, but Lazarus was one of those who sat at the table with Him. Then Mary took a pound of very costly oil of spikenard, anointed the feet of Jesus, and wiped His feet with her hair. And the house was filled with the fragrance of the oil. John 12:1–3

1. Describe the time frame of this encounter and its importance.

2. What village did Jesus enter? In the above Scripture, circle the names of those who lived there.

3. Recount the miracle that occurred in the life of Lazarus. How might this have affected his life?

4. Underline and record the position each of the siblings assumed.

5. Describe what Mary did at the feet of Jesus.

6. In your own words, give a detailed description of the oil.

LIVE OUT ...

7. After his encounter with Jesus, Lazarus carried a tag line: "Raised from the dead." Read Romans 6:3–11.

   a. Explain what water baptism represents (vv. 3–4).

   b. How should this baptism affect our lives (vv. 5–6)?

   c. Describe the benefits of those who are "in the likeness of His resurrection" (v. 5; see vv. 7–11).

8. Anointing carried a variety of meanings. Fill in the following chart to discover others who were anointed.

SCRIPTURE	THOSE ANOINTED
1 Samuel 16:13	
Ezekiel 28:13–17	
Luke 4:18	
2 Corinthians 1:21	

9. The room filled with the fragrance of Mary's perfume. Paul said, "For we are to God the fragrance of Christ among those who are being saved and among those who are perishing" (2 Cor. 2:15).

   a. What is your favorite fragrance? Describe its scent, cost, and origin.

   b. Spray some of your perfume on this page as an offering to the Lord.

LEARN ABOUT ...

5 A Practice

Anointing (pouring oil on) someone was a rite to set that person apart. It was done at the inauguration or appointing of prophets, priests, and kings. Jesus was the Messiah, which meant "Anointed One." Anointing was also employed during hospitality or burial rites. In the New Testament, it is associated with the Holy Spirit.

6 A Fragrance

Spikenard, a famous perfume, came from distant areas such as Persia, Africa, and the Himalayan Mountains. The plant was sealed in alabaster boxes, and transport was costly. It was among the most desired plants of the ancients.

7 A Reputation

Like Lazarus, many characters in the Bible possessed a "tag line" that represented their reputation. Four times in John's gospel, John is described as the apostle "whom Jesus loved." James and John were known as the "sons of thunder." Imagine the honor of possessing a nickname from Jesus. What would yours be?

Learn About ...

9 An Aroma

Psalm 45, a messianic psalm, extols the coming of the great Bridegroom to receive His bride, the church. Verse 8 says, "All your garments are scented with myrrh and aloes and cassia." I believe when Jesus returns we will be in awe of the sights and sounds and the aromatic fragrance of His clothing.

c. Journal your praise to the King of Kings, the Anointed One. Let your hair down, your tears loose, and the fragrance flow.

○ ○ ● ○

Perfume traces its beginnings through antiquity. Earliest records of this sweet-smelling substance rise from ancient Egypt.[5] Burning the incense of aromatic herbs for religious services produced the Latin term *per fumus* (perfume), which means "through smoke."[6] It is believed that Tapputi, a chemist from Mesopotamia, was the first to refine the art.[7] In 2004, archaeologists uncovered a four-thousand-year-old perfumery in Cyprus that had the capacity to produce industrial amounts of the luxury liquid.[8] Frequently at the Roman games, emperors sprinkled sweet perfumes on the crowds through the awning in the amphitheater. It is said that Nero often showered his guests with specially blended potions. Perfume, like caviar or truffles, is costly to produce because of its scarcity.

Holding nothing back, Mary broke her prized alabaster box of rare perfume to pour on the Lord's feet. Once spilled, its fragrance was lost forever. Her tears, no doubt, flowed from the recesses of her heart. This was poetry in motion: broken vessels of earth and flesh streaming onto the Savior.

What is the most valuable item you possess? Grandma's china? Wedding silver? Framed art? Love letters? Imagine lavishly casting them before the Lord, never to be seen again. Shatter the china. Melt down the silver. Smash the art. Burn the letters like incense. Could you do this in adoration for the Lord? Like Mary's gift, it could be historic.

Listen To ...

If through a broken heart God can bring His purpose to pass in the world, then thank Him for breaking your heart.

—*Oswald Chambers*

DAY 4

Friend or Foe?

The term *friend or foe* originated during World War II. The invention of radar allowed the military to detect approaching aircraft before they were visible. The identification friend-or-foe system (IFF) enabled the radar to verify the aircraft as friendly.[9] If the IFF system received no reply or an invalid reply, it could be an enemy, or it could be friendly aircraft with battle damage or equipment failure.

Wouldn't it be great if humans possessed IFF systems? Have any of your former friends changed to foes? One day you're fellowshipping side by side, and the next you're the victim of their unkind gossip. The point of transition may go undetected, but the sudden realization is devastating: your friend was really a foe.

In his teaching, "Strong to the Finish," Craig Brian Larson states, "Think of Judas. Judas decided to follow Jesus. Judas heard Jesus teach. He went out two by two with the others, healing the sick and exorcising demons. Judas did a lot of disciple kinds of things. Yet he is remembered solely for how his relationship with Jesus ended. How a life, a ministry, or a relationship ends is absolutely crucial to everything that goes before it."[10] Sadly, in today's text we witness the relationship between Jesus and Judas decline from friend to foe.

LIFT UP ...

Lord Jesus, nothing hurts as much as the betrayal of a friend. I can't control what is done to me by others, but make me a loyal friend to my friends. In Jesus' name. Amen.

LOOK AT ...

Yesterday we focused on Mary's extravagant act of worship as she broke a priceless box of perfume for Jesus. Her actions equaled the offering as she humbly fell at His feet to wipe the oil with her hair—heart and hands in complete unity.

LEARN ABOUT ...

2 Betrayer

The Greek word translated "betray" is *paradidomi*, which literally means "to give into the hands." In the Bible, it usually applies to the actions of Judas: "For Jesus knew from the beginning who they were who did not believe, and who would betray Him" (John 6:64).

---

4 Barterer

A denarius was a Roman silver coin dated to the time of Jesus. Its original worth was the equivalent value of ten donkeys. During the New Testament era, the coin was valued at a laborer's daily wage: "He had agreed with the laborers for a denarius a day" (Matt. 20:2). Three hundred denarii equaled one year's income.

---

6 Banker

John revealed a secret: Judas stole from the ministry monies since he controlled the purse. Often we think our secret sins go unnoticed. But "there is nothing hidden which will not be revealed, nor has anything been kept secret but that it should come to light" (Mark 4:22).

Today we meet a disciple who was the opposite of this heroic woman: Judas Iscariot. His name derived from his hometown of Kerioth in southern Judah. This moniker distinguished him from the other disciple named Judas. Judas was the only Judean; all the others were Galileans. In a modern analogy, he was a city slicker surrounded by country bumpkins. Jesus must have seen something promising in Judas to include him as a follower. Notably, his name always comes last in the lists of the twelve disciples (Matt. 10:2–4 and Mark 3:16–19). His life tragically ended in suicide.

READ JOHN 12:4–6.

But one of His disciples, Judas Iscariot, Simon's son, who would betray Him, said, "Why was this fragrant oil not sold for three hundred denarii and given to the poor?" This he said, not that he cared for the poor, but because he was a thief, and had the money box; and he used to take what was put in it. John 12:4–6

1. Who spoke next?

2. Describe what we learn about him.

3. What question did Judas pose?

4. In your opinion, does his recommendation for the oil seem reasonable or spiritual? Explain.

5. Explain the motives behind Judas's murmuring.

6. In your own words, write a short obituary for his life.

LIVE OUT ...

7. Betrayal breaks the bond of intimacy. Only someone close to us possesses the potential to betray. Journal about a time one of your friends became a foe. How did it make you feel? What was the outcome?

8. Judas spiritualized his accusation against Mary by suggesting her extravagant gift should be donated to the poor. Read Luke 18:9–14.

   a. Why did Jesus tell this parable (v. 9)?

   b. Describe the Pharisee's actions and motives (vv. 10–12).

   c. Describe the tax collector's actions and attitude (v. 13).

   d. Who walked away justified? Explain why (v. 14).

9. Jesus holds Christians to a higher standard than unbelievers. He told his followers, "Forgive us our debts, as we forgive our debtors" (Matt. 6:12). Rewrite the following passage into a prayer for your enemies:

   > You have heard that it was said, "You shall love your neighbor and hate your enemy." But I say to you, love your enemies, bless those who curse you, do good to those who hate you, and pray for those who spitefully use you and persecute you, that you may be sons of your Father in heaven; for He makes His sun rise on the evil and on the good, and sends rain on the just and on the unjust. (Matt. 5:43–45)

LEARN ABOUT ...

7 Blocker

Although Judas possessed intimate access to Jesus, he opened his heart to Satan's influence. Each of us controls the door to our hearts. No one has access without our permission. Jesus beckons: "Behold, I stand at the door and knock. If anyone hears My voice and opens the door, I will come in to him" (Rev. 3:20).

8 Boaster

Man looks at the outward appearance, but God examines the heart (1 Sam. 16:7). On the outside, Judas seemed righteous in his request to help the poor. And Mary seemed reckless in wasting a year's wage in one gesture. The defining difference was motive. Mary moved out of adoration. Judas acted out of avarice. Jesus recognized the difference.

∘ ∘ ● ∘ ∘

In some cultures, during Easter weekend, a celebration known as "The Burning of Judas" takes place. On Good Friday, children build an effigy of Judas similar to a straw man. The stuffed figure is affixed to a pole and marched through the streets as the children beg, "A penny for Judas." They fill a bag with the collected coins and stuff it into the life-sized figure. Next they parade the dummy to a public arena while participants jeer, jab, and jostle the figure in what they call punishing Judas. Once they arrive at their destination, the effigy is hung and burned. Children scramble to pick up the coins as they fall from the flaming remnants.[11]

What a horrific way to be remembered. Judas began with great potential and ended his life in shame and scorn. What turned the heart of a person so close to Jesus? Scripture reveals no evidence that Judas was shunned by the other disciples or cold-shouldered by Jesus. In fact, Jesus dipped his bread in the same bowl as Judas, eating side by side. In the end, money caused his madness. Orin Philip Gifford wrote, "Ahab sold himself for a vineyard; Judas, a bag of silver; Achan, a wedge and a garment; Gehazi, silver and raiment. Are you for sale?"[12] Guard your heart from the things that might steal it away from Jesus.

LISTEN TO ...

To say the truth, so Judas kiss'd his Master, and cried, "All hail," whereas he meant all harm.

—*William Shakespeare*

Oil and Vinegar

O. Henry's short story "The Gift of the Magi" tells of a young couple living in a shabby flat. It was the day before Christmas, and Della had only $1.87 to buy a gift for her husband, Jim. She loved him more than anything in the world. What to do?

Jim and Della had only two items of value: Jim's gold watch inherited from his grandfather, and Della's cascade of brown hair that fell below her knees. To buy a platinum chain for his watch, Della determined to sell her precious hair to a wig store. At the same time, Jim sold his gold watch to buy her jeweled tortoiseshell combs for her hair. When Jim walked through the door, her sacrifice was obvious. Their dearest possessions were gone and the new gifts useless, yet they rejoiced in their obvious love and mutual sacrifice.[13]

Sometimes, despite our best efforts, we buy gifts that miss the mark. There is an art to gift giving, and it's as joyful to give the perfect gift as it is to receive it. What makes a good giver? A good gift-giver is usually an observant person who notices a need and reflects on how to creatively meet it. Timing is crucial; too much pondering, and the opportunity can be lost. Worse yet, becoming attached to the gift can mean the joy of giving and receiving were never realized.

Today we have the privilege of witnessing a wise woman who gave the perfect gift at the perfect time.

LIFT UP ...

Lord Jesus, make me sensitive to the Spirit's leading in my giving, my timing, and my works. In Jesus' name. Amen.

LOOK AT ...

Yesterday we took a somber look at Judas Iscariot. Although he occupied a privileged position in Jesus' group of confidants, he used his position to further his own interests and his

LEARN ABOUT ...

2 Burial

At burial it was customary to wrap the body in a cloth with spices, oils, and perfumes applied within the folds. After Jesus' birth, the magi gave Him the gift of myrrh, a burial spice, and once again, at the end of His earthly life, He was gifted with a burial substance.

---

3 Kept

We don't know how long Mary owned the treasured oil before this unprecedented moment. She may have kept it as a secret savings account should times get difficult, or maybe she was saving it for her own eventual burial. The Holy Spirit most certainly directed her to use it at this time in this way.

---

4 Legacy

Mary used her treasure at the perfect time, in the perfect way, for the perfect reason. Jesus promised her actions would be remembered: "Assuredly, I say to you, wherever this gospel is preached in the whole world, what this woman has done will also be told as a memorial to her" (Matt. 26:13).

own wealth. Judas was a "poser," pretending to be something he wasn't in order to obtain something he wanted.

Today, we once again consider Mary, the sister of Martha and Lazarus. Mary, who worshipped Jesus in lavish abandon, was now the object of judgment and criticism from none other than Judas. No surprise. As a thief in the convenient position of treasurer, he hated seeing something that could pad his pocket poured out on Jesus' feet. He was quick with self-righteous criticism. Jesus saw through this and defended Mary's actions. It's important to remember that when we are glorifying Him in our worship and giving, Jesus also defends our actions. Jesus promised that Mary's actions would be long remembered.

READ JOHN 12:7–8.

But Jesus said, "Let her alone; she has kept this for the day of My burial. For the poor you have with you always, but Me you do not have always." John 12:7–8

1. Who jumped to Mary's defense?

2. Jesus knew the significance of this particular gift given at this particular time. What was the significance of the oil?

3. Scripture tells us Mary *kept* the fragrant oil. Why would she own such an expensive and unusual item? Is there something you have been holding on to that the Holy Spirit is urging you to give?

4. We will all leave a legacy when we depart this earth. Check the boxes that could be what you are most remembered for.

   ❏ A forgiving spirit   ❏ Generous giving
   ❏ Real-estate portfolio   ❏ Banking portfolio

❑ Loving others   ❑ Being a great listener
❑ Gold and silver   ❑ A worshipful attitude
❑ Stocks and bonds   ❑ Debt

5. Loving Jesus came at a cost to Mary. Her adoration of the Lord brought a mixed bag of responses. We are told in the Scripture to count the cost (Luke 14:27–29). Draw a line from what Mary gave to what it cost.

WHAT SHE GAVE   **WHAT IT COST**
Timely worship   Judgment from others
A costly possession   Anger from family
Adoration over obligation   A legacy through the ages

LIVE OUT ...

6. Think about a time when the Holy Spirit prompted you to give up something that was holding you back. Mark those items that apply to you, and journal about what God gave you in return for your sacrifice.

❑ A harmful habit: _____

❑ A bad attitude: _____

❑ Unforgiveness/bitterness: _____

❑ The need to control: _____

❑ A destructive behavior: _____

❑ A hidden sin: _____

7. Look at your answers in the previous question. Are you holding on to something God is asking you to release? Write a prayer asking for His power to be perfected in your weakness (2 Cor. 12:9). Remind yourself that you can do all things through Christ who strengthens you (Phil. 4:13).

LEARN ABOUT ...

8 Listen

Mary was "tuned in" spiritually. The disciples were unable to absorb Jesus' prediction of His imminent death: "You know that after two days is the Passover, and the Son of Man will be delivered up to be crucified" (Matt. 26:2). Mary heard Jesus and acted in accordance with her faith in Him.

8. Mary was not only a listener; she was a "hearer." She had no ulterior motive by gifting Jesus with the oil. She was simply hanging on His every word and treasuring every moment. How are your listening, hearing, doing, and being skills?

a. Write about a time when listening to another was interrupted because you were busy planning what you were going to say next.

b. Sometimes giving requires letting go of something important. Have you missed an opportunity to give to someone because you resisted the urging of the Holy Spirit?

c. Regret has a long memory. Is there something you've thought about doing for someone? Do it now. Is there someone you need to speak to about the Lord? Speak now. Is there someone you need to forgive? Forgive now. Is there someone to whom you need to show love? Love now.

9. *Carpe diem* is the Latin phrase for "seize the day." The Bible tells us, "Today, if you will hear His voice, do not harden your hearts as in the rebellion" (Heb. 3:15). If you haven't done it before, give yourself the best gift ever. Journal a prayer asking Jesus to come into your heart and be Lord and Savior of your life.

o o • o o

Remember hope chests? For many years it was customary for young girls to keep a cedar chest filled with special things, often handmade, that would follow them into their own homes when they married. Sometimes those items took on such a special quality that the embroidered pillow slips never covered a pillow, grandma's hand-tied quilt remained folded in tissue paper, and the special silver candlesticks never held candles that would cast a warm glow across the dinner table.

When we value something greatly, we may be inclined to pack it away and save it for a day that never comes. And if we are not careful, our possessions can subtly begin to possess us.

Not Mary. She disregarded the potential judgment, criticism, and expense when she gave her lovely gift. She listened to her Lord and responded with decisive action and committed love. It's interesting to note that Mary was not among the women who came to the tomb to anoint Jesus' body and prepare Him for burial. They found He was not there. Mary seized her opportunity, gave her best, and is still remembered for it.

For the record: furniture stores no longer carry hope chests. Instead, the fragrant cedar boxes are now called "memory chests" or "blanket chests." I like *hope* a lot better.

If you haven't done it already, pull out the embroidered pillow slips and put them on your pillows, light the candles, and cuddle under the quilt. Gifts are for being used.

LISTEN TO ...

Do not keep the alabaster boxes of your love and tenderness sealed up until your friends are dead. Fill their lives with sweetness. Speak approving, cheering words while their ears can hear them and while their hearts can be thrilled by them.

—Anonymous

Red Lentil Soup

Esau sold Jacob his birthright for a bowl of red lentil stew (Gen. 25:34). In both the Old and New Testament eras, legumes were incredibly popular—the most desirable being lentils. Historians believe that after grains, beans held the highest place in most diets because of their protein content. Lentils grow annually and can be eaten fresh. Often dried and stored for later, they served as a staple for ancient kitchens. Lentils can also be served sweet. First the lentils are toasted, then ground and rolled in honey. Finally the balls are fried and served warm.

Both Egypt and Syria produce lentils of the red variety. The Hebrew word for red is *edom*. In the land of Edom, the ground consisted largely of red rock and soil. Lentils grew plentifully, and they may explain the origin of the land's name.

Preparation Time: 15 minutes
Cook Time: 45 minutes

Ingredients:

> 6 cups chicken stock
> 1 1/2 cup red lentils
> 3 tablespoons olive oil
> 1 tablespoon minced garlic
> 1 large onion, chopped
> 1 leek, chopped
> 1 tablespoon ground cumin
> 1/2 teaspoon cayenne pepper
> 1/2 teaspoon of turmeric
> 1/2 cup chopped cilantro
> 3/4 cup fresh lemon juice

Instructions:

1. Bring chicken stock and lentils to a boil in a large saucepan over high heat, then reduce

heat to medium-low, cover, and simmer for thirty minutes or until lentils disintegrate. If too thick, add more water (some prefer their lentils soft yet retaining their shape).

2. Meanwhile, heat olive oil in a skillet over medium heat. Stir in garlic and onion, and cook until the onion has softened and turned translucent, about three minutes.

3. Stir onions into the lentils and season with cumin and cayenne. Continue simmering until the lentils are tender, about ten minutes (some serve their soup at this stage while others serve it pureed as in step 4).

4. Carefully puree the soup in a standing blender or with a hand blender until smooth. Garnish with cilantro, lemon juice, and croutons before serving. Alternate garnish of sour cream or plain yogurt is recommended.

GRACE NOTE

Lord,

   Esau traded his birthright for a bowl of soup. Our earthly needs and hunger can blind us to long-term logic and wisdom. Help us remain so fixed on You that we avoid impulsive and foolish decisions. In Jesus' name. Amen.

LESSON SIX

Guess Who's Coming to Dinner?

Luke 19:1-27

Being a pastor's wife for over thirty years has taught me to go with the flow. On occasion my husband has surprised me with unexpected guests. The first time I met Franklin Graham, Skip called from the airport to let me know *they* were on their way home for dinner. I scrambled to clean up a mess here and stir up a pot there. However, Skip's not the only one to welcome in strangers without advance warning. Once, I ran to the market while dinner cooked in the oven. Outside the store stood a homeless man with a "Will Work for Food" sign. God nudged me to invite him home. The shock on Skip's face was priceless. Naturally, our son, Nathan, comes by this trait honestly. He's invited complete unknowns to join him for lunch at fast-food restaurants.

Scripture reminds us, "Do not forget to entertain strangers, for by so doing some have unwittingly entertained angels" (Heb. 13:2). Likely, Jesus referred to Abraham, who received two visitors at dinnertime who were on their way to Sodom. The patriarch prepared them a meal fit for a king. Only after eating did the strangers reveal who they were, where they were going, and what they were doing.

As we look at today's text, we'll notice that Zacchaeus received the unexpected joy of dining with Jesus. Does the idea of inviting a stranger in for supper seem outside your comfort zone? Let me encourage you to take a couple of baby steps. How about buying fast-food gift cards to hand out to the homeless? Or you could prepare a couple of nonperishable sack lunches to carry in your car for those in need. You never know who's coming to dinner.

DAY 1

What's for Dinner?

LIFT UP ...

Father God, I want to be Your ambassador—a woman of grace and acceptance. My tendency is to incline myself to what is comfortable and predictable. Expand my vision to see the needs of others and to take tangible actions. In Jesus' name. Amen.

LOOK AT ...

So far in our study, we've seen Jesus and His disciples drop in for several unexpected meals. It's uncertain whether Jesus' disciples were included on the wedding list in Cana. The woman at the well never dreamed her day would include refreshments with the Savior. In lesson 5, Mary and Martha welcomed the Lord's interruption like a grand invitation. Today, Zacchaeus joins the list of those whom the Lord surprised at suppertime.

Whether you realize it or not, Jesus joins you at every meal. The question is, do you acknowledge Him? Christians say grace not just to thank God for His provision, but also to praise Him for His presence. A plaque reads: "Christ is the head of this house, the unseen guest at every meal, the unseen listener to every conversation." What a privilege!

READ LUKE 19:1–5.

Then Jesus entered and passed through Jericho. Now behold, there was a man named Zacchaeus who was a chief tax collector, and he was rich. And he sought to see who Jesus was, but could not because of the crowd, for he was of short stature. So he ran ahead and climbed up into a sycamore tree to see Him, for He was going to pass that way. And when Jesus came to the place, He looked up and saw him, and said to him, "Zacchaeus, make haste and come down, for today I must stay at your house." Luke 19:1–5

LEARN ABOUT ...

1 The Place

Jericho was where the walls came tumbling down when Joshua and the children of Israel entered the Promised Land. It is one of the oldest cities in the Jordan plain. Jericho is known as "the city of palms," since the region is filled with date palms, which were included in the many fruits of Canaan.

2 The Person

Zacchaeus seemed the least likely candidate to host the Savior during His stay in Jericho. The Jews considered tax collectors enemies. Tax collectors served Rome and often overtaxed residents to line their own pockets with wealth. Jesus said, "I did not come to call the righteous, but sinners, to repentance" (Mark 2:17).

6 The Purpose

Jesus loves relationships. When He passed through towns and villages, He called out specific citizens he might greet and meet and eat with. Sharing a meal differs vastly from spending a moment in passing. Time in the Savior's presence is always transformative. Zacchaeus would never be the same—because Jesus tarried with him.

1. Where did this encounter take place?

2. Describe the man who lived in Jericho.

3. What phrase describes this man's intent?

4. Describe the obstacles he encountered.

5. How did he overcome these obstacles? What does this reveal about his heart?

6. Describe the Lord's response to him, and explain why He responded this way.

LIVE OUT ...

7. Jesus spotted Zacchaeus up a tree. Often in life's extreme situations, we feel forsaken. Instead, these are the perfect places to gain God's attention. Rewrite the following passage into a personal prayer:

> Hear my cry, O God;
>> Attend to my prayer.
> From the end of the earth I will cry to You,
>> When my heart is overwhelmed;
>> Lead me to the rock that is higher than I.
> For You have been a shelter for me,
>> A strong tower from the enemy. (Ps. 61:1–3)

8. a. Zacchaeus overcame several obstacles to encounter Jesus. He was short in stature, the object of discrimination, and a cheat. List some obstacles you face in your pursuit of God.

b. Journal a prayer asking God for strength to rise above roadblocks. Praise Him for giving you grace for today.

9. James said, "Draw near to God, and He will draw near to you" (James 4:8). When Zacchaeus reached out to Jesus, the Lord responded with a dinner invitation. Using the word DRAW as an acrostic, list the ways you will draw closer to God:

D

R

A

W

° ° ● ○ ○

Imagine if Jesus visited your hometown. What price would you pay to see Him? Would you ...

... rise early or stay up late?

... stand in long lines for hours?

... fight enthusiastic crowds?

... sit in the cheap seats?

... risk public disapproval?

... suffer hunger or discomfort?

... walk a long distance?

... lose a day's wage?

My heart cries a resounding, *Yes!* But my flesh fights. Deep inside I hedge. Perhaps I'd turn off the alarm to get a few extra winks. The long lines and crowded streets might discourage. And if the throngs disliked me, I'd shrink back. Let's face it: Jesus offers to meet us daily. But do we make the appointment, or do we allow hurdles to hinder us? Zacchaeus, a social outcast, overcame all obstacles to get a glimpse of the Savior. His zeal makes me jealous.

LEARN ABOUT ...

7 The Point

Jesus visited Jericho. Perhaps the sole reason for the Savior to pass by was His meeting with Zacchaeus. The Lord found Hagar in the wilderness, seeking solace under a shrub. Moses met the Lord on the back side of the desert beside a burning bush. When you're out on a limb—God's ready to rescue!

8 The Problem

Zacchaeus had self-inflicted problems. His hoarded gold and chosen profession brought neither pleasure nor gratification. Instead, they isolated him from others. But he had heard of the One who welcomed sinners and satisfied empty hearts.

Thankfully, Jesus understood that: "The spirit indeed is willing, but the flesh is weak" (Matt. 26:41). Several saints faced this same struggle. The Lord warned Peter that haters would make him a traitor. David, the man after God's heart, lamented over his fragile humanity. Paul admitted, "For I know that in me (that is, in my flesh) nothing good dwells; for to will is present with me, but how to perform what is good I do not find" (Rom. 7:18).

What is the solution to conquer our bothersome bodies? The Spirit of God! The same Spirit that raised Jesus from the dead breathes resurrection life into your soul (Rom. 8:11). Without God we accomplish nothing—but with Him, all things are possible.

LISTEN TO ...

Living one day in the Spirit is worth more than a thousand lived in the flesh.

—*Richard Owen Roberts*

DAY 2

Lost and Found

Recently, I went to a nice department store to help a friend accessorize an outfit for a special occasion. I took off one of my diamond stud earrings to try on a funky piece of costume jewelry. As I untwisted the back of the earring, I thought, *Lenya, don't put this on the counter. You'll forget to pick it up.* Ignoring the cautionary voice within, I fell in love with the shiny baubles, paid for them, and promptly left the store—and my diamond earring—behind. Hours later, as our family ate dinner, I remembered: "Oh no! I left my diamond earring at the store."

My son said, "Mom, that was dumb. You'll never get it back."

"Oh yes I will," I responded. "I believe in prayer and that people do good things."

After prayer, I called the store to share my plight. And wouldn't you know it—the earring was behind the counter, safely tucked away in a bag. I retrieved it first thing the next day.

Jesus understood that something more valuable than a diamond earring waited in the lost and found of life. He came to seek and save lost human beings. You might say these people (including me) were diamonds in the rough. They included prostitutes, murderers, and thieves. Before salvation, we wallowed at the bottom of the lost-and-found heap: a single mitten, a broken pair of glasses, a tattered paperback book. But when the Master retrieved us, we became jewels of joy.

Lift Up ...

Dear Lord, I am drawn to the smart, the shiny, the lovely, and the tidy. I'm not sure I would notice someone who was a diamond in the rough—a person just waiting to be cut and polished into Your divine image. Give me Your Jeweler's eye to recognize and nurture those people. In Jesus' name. Amen.

LEARN ABOUT ...

1 Action and Attitude

Zacchaeus didn't need
to be asked twice. He
quickly descended from his
lofty perch at the Lord's
invitation. His attitude
matched his actions; he
received the Savior joyfully.
Feelings follow acts of
faith. Previously, sin held
Zacchaeus in sorrow.
But obedience made him
overjoyed. What do your
actions and attitudes reveal?

---

5 Repent and Restore

The Mosaic law introduced
an additional response to
repentance. If a thief stole
property, true repentance
included making restitution.
For instance, if property was
stolen, the item had to be
returned with 20 percent
interest. Zacchaeus offered
double the amount required
by the law. His repentance
matched the severity of his
crime.

LOOK AT ...

Previously, we witnessed a small man with a huge heart refuse to let
anything block his access to the Savior. The tax collector behaved like a
schoolboy as he scrambled up the sycamore tree. The Bible encourages
us to have childlike hearts. Jesus said, "Unless you are converted and
become as little children, you will by no means enter the kingdom of
heaven" (Matt. 18:3).

The great thing about children is that they are teachable, tender, and
turnable. Teachable just means receptive. Kids don't have lots of precon-
ceived prejudices that block the Lord's instruction. With tender, humble
hearts, children don't mind showing their inner feelings outwardly. And
finally, they turn around quickly when corrected for wrong behavior. As
an adult, do you possess a childlike heart like Zacchaeus?

READ LUKE 19:6–10.

*So he made haste and came down, and received Him joyfully. But when
they saw it, they all complained, saying, "He has gone to be a guest with a
man who is a sinner."*

*Then Zacchaeus stood and said to the Lord, "Look, Lord, I give half
of my goods to the poor; and if I have taken anything from anyone by false
accusation, I restore fourfold."*

*And Jesus said to him, "Today salvation has come to this house, because
he also is a son of Abraham; for the Son of Man has come to seek and to save
that which was lost." Luke 19:6–10*

1. Underline the three things Zacchaeus did in response to the Lord's
    invitation. List them below.

2. Describe who witnessed this and how they responded.

3. In your own words, explain the accusation they made.

4. What action on the part of Zacchaeus makes you think he overheard the crowd?

5. What two things did Zacchaeus offer as a sign of his repentance?

6. Explain how the Lord responded to the repentance of Zacchaeus.

7. What reasons did the Savior give for His interaction with Zacchaeus?

LIVE OUT ...

8. The faith of Zacchaeus led to feelings of jubilation. Fill in the following columns with your acts of faith that led to positive feelings.

FAITHFUL ACTS   **FEELING GOOD**

9. The Bible instructs us about sins of commission (wrongs that we do) and sins of omission (rights that we don't do). To repent, we must not only stop doing wrong but also start doing right. Fill in the appropriate columns to repent of your sins.

STOP WRONG   **START RIGHT**

LEARN ABOUT ...

7 Seek and Save

Jesus came to seek and save the lost. Some search for God as though He were lost. Instead, the sinner is lost. You did not find Jesus—He found you: "If a man has a hundred sheep, and one of them goes astray, does he not leave the ninety-nine and go to the mountains to seek the one that is straying?" (Matt. 18:12).

8 Feelings and Faith

Feelings rarely lead us in the right direction. That's why the prophet Jeremiah warned, "The human heart is the most deceitful of all things, and desperately wicked. Who really knows how bad it is?" (Jer. 17:9 NLT). If we act according to our emotions, we'll be led astray. But living by faith leads to peace, joy, and happiness.

9 Stop and Start

True repentance stops doing wrong and starts doing good. Paul said, "Let him who stole steal no longer, but rather let him labor, working with his hands what is good.... Let no corrupt word proceed out of your mouth, but what is good for necessary edification" (Eph. 4:28–29). Through his changed life, Zacchaeus proved his repentance was real.

10. Jesus went to great lengths to seek and save you. In response, He wants you to seek Him always. Rewrite the following Scripture into a personal prayer:

> And do not seek what you should eat or what you should drink, nor have an anxious mind. For all these things the nations of the world seek after, and your Father knows that you need these things. But seek the kingdom of God, and all these things shall be added to you. (Luke 12:29–31)

○ ○ ● ○ ○

I was a thief. I can't believe I just typed those four words. For several moments I left that sentence hanging … I squirmed. I contemplated deleting those words. I felt raw and exposed. What would you think about me after reading them? Then I remembered a phrase from my past: our repentance must be as notorious as our crime.

The robbery happened a long time ago, over thirty years, back in my college days. I worked for a music store, and a friend worked in a clothing store in the same mall. We made a pact to turn a blind eye as each shoplifted items from the other's place of business. I guess that makes me a conspirator, too. We never got caught, yet I wonder if my friend remembers this with similar shame and sadness.

During my sophomore year I got radically saved—just like Zacchaeus. One Sunday my pastor taught on the principles of repentance and restitution. I'd confessed that sin and many others months earlier. But the idea of restitution plagued me. While revisiting my college alma mater, I knew I must go to the store and offer to pay for my crimes. How humiliating! Honestly, I didn't have a dollar amount. I couldn't remember. Amazingly, the manager refused my offer, saying something about the register not balancing at the end of the night. I left with a sense of liberty—amazed at the grace that saved a wretch like me.

LISTEN TO …

Honest restitution is a mark of honest repentance.

—Anonymous

DAY 3

Dinner Conversation

We plan our menus for mealtime; why not plan our conversations, too? Good food and good conversation complement one another. Whether it's fast food with the family, roast turkey with relatives, or dinner on a first date, your discussions can leave a sweet or sour aftertaste.

Here's some advice:

- Know your audience, whether office associates or next-door neighbors.
- Agree to one conversation at a time. Cross-table talk is rude and distracting.
- Turn off all electronic devices. Give those present your undivided presence.
- Discussions begin and end at the table. The meal is finished when all are finished.
- Ask open-ended questions instead of those that require yes-or-no answers.
- Show your interest by asking a follow-up question instead of regaining attention.

Open-ended questions may include: What superpower would you like to possess and why? If you could invite a historical figure to dinner, who would it be? Where in the world would you like to visit? You might choose a word for the day. For example, *enthrall.* Discussion follows a definition with the challenge to use the word in a sentence the next day.

Dinnertime conversation shouldn't be a strain. While it is natural to talk about your day or the meal, there are many other great topics that can fill the void. Use these ideas to avoid awkward silences. Jesus was an excellent conversationalist. He knew how to engage those at the dinner table with questions and direct attention. Today, we'll see Him tell a story.

LIFT UP ...

Lord Jesus, cultivate in me the art of conversation. Through my words, allow Your love and interest in others to flow through me. Teach me to be a quiet listener, a kind questioner, a respectful thinker, and a loving friend. In Jesus' name. Amen.

LEARN ABOUT ...

2 Parables

The intent of a parable is to lay alongside parallel truths for comparison. These earthly stories always included a heavenly meaning. Veiled to the hearts of unbelievers, they served to enlighten believers to greater kingdom insight: "I will open My mouth in parables; I will utter things kept secret from the foundation of the world" (Matt. 13:35).

3 Perceptions

Most people misunderstood the meaning of our Lord's first coming. Many expected that Jesus brought political salvation to overthrow the Romans who oppressed the Jews in Palestine. Because He neared Jerusalem, the crowds thought earthly freedom and splendor drew close. Instead, Jesus met His persecutors and brought freedom from sin on the cross.

LOOK AT ...

Salvation came to the house of Zacchaeus through the words of the Savior. Out in the open (rather than behind closed doors), Jesus emphasized that deliverance had arrived "today." Likely the Lord made this public display because the accusers of Zacchaeus were so outwardly vocal. While others gossiped, Jesus gave absolution. Salvation implied deliverance or rescue and carried the idea of safety.

Now we'll see a further contrast between those invited to dinner. Jesus told a parable that revealed the intent in the hearts of those who accused Zacchaeus. Simultaneously, Jesus exposed souls—those who were repentant and those who were self-righteous. While comforting some, He condemned others.

READ LUKE 19:11–14.

Now as they heard these things, He spoke another parable, because He was near Jerusalem and because they thought the kingdom of God would appear immediately. Therefore He said: "A certain nobleman went into a far country to receive for himself a kingdom and to return. So he called ten of his servants, delivered to them ten minas, and said to them, 'Do business till I come.' But his citizens hated him, and sent a delegation after him, saying, 'We will not have this man to reign over us.'" Luke 19:11–14

1. Review yesterday's lesson. What things were heard and by whom?

2. What teaching technique did Jesus employ?

3. What reason did Luke give for this teaching method?

4. Describe the main character of this parable and his circumstances.

5. In your own words, explain the arrangement he made with his servants.

6. Describe how the servants felt and why.

7. Explain how they responded to their feelings.

Live Out ...

8. Jesus shared kingdom parables that taught principles of His coming kingdom. Fill in the following chart to discover more about the kingdom of heaven.

SCRIPTURE	KINGDOM OF HEAVEN
Matthew 5:3	
Matthew 5:19	
Matthew 7:21	
Matthew 13:44–47	

9. John's gospel underscores Jesus' tragic rejection at His first coming. Read John 1:10–13.

a. In your own words, summarize verse 10.

b. Who do you think "His own" included? What did they do (v. 11)?

c. Who received the Lord and what was the outcome (v. 12)?

d. Compare and contrast the two bloodlines described in v. 13.

LEARN ABOUT ...

6 Portrayed

Jesus portrayed Himself as a royal nobleman, the son of David who came from heaven to the "far country" earth in order to gain His inheritance. Before returning to glory, He entrusted His servants with treasure. Sadly, they "hated" Him and refused His rule. The rebellious Jewish leaders were exposed while the grateful sinners were enfolded in grace.

8 Paradox

The kingdom of heaven is a paradox. In fact, heaven's rules often run in direct opposition to the world's order. For instance: The poor become rich. The weak are made strong. The first are last. And the meek inherit the earth. Godly advice? "The kingdom of God is at hand. Repent, and believe in the gospel" (Mark 1:15).

9 Populace

Jesus was not well received by religious and political leaders. Shockingly, "the common people heard Him gladly" (Mark 12:37). Often it was not the white-collar executives that accepted the Lord, but the blue-collar, hardworking people that gladly received Him. Make sure that titles, degrees, or bank accounts don't hinder your faith.

10. If Jesus is not Lord of all, He is not Lord at all. Have you surrendered your entire life to Jesus, the King of Kings? List the various areas of your life that you have submitted to God:

· · • · ·

Black Like Me documents the true story of John Howard Griffin, a white man who believed he could never understand the plight of African Americans unless he became like one. During the tumultuous civil rights era, under a doctor's supervision, John darkened his skin with medication, sun lamps, and stains. He went so far as to crop his hair to the scalp and shave his hands. Afterward he traveled the racially segregated states of Louisiana, Mississippi, Alabama, and Georgia by hitchhiking or riding a Greyhound bus.

At a diner, a black man commiserated with John about the difficulties in finding a public restroom. On another occasion, John refused to yield his seat to a white child while African Americans on the bus glared at him. The mother blurted aloud how uppity black people were becoming. By the 1970s, the hostility and threats against Griffin and his family forced them to move away from America to Mexico.[1]

This classic book helped Caucasians empathize with the humiliation and discrimination that African Americans faced daily. In like manner, Jesus became flesh and dwelt among us. He left heaven, His Father, and adoring angels to become one of us. He walked dusty roads, ate meager meals, and was rejected by those He came to meet. The prophet Isaiah predicted, "He [was] despised and rejected by men, a Man of sorrows and acquainted with grief" (Isa. 53:3). Discrimination hurts, whether racial, religious, or social. And it hurts the heart of God, too. He knows the stinging pain of rejection. But His rejection brought our acceptance.

LISTEN TO ...

Try Jesus before you reject him.

—*Anonymous*

DAY 4
Awkward Moment

The phrase *awkward moment* has really caught on. When I did a web search, over half a million hits popped up. Certain sites asked the viewer to blog their most awkward moment with the promise of no judgment. Facebook records a list of "Ten of the Most Awkward Moments." Even Oprah felt compelled to share her most awkward moment. In 2008 *TIME* magazine got in on the act, reporting that George Bush dancing while waiting for John McCain was the year's number one awkward moment.[2] Do you have a memorable moment of awkwardness?

Recently, I experienced this phenomenon. I busted out my flip-flops on the first warm day of spring. While running late for a hair appointment, I burst out of my car, hit the curb with my sandal, and flew several feet forward before doing a full body plant on the sidewalk. I jumped up to look this way and that. Whew! No one was in sight. When I walked into the salon I asked, "Did you see that?" Everyone nodded and pointed to the huge window. Awkward!

Today, we'll witness the nobleman as he requires an accounting for the investment he left with three servants. One servant in particular gets publicly reprimanded. It's likely he never lived down the disappointment of that day. Don't let your most awkward moment occur before the judgment seat of God. What a shame to realize you squandered salvation or the opportunity to store riches in heaven.

LIFT UP ...

Lord, I can't help the occasional trip and fall that comes with life, but I want to stand steady and sure in Your presence. Make me mindful and sensitive to serving You in light of Your standards and Your power. In Jesus' name. Amen.

LOOK AT ...

Jesus told this story in Jericho, where Herod Archelaus possessed a palace. He had been proclaimed ruler of the region of Judea when his father, Herod the Great, died in 4 BC and

LEARN ABOUT ...

2 Mina

A mina was both a weight and a unit of money. It weighed about a pound and was equivalent to about sixty shekels. During this time, one mina was worth "about one hundred days of an average working wage." Although not as valuable as a *talent*, described in another parable, the minas revealed whether the servants could be trusted to increase the nobleman's treasure.

divided his kingdom among four men. However, before Archelaus could inherit his kingdom, Rome had the right to ratify the division since Palestine fell under its jurisdiction. The Jews of Judea sent fifty ambassadors to Caesar Augustus, asking him to refuse the kingship of Archelaus. Caesar confirmed his inheritance but withheld the title of king. All of those listening to Jesus' parable understood this historical precedent.[3]

This parable had a heavenly parallel. Just as the Jews rejected Rome's king, they would reject the King of Kings. After the crucifixion, Stephen reminded the religious leaders of their stiff-necked attitude toward Jesus: "Which of the prophets did your fathers not persecute? And they killed those who foretold the coming of the Just One, of whom you now have become the betrayers and murderers" (Acts 7:52).

READ LUKE 19:15–24.

And so it was that when he returned, having received the kingdom, he then commanded these servants, to whom he had given the money, to be called to him, that he might know how much every man had gained by trading. Then came the first, saying, "Master, your mina has earned ten minas." And he said to him, "Well done, good servant; because you were faithful in a very little, have authority over ten cities." And the second came, saying, "Master, your mina has earned five minas." Likewise he said to him, "You also be over five cities."

Then another came, saying, "Master, here is your mina, which I have kept put away in a handkerchief. For I feared you, because you are an austere man. You collect what you did not deposit, and reap what you did not sow." And he said to him, "Out of your own mouth I will judge you, you wicked servant. You knew that I was an austere man, collecting what I did not deposit and reaping what I did not sow. Why then did you not put my money in the bank, that at my coming I might have collected it with interest?"

And he said to those who stood by, "Take the mina from him, and give it to him who has ten minas." Luke 19:15–24

1. Think back to yesterday's lesson. Where did the nobleman travel, and for what purpose?

2. What did he do upon his return, and why?

3. Describe the results of the first servant's actions.

4. How did the nobleman respond? Why?

5. Describe the results of the second servant's actions.

6. How did the nobleman respond? Why?

7. Describe the actions and underline the attitude of the third servant.

8. How did the nobleman respond? Why?

Live Out ...

9. The mina represented a test of trust. Could the servants be trusted with treasure? Read Luke 16:10–13.

   a. Describe the test. What terms are used to describe those who passed or failed the test (v. 10)?

   b. List the two entities that God used to test hearts (vv. 11–12).

   c. List the three opposites that Jesus contrasted in this text (v. 13).

Learn About ...

4 Many

God rewards us for financial faithfulness as well as for our stewardship over time, spiritual fruit, and sacrifice: "Everyone who has left houses or brothers or sisters or father or mother or wife or children or lands, for My name's sake, shall receive a hundredfold, and inherit eternal life" (Matt. 19:29).

7 Master

The word *master* means "superintendent or overseer." It describes someone who possesses complete control, authority, or power over another individual. The disciples often called Jesus, "Master": "Simon answered, 'Master, we've worked hard all night'" (Luke 5:5 NIV). This parable reminds us that as Lord, Jesus is the Master of our lives.

9 Mammon

Mammon represents wealth or riches. Jesus contrasted the two: "No one can serve two masters; for either he will hate the one and love the other, or else he will be loyal to the one and despise the other. You cannot serve God and mammon" (Matt. 6:24).

10. a. Place a check in the box that corresponds to items over which you've been a good steward:

❑ Your time   ❑ Your church

❑ Your finances   ❑ Your calling

❑ Your resources   ❑ Your family

❑ Your opportunities   ❑ Your talents

❑ Your health   ❑ Your community

❑ Your soul   ❑ Other _____

b. Journal a prayer asking God to help you to be a more faithful steward. Commit all that He's given you to build up His kingdom.

11. Our Master is an excellent mathematician. Fill in the following charts to discover His equations.

SCRIPTURE	MATHEMATICAL METHOD
Genesis 1:4	
Exodus 1:20	
Deuteronomy 1:10	
Psalm 136:13	
Proverbs 10:22	

o o ● o o

"Use it or lose it" encapsulates the lesson of this parable. This principle rings true in several realms. When we exercise, we gain muscle mass. The more we work out, the firmer we get. But once we stop, everything slips. The lazier we are, the flabbier we become.

The same principle relates to language. In high school, I took two years of Spanish. When our class traveled to Spain, I conversed reasonably well. Decades later, I can barely remember *por favor* and *gracias*. However, Schwarzenegger ensured I'd never forget *Hasta la vista, baby*. Practice makes perfect.

"Use it or lose it" applies spiritually, too. I saw a sign on a church that read, "Seven Days Without the Word of God Makes One Weak." So true! Jesus encouraged us to pray, "Give us this day our daily bread" (Matt. 6:11). Job said, "I have treasured the words of His mouth more than my necessary food" (Job 23:12). We must never take a spiritual diet.

But hearing God's Word is not enough. We must also be "doers" who live out what we hear. Faith in God's Word is like a muscle: the more we act on it, the more spiritual stamina we develop. Praying leads to answered prayers. Claiming God's promises makes us spiritually rich; but if we neglect His Word, refrain from prayer, and leave His promises unclaimed, we lose ground and weaken our faith. Paul said, "For bodily exercise profits a little, but godliness is profitable for all things" (1 Tim. 4:8).

Listen To ...

The possessor of heaven and earth ... placed you here not as a proprietor but a steward.

—*John Wesley*

DAY 5
Turning the Tables

Three servants received one mina. The first increased his amount tenfold. His reward wasn't rest, but more work. Ruling over ten cities increased the commitment and opportunity for fruitfulness. William Barclay wrote, "The greatest compliment we can pay anyone is the offer of even greater and harder tasks to do. The great reward of God to the person who has satisfied the test is more trust."[4]

The second servant multiplied his inheritance, but to a lesser degree. He was rewarded similarly by receiving the rule of five cities for the increase of five minas. This is like the parable of the sower: "But he who received seed on the good ground is he who hears the word and understands it, who indeed bears fruit and produces: some a hundredfold, some sixty, some thirty" (Matt. 13:23). We produce according to our individual capacity.

The third servant squandered the opportunity to increase his investment. He did not lose the mina; he simply hoarded it. Commentator Norval Geldenhuys explained, "Whosoever neglects his opportunities and is unfaithful in the Lord's service will become spiritually impoverished, will receive still fewer opportunities for service and will appear poor and naked before His throne at his second advent."[5]

Today we'll observe the end of those who refused the king's rule. The tables will turn on them. The rejecters will be rejected.

Lift Up ...

Heavenly Father, help me understand that miserly actions and timid thinking yield miserly and timid results. Remind me that it's Your wealth and Your courage at my fingertips—not my own. Thank You, Father. In Jesus' name. Amen.

3 Unfair

The crowd claimed the king's justice was unfair. Paul spoke of a judgment seat not of sin, but of works: "If anyone's work is burned, he will suffer loss; but he himself will be saved, yet so as through fire" (I Cor. 3:15). The Christian's works will be tried by fire. The danger is to be left with nothing but salvation.

5 Unwilling

Those who refuse God's reign find themselves excluded from His kingdom. God does not force Himself upon sinners. Jesus said, "Behold, I stand at the door and knock. If anyone hears My voice and opens the door, I will come in to him and dine with him, and he with Me" (Rev. 3:20).

LOOK AT ...

We've learned that the mina in this parable represented various things, the most obvious being treasures and the most important being the gospel. God expects us to invest our time and talents wisely for the kingdom's sake. In this parable, unlike the parable of the talents, each person received the same amount. Salvation is equal to all who receive it. But what do we do with so great a salvation? When we share this free gift with those around us, we multiply God's family. We must fulfill the Great Commission: "Go into all the world and preach the gospel to every creature" (Mark 16:15).

We should not be content to go to heaven alone. Jesus issued a broad invitation when He said, "For God so loved the world that He gave His only begotten Son, that whoever believes in Him should not perish but have everlasting life" (John 3:16). Are you a good steward of the gospel of grace?

READ LUKE 19:25–27.

(But they said to him, "Master, he has ten minas.") "For I say to you, that to everyone who has will be given; and from him who does not have, even what he has will be taken away from him. But bring here those enemies of mine, who did not want me to reign over them, and slay them before me." Luke 19:25–27

1. Review yesterday's lesson, and summarize the story we're examining.

2. What did the nobleman do with the mina squandered by the third servant? Why?

3. How did the crowd respond to this action?

4. Describe the two outcomes possible for those given responsibility.

5. Who did the nobleman request be brought before him? Explain who they represented.

6. Why were they brought forward?

7. What was their fate?

LIVE OUT ...

8. The three servants were rewarded according to their outcome. The more they gained, the more they received. However, a reward was withheld from the servant with no returns. Instead he lost his original investment. In your own words, describe the difference between fairness and justice. Give an illustration of this principle from your own life.

9. This parable highlighted those who say, "No, Lord," whether in outright rebellion or passive resistance. Is God telling you to do something that you are answering with, "No"? If so, journal a prayer of repentance, surrendering your will to your Master. Let Him rule in every realm of your life.

10. The gospel has the ability to turn us from enemies of Christ into heirs in Christ.

    a. Make a list of those you know who are enemies of Christ (James 4:4).

LEARN ABOUT ...

7 Undone

Those brought to the king are those who refused his reign. The imagery of slaying enemies before a potentate comes from ancient Eastern custom: "For judgment is without mercy to the one who has shown no mercy" (James 2:13). Jesus will return with a sword and a robe dipped in blood to subdue His enemies.

8 Unwise

Only when we compare ourselves to others do things seem unfair. Paul warned the Corinthians, "For we dare not class ourselves or compare ourselves with those who commend themselves. But they, measuring themselves by themselves, and comparing themselves among themselves, are not wise" (2 Cor. 10:12). Life is not fair—but God is good!

9 Unyielding

No and *Lord* are contradictory words in the context of God's leading. The word *Lord*, similar to *master*, implies ownership, rule, possession, and authority. If Jesus is your Lord, then the only proper response to His requests is, "Yes." Remember when Peter said, "Not so, Lord!" (Acts 10:9–17)? The Lord repeated the command three more times before Peter yielded.

b. Dedicate a consistent time to pray for them (such as every Monday morning).

c. Decide how and when you will share the good news of Jesus Christ with them.

∘ ∘ • ∘ ∘

Do you have any enemies? Your first instinct may be to say no. Sadly, we all have people in our past or present who wish us harm or avoid our company. Have you ever lost a friend over a squabble? Do any of your relatives rub you the wrong way? Are there celebrities or politicians you despise? An enemy can simply be one who harms or opposes us.

Jesus had enemies. And He predicted that we would too. He went so far as to say, "Your enemies will be right in your own household" (Matt. 10:36 NLT)! In fact, before salvation, we were God's enemies (Rom. 5:10). It is often said that you can know a person by their friends. Well, you can know a person by their enemies, too. Scottish poet Charles Mackay wrote:

> You have no enemies, you say?
> > Alas! my friend, the boast is poor;
> He who has mingled in the fray
> > Of duty, that the brave endure,
> *Must* have made foes! If you have none,
> Small is the work that you have done,
> You've hit no traitor on the hip,
> You've dashed no cup from perjured lip,
> You've never turned the wrong to right,
> You've been a coward in the fight.[6]

However, we are never to mistreat our enemies. That's what makes Christianity different from all other religions. Jesus tells us, "Love your enemies, do good, and lend, hoping for nothing in return; and your reward will be great, and you will be sons of the Most High. For He is kind to the unthankful and evil" (Luke 6:35). Perhaps your love will change an enemy into a friend.

LISTEN TO ...

The enemies a person makes by taking a stand will have more respect for him than the friends he makes by being on the fence.

—*Proverb*

Veal (Fatted Calf) Stew

Ancient Hebrews considered "fatted calf" the choicest among food. These stall-fed animals were reserved for holidays or religious ceremonies. The prodigal's father bestowed approval on his returning son by preparing this expensive, extravagant meal. Today the phrase *killing the fatted calf* describes a long-awaited homecoming celebration. During the life of Jesus, slaughtering animals (whether cow, lamb, or goat) was rare because livestock provided the daily needs of milk, butter, and cheese. Therefore, they were more valuable alive. A proverb confirmed their rarity: "Better a meal of vegetables where there is love than a fattened calf with hatred" (Prov. 15:17 NIV). In other words, better to eat like a pauper with harmony than to eat like a king with strife.

Preparation Time: 30 minutes
Cook Time: 3 1/2 hours

Ingredients:

> 3 large onions, sliced
>
> 1 1/2 pounds veal, cut into stewing cubes
>
> 2 garlic cloves, minced
>
> 2 small quinces, cored
>
> 1 small eggplant, cubed
>
> 2 carrots, peeled and sliced
>
> 3 tomatoes, cubed
>
> 2 large potatoes, cubed
>
> 4 tablespoons olive oil
>
> 1 cup pitted prunes, diced
>
> 1/2 teaspoon cinnamon
>
> 1/2 teaspoon cardamom
>
> 1/4 teaspoon turmeric
>
> 2 teaspoons salt
>
> 1/4 teaspoon pepper

1 tablespoon tomato paste, dissolved in 2 tablespoons hot water

1/4 teaspoon saffron, ground and dissolved in 1 tablespoon hot water

Juice of 1 lime

Instructions:

1. Pour two tablespoons of oil into a large, heavy Dutch oven. Layer the first eight ingredients in the pot in the order they're listed.

2. Top with the prunes, and then pour in the remaining oil. Sprinkle with remaining spices, dissolved tomato paste, saffron, and lime juice. Cover and cook for two hours on low heat. After two hours, remove the lid and mix the contents around a little. The veggies release their juices, forming a succulent broth. Bring the broth to a gentle simmer, re-cover, and continue to cook until done, around another one and a half hours. Recommendation: serve over couscous and garnish with sour cream.[7]

GRACE NOTE

Gracious Father,

When we are wayward and then return home to You, nothing is spared to demonstrate Your pleasure—even the angels in heaven rejoice. You are not a disconnected, detached, or distracted Father. When we come to You, You run down the road to meet us. Thank You, Father. In Jesus' name. Amen.

Wedding Fit for a King
Matthew 22:1–14

Americans aren't the only ones obsessed with British royalty and their elaborate weddings. Over two billion people watched in awe as Prince William married commoner Catherine Middleton on April 29, 2011. Catherine, dressed in a simple yet elegant gown, and her prince were the picture of grace and royalty. Their every word, facial expression, and movement was scrutinized, analyzed, and relished. These modern royals adhered to long-held traditions while bringing their individual style to the event—including an unprecedented *two* kisses on the balcony of Buckingham Palace.

It wasn't that long ago when twenty-eight million viewers watched the wedding of Prince William's parents: Prince Charles and Lady Diana Spencer. As Lady Diana walked down the aisle of St. Paul's Cathedral, her dream wedding became the vicarious fulfillment of many a young girl's longing to find her own Prince Charming. Yet even the most elaborate ceremony doesn't guarantee a successful marriage. The world watched again as the marriage of Prince Charles and Princess Diana gradually eroded and collapsed in divorce—and ultimately, tragedy. No amount of jewels, palaces, gowns, or lineage could preserve what never existed.

Generally, the least of all wedding worries is finding enough people to invite. Many stressed-out brides and grooms have edited their desired guest list to fit their budgets. However, that's not the case in the parable we'll be studying. On the contrary, everything was in place *except* the invited guests.

Day 1: Matthew 22:1–3   **ROYAL WEDDING**

Day 2: Matthew 22:4–6   **NO RSVP**

Day 3: Matthew 22:7–9   **THE B-LIST**

Day 4: Matthew 22:10–12   **NO SHIRT, NO SERVICE**

Day 5: Matthew 22:13–14   **BLACKLISTED**

DAY 1
Royal Wedding

LIFT UP ...

Lord, thank You for loving me and desiring my presence. I am unworthy to be invited into Your kingdom. Please give me a heart that recognizes You as my Lord and Savior and faithfully responds to Your call. In Jesus' name. Amen.

LOOK AT ...

This week's parable is part of a set that begins in Matthew 21. These parables are all directed to the Pharisees and chief priests who refused to recognize Christ's authority. The one we'll study depicts a king (God the Father) who arranged a wedding feast for his son (Jesus) and his bride (true believers). The servants were sent out to hand-deliver personal invitations to a select group of guests (the unbelieving Jews). By virtue of the king's selection of the guests, he expressed his desire for a personal relationship with these chosen people.

What an honor! Yet they responded by refusing the invitation. This was not a simple inability to work out a conflict in their busy schedules—it was a deliberate, hostile decision to turn their backs on the grace and hospitality extended to them by the king.

READ MATTHEW 22:1–3.

And Jesus answered and spoke to them again by parables and said: "The kingdom of heaven is like a certain king who arranged a marriage for his son, and sent out his servants to call those who were invited to the wedding; and they were not willing to come." Matthew 22:1–3

LEARN ABOUT ...

1 People

The word *Pharisee* means "one who is separated." This group of prideful men believed the way to God was through strict adherence to the law, which put them at odds with Jesus' message of repentance and forgiveness (Matt. 23:13). It's odd that the religious leaders—instead of the average citizens—rejected the Messiah.

2 Parable

The word *parable* means "to lay beside so as to compare." Jesus picked an example from everyday life and compared it with a spiritual truth in order to reach His audience. Others besides Jesus also employed parables. For example, Nathan the prophet told the parable of the stolen lamb to King David.

5 Priority

In Jesus' time—as in our time—wedding etiquette meant extending the invitation early enough to give the guests enough time to arrange to attend the celebration. When the wedding preparations were complete, the host informed the invited guests that the celebration was commencing.

1. Looking back at Matthew 21:45–46, to whom did Jesus speak?

2. "Jesus … spoke to them again by parables" indicates that Jesus previously used parables to illustrate spiritual truths to these men.

   a. Look back at the first parable of this set in Matthew 21:28–31. Which character did the Pharisees believe represented them?

   b. Review the second parable in Matthew 21:33–40. Who characterized the unbelieving religious leaders?

3. What did the phrase *a certain king who arranged a marriage for his son* symbolize?

4. Describe who the king sent to invite the guests.

5. Who was included on the invitation list?

6. How did the invited guests in the parable respond?

7. Who do you think the invited guests represent today?

LIVE OUT ...

8. In this parable, Jesus compared the royal wedding feast to the kingdom of heaven. What other insights into the kingdom of heaven can we glean from the following Scriptures?

SCRIPTURE	KINGDOM INSIGHTS
Matthew 13:31–32	
Matthew 13:44	

Matthew 13:47–49

Matthew 18:1–4

Matthew 19:23–24

LEARN ABOUT ...

8 Presence

Jesus often referred to the kingdom of heaven in His parables. This describes both His eternal kingdom and His presence in the hearts of those who trust in Him: "The kingdom of God does not come with observation…. For indeed, the kingdom of God is within you" (Luke 17:20–21).

10 Preference

God's invitation went first to His chosen people, the Jews, but they rejected the invitation. According to *The New Daily Study Bible,* "Ages ago the Jews had been invited by God to be His chosen people but when His Son came into the world and they were invited to follow Him, they refused."

9. God wants His people to think of the kingdom in terms of His provision and blessing rather than simple geography. Romans 14:17 says, "For the kingdom of God is not eating and drinking, but righteousness and peace and joy in the Holy Spirit."

a. Draw a line connecting the heavenly kingdom provision to its worldly opposite.

KINGDOM PROVISION	WORLDLY OPPOSITE
Eternal Life	Uncertainty
Security	Unrest
Hope	Judgment
Peace	Despair
Grace	Death

b. From the list above, choose a kingdom provision that is evident in your life today. Thank the Lord for His generous blessing.

10. Matthew 22:3 makes clear that the invited guests were not willing to attend the wedding feast of the king's son. Their choice brought serious consequences.

a. Take a moment to consider the phrase *not willing*. How do you define this phrase?

b. In your life right now, is God inviting you to do something you are not willing to do? What is it?

❑ Forgive someone

❑ Make a difficult change

❑ Draw closer to Him

❑ Give something up

❑ Other: _____

c. Ask the Lord to reveal the impact of this choice in your life. Write your thoughts below.

○ ○ ● ○ ○

Life in the twenty-first century is fast and furious. In this day of smartphones and social networking, everything seems to require an immediate response. We are constantly prioritizing and making choices as to how we spend our time.

In Jesus' time people were busy too. Luke 14 says they had land to care for, marriages and families to nurture, and businesses to manage. Yet a wedding invitation from a king took precedence over daily chores and responsibilities. Would the king really understand if one failed to attend because something else was more important?

Apply this mind-set to receiving an invitation from King Jesus. He has invited you to make a priority and commitment to honor Him with your presence. The invitation is not open-ended. There comes a point when the opportunity passes, and you must then live with the consequences.

Consider the scenario of a steamship taking on water in mid-ocean. A nearby vessel responds to her distress call and proceeds toward the troubled steamship. The captain offers to take the passengers on board immediately, but the commander hesitates, fearing the dangers of transporting the passengers at night. He decides to wait until morning. An hour later, the steamship's lights disappear beneath the sea. All on board perish, because they postponed responding to the invitation for rescue until a more convenient time.[1] The time to respond is now.

LISTEN TO ...

There are only two kinds of people in the end: those who say to God, "Thy will be done," and those to whom God says, in the end, "Thy will be done."

—*C. S. Lewis*

No RSVP

The world is culturally diverse, yet there is an interesting area of common ground: weddings. In most societies, a marriage warrants special attention. The festivities, whether grand or simple, are designed to honor the couple and make the guests feel welcomed and satisfied.

Consider some of the grand weddings of the rich and famous. Vanisha Mittal, daughter of a wealthy steel tycoon, sent her thousand wedding guests a silver book containing airline tickets and room reservations at a five-star Paris hotel. Then there was Liza Minelli's wedding. The guests were served by a staff of five hundred and entertained by Tony Bennett and Stevie Wonder. The lucky individuals who attended Sir Paul McCartney's wedding stayed in an Irish castle and were treated to an elaborate fireworks display.[2]

In these grand weddings, the hosts made special efforts to pamper their guests. The king in this parable did the same. The best and richest foods were served. Nothing was held back for a more important occasion—there was nothing more important than the wedding of his son.

The parallel is obvious. God invites us to the wedding feast of His Son. He gifts us with the "fatted calves" of blessings, opportunities, grace, mercy, eternal life, and eternal joy: "Oh, taste and see that the LORD is good; blessed is the man who trusts in Him!" (Ps. 34:8).

LIFT UP ...

Thank You, Lord, for Your lavish generosity. You provide all I need in this life and for life eternal. Help me to gratefully and gracefully accept Your provisions. In Jesus' name. Amen.

LOOK AT ...

Yesterday we observed the reactions of some fortunate folks who were invited to a royal wedding. This was an incredible honor. In the East, wedding feasts were inseparable from the wedding itself and involved a minimum weeklong procession of meals and festivities. This was the pinnacle of social life and celebration.

LEARN ABOUT ...

1 Mercy

Although the king showed great mercy, grace, and patience, he was disregarded and disrespected. "The Lord is not slack concerning His promise, as some count slackness, but is longsuffering toward us, not willing that any should perish but that all should come to repentance" (2 Peter 3:9).

3 Meal

Serving the fatted cattle was an enticement to cause those invited to reconsider coming to the wedding. These fatted calves had been culled from the herd as the best of the best. They were housed separately, fed meticulously, and raised for special occasions like the marriage of the eldest son or dinner with dignitaries.

4 Move

All that was required of the guests was to come to the wedding. Essentially, God does the same for us. We are not asked to make arrangements or preparations; we are not asked to be good and worthy. Jesus simply invites us to come to Him—all we need do is accept His invitation (Luke 9:23–24).

The guests of a royal wedding were invited to stay at the house of the groom's parents—in other words, they stayed in the palace! The festivities sometimes lasted weeks. Understandably, invitations to a royal wedding were coveted because the king could afford the most elaborate party of all. On these rare occasions, commoners invited to the festivities sampled exotic foods and spices they had previously only heard about.

A wedding feast prepared by the king for his son was the feast of all feasts. So in this parable, Jesus portrayed the most elaborate celebration conceivable. This directly parallels the marriage supper of the Lamb. At this grandest feast in heaven, Christians (the bride of Christ) will dine in a banquet beyond our wildest dreams. Our glorified taste buds will dance with delight.

READ MATTHEW 22:4–6.

Again, he sent out other servants, saying, "Tell those who are invited, 'See, I have prepared my dinner; my oxen and fatted cattle are killed, and all things are ready. Come to the wedding.'" But they made light of it and went their ways, one to his own farm, another to his business. And the rest seized his servants, treated them spitefully, and killed them. Matthew 22:4–6

1. The king persisted in enticing his guests. What did he do "again"?

2. Why do you think the king sent different servants this time?

3. What additional information were the servants to give the marriage guests?

4. What did the king want the guests to do?

5. What did the uninterested guests do rather than attend the wedding?

6. How did the remaining people treat the servants?

LIVE OUT ...

7. Just as the king requested the presence of the wedding guests, the Lord asks us to come to Him. In the following verses, what is His purpose in asking?

SCRIPTURE	HIS PURPOSE IN ASKING
Matthew 11:28	
Mark 1:17	
Mark 10:21	
John 7:37–38	

8. Once again, the invited guests refused to attend the wedding feast. They had a variety of reasons and excuses. Some *disregarded* the invitation, and others *discarded* it.

a. Those who *disregarded* the invitation apparently had other things to do. Prayerfully examine your schedule. Below, make a list of five activities that occupy the majority of your time. Are you pleased with this list? Do you think the Lord is pleased?

(1)

(2)

(3)

(4)

(5)

LEARN ABOUT ...

8 Mocked

God knows your heart. No excuse will convince Him, and He would rather receive a blatant refusal than a weak excuse: "I know your works, that you are neither cold nor hot.... So then, because you are lukewarm, and neither cold nor hot, I will vomit you out of My mouth" (Rev. 3:15–16).

LEARN ABOUT ...

9 Mystery

God has blessings planned for us that we can't begin to comprehend. Don't be lulled by the day-to-day sameness of life. This is just the beginning: "Eye has not seen, nor ear heard, nor have entered into the heart of man the things which God has prepared for those who love Him" (I Cor. 2:9).

b. Are you making excuses for disregarding or avoiding God's invitation to come to Him or spend time with Him? If so, take a moment now to confess your excuses to the Lord.

c. Those who *discarded* the invitation had blatant disdain for the invitation, the messengers, and for the king himself. Record a time when you justified rejecting an invitation or directive from the Lord.

d. Have you ever blamed or punished the messenger for your refusal? How did you justify that response?

9. The king represents God calling us into a personal relationship with Him. He invites us to linger in His presence and enjoy the blessings of His grace. Journal a prayer of acceptance or renewed commitment to the Lord.

∘ ∘ • ∘ ∘

Every year, millions of Americans open invitations to various functions and wonder, *what on earth does* RSVP *mean?* First of all, it doesn't mean: Refreshments Served Very Properly. Nor does it mean respond only if you're not coming, or respond the day of the party, or respond and then fail to show up, or show up with an uninvited friend.

The concept of RSVP was initiated in France and later adopted by Western society. *RSVP* is the abbreviation for the French term *respondez, s'il vous plait,* which means "please reply" or "please respond." Simply speaking, RSVP allows the event planner to know how many people will be in attendance so appropriate arrangements can be made. The appropriate response to an RSVP is immediately upon receipt of an invitation.

We've learned that the invitation in this passage represents God's offer of salvation. Just as in the New Testament era, people today who refuse the invitation have three main excuses:

Apathetic: "But they made light of it and went their ways" (Matt. 22:5). These people act as if this feast were of no consequence—no big deal! They mocked rather than honored the king.

A-Type: "Went their ways, one to his farm, another to his business" (Matt. 22:5). These were preoccupied people, obsessed with daily living and personal pursuits. They were materialistic—primarily interested in accumulating things and ambitiously trying to get ahead. While not necessarily antagonistic to the things of God, they simply did not have time for them.

Antagonistic: "The rest seized his servants, treated them spitefully, and killed them" (Matt. 22:6). Those who are actively hostile to the gospel invariably are involved in false religion, whether Muslim or mysticism. The history of God's people testifies to the fact that persecution comes from *very* religious people whose elevation of error makes them aggressive enemies of the truth.

LISTEN TO ...

We can be so busy making a living that we fail to make a life.

—*Anonymous*

DAY 3

The B-List

Prior to the wedding of Prince William and Kate Middleton, the couple made the unique gesture of randomly issuing invitations to one hundred lucky Londoners. The invitations arrived hand-delivered to their doorsteps. Can you imagine the thrill of being inside Westminster Abbey for this exclusive occasion? Certainly these guests did their best to dress in a manner befitting a royal wedding. As Prince William was described when his upcoming marriage was announced, certainly these honored guests were "over the moon."

If the A-list guests include the highest level of society, excellence, or eminence, then who's on the B-list? I believe they're people like you and me. I know my own family tree was not planted in royal soil, nor were we members of the upper crust.

In our parable, the king's goodness was not quenched by the evil ingratitude of the previously invited guests. The Jews scornfully rejected the grace of God, so the invitation went out to the Gentiles—those deemed unworthy by the Jews. Paul wrote, "Blindness in part has happened to Israel until the fullness of the Gentiles has come in" (Rom. 11:25).

The Old Testament predicted that God would go outside the confines of the Jewish people: "Then I will say to those who were not My people, 'You are My people!' And they shall say, 'You are my God!'" (Hos. 2:23). Although unworthy, we are among those invited to the marriage feast of the Lamb.

LIFT UP ...

Heavenly Father, You are the King and God of all. Your love reaches out to all. Thank You for the invitation to be part of Your family. Please give me the wisdom and grace to respond readily to any invitation You extend. In Jesus' name. Amen.

LEARN ABOUT ...

2 Purpose

Whether Matthew 22:7 refers to the destruction of Jerusalem in AD 70 or to the ultimate battle at the end of the age, God is in control. He is Lord and Commander of all—both earthly or heavenly armies. He will enlist whomever He desires to achieve His purposes.

LOOK AT ...

Previously we witnessed the king's gracious and compelling invitations to attend the marriage feast of his son; yet his chosen people rejected the invitations. Today we learn that rejecting those invitations brought consequences. Whether a person is too busy or too proud, a refusal results in judgment. From this parable we learn the necessity to stand ready to clear our calendar when God calls us to action. It won't come as an engraved invitation—it comes as a prompting of heart and mind.

In our text, Matthew said, "And he sent out his armies, destroyed those murderers, and burned up their city" (22:7). Biblical scholars generally agree this verse refers either to the invasion of Israel by the Roman army in AD 70 (the most common interpretation) or the ultimate battle at the end of the age. Either way, Jesus emphasized that ignoring His invitation results in judgment.

READ MATTHEW 22:7–9.

But when the king heard about it, he was furious. And he sent out his armies, destroyed those murderers, and burned up their city. Then he said to his servants, "The wedding is ready, but those who were invited were not worthy. Therefore go into the highways, and as many as you find, invite to the wedding." Matthew 22:7–9

1. Why do you think the king was angry?

2. Verse 7 is believed to be prophetic. Jesus informed the religious leaders that their rejection would ultimately bring consequences. What three actions did the king take?

    (1)

    (2)

    (3)

3. Who did the king call to action concerning the wedding guests (v. 8)?

4. What was the status of the wedding feast preparations?

5. What was the king's opinion of the invited guests (v. 8)?

6. Where were the servants instructed to go?

7. What were the servants to do when they reached the highway?

LIVE OUT ...

8. In verse 8 the king called the invited guests "not worthy." The following verses emphasize elements of "worthiness," or qualities the invited guests may not have possessed. Below, make note of these qualities.

SCRIPTURE	ASPECTS OF WORTHINESS
Ephesians 4:1–3	
Colossians 1:10	
1 Thessalonians 2:12–13	
Hebrews 11:6	

b. From a worldly perspective, it seems the randomly invited guests were less desirable than those who received the initial invitation, but Scripture doesn't call this group unworthy. Journal about what this tells us about God's perspective on the worthy and the unworthy.

LEARN ABOUT ...

4 Preparation

The Greek word *hetoimos* means "ready, prepared." The wedding was ready for the people—but the people weren't ready for the wedding. Luke 12:40 tells us, "Therefore you also be ready, for the Son of Man is coming at an hour you do not expect."

6 Public Places

Highways were (and are) busy roads or intersections where people traveled or gathered. This implies that the wedding invitation is now offered indiscriminately to all, not just to the Israelites. Romans 3:29 reassures us that God is the God of both Jews and Gentiles.

9. Use the acrostic below to record aspects of worthiness in your own life that may require attention.

W

O

R

T

H

Y

10. Two groups were invited to the wedding. The first group didn't appreciate the invitation; the second group didn't expect it. For both, it was undeserved. Take a moment to meditate on the following words. How do these words describe your response and commitment to God's call in your life?

Unappreciated

Unexpected

Undeserved

· · ● · ·

In reality, we are all unworthy to be in the presence of the King. Today we learned that some people recognize their unworthiness and seek to change it, while others blindly proceed with their lives. We are not the judge of either response. We can only ask God to work in our own lives.

Chuck Smith recalled an incident from the early days of Calvary Chapel Costa Mesa that exemplifies this concept. The church was growing, and God was moving in the lives of the local hippies. This caused a rift between those who viewed the church as a sanctuary of respectability and those "long-haired, barefooted hippies."

Push came to shove with the installation of new carpeting in the sanctuary. The skeptics used this as an excuse to bring those radical converts into line by posting a sign saying "No Bare Feet Allowed." Pastor Chuck responded by saying, "If, because of our plush carpeting, we have to close the door to one young person who has bare feet, then I'm personally in favor of ripping out all the carpeting and having concrete floors.... Let's not ever, ever, close the door to anyone because of dress or the way he looks."[3]

Out of this group of hippie converts grew a work of God that brought untold numbers of individuals into a saving relationship with Jesus Christ. Skip and I were two of those people. God's invitation is an undeserved gift of grace—and He alone will judge our response as worthy or unworthy.

LISTEN TO ...

Never be afraid to trust an unknown future to a known God.

—*Corrie ten Boom*

No Shirt, No Service

There was a great deal of speculation about what foods would be served at the reception of William and Kate. The six hundred guests were indulged with a variety of ten thousand hot and cold canapés and endlessly flowing champagne. The eight-tiered wedding cake was the traditional English fruitcake topped with cream and white icing. Simple, elegant … and costly!

Weddings are a big business! In the United States alone, a conservative estimate of $71 billion is spent on weddings every year. This figure doesn't include the $8 billion spent on honeymoons and the average of $5,780 per wedding received in gifts. Based on an average wedding of 170 guests, the typical wedding in the United States costs around thirty thousand dollars. Of that figure, the largest expenses are the reception and rings, followed by formal wear for the bride and groom. The typical bridal gown averages $1,500.[4]

It's doubtful we will ever know the cost of Kate Middleton's wedding dress, but the influence of Hollywood royalty was evident. In 1956, Grace Kelly married Prince Rainier of Monaco. Like Grace Kelly's gown, Kate's dress had a lace appliquéd bodice and sleeves, full skirt, sheer veil, and diamond tiara. Kate's wedding dress choice will surely influence many future brides.

In our Bible text today, the wedding garment is also fundamental. In fact, it is the essential covering required to make one worthy to stand in God's presence. It represents the sacrifice and righteousness of Jesus Christ.

LIFT UP …

Lord, thank You for providing the covering I need to stand in Your presence: the blood of Your Son. In Jesus' name. Amen.

LOOK AT …

In this parable, the king twice beseeched the chosen guests to attend the feast in honor of his son's marriage. Two times he asked; two times they refused. Now he extended the invitation

LEARN ABOUT ...

1 Masses

The word *all* encompasses the whole—the entirety. All are invited, and no one is disqualified except those who choose to be. First Timothy 2:4 says God has an inclusive heart. He is One "who desires all men to be saved and to come to the knowledge of the truth."

2 Mean

Poneros is translated "bad" in this context and refers to humankind's depravity of mankind—our wicked behavior, or evil nature. According to John Phillips, "The gospel reaches bad people. It also reaches good, moral, upright, religious people. All kinds of people are called and all kinds of people respond."

to strangers from the busiest intersection in town. Everyone encountered was invited. The wedding hall filled with these newly invited guests.

The king's inclusive invitation was not at the expense of proper protocol or inappropriate attire. All but one of them dressed in accordance with the dignity of the occasion.

When we accept the invitation to be included in the Lord's family we, too, must have a heart of surrender and an attitude of submission. Our willingness to examine our readiness is a requirement to attend the marriage feast. As you study today, be prepared to evaluate your own heart: "The LORD is near to those who have a broken heart, and saves such as have a contrite spirit" (Ps. 34:18).

READ MATTHEW 22:10–12.

So those servants went out into the highways and gathered together all whom they found, both bad and good. And the wedding hall was filled with guests. But when the king came in to see the guests, he saw a man there who did not have on a wedding garment. So he said to him, "Friend, how did you come in here without a wedding garment?" And he was speechless. Matthew 22:10–12

1. In verse 10, what phrase describes the selection criteria for the wedding guests?

2. How does Jesus describe the moral condition of the people found along the highway?

3. How many guests were the servants able to assemble?

4. Who came in to see the guests? What was his concern?

5. What expression of familiarity did the king use to address the man?

6. How did the man respond?

LIVE OUT ...

7. Do you think the king was disappointed or dishonored by the guests who ultimately attended the wedding feast? Is God ever dishonored by those who accept His invitation? Read the following verses, and note to whom God extends His invitation.

SCRIPTURE	RECIPIENTS OF GOD'S INVITATION
Matthew 18:11	
John 1:11–12	
John 6:40	
1 Corinthians 1:27	

8. John Phillips wrote, "The man without the wedding garment *professes* salvation but does not *possess* salvation."[5]

   a. In your own words, define and compare these two words as they pertain to salvation:

   Profess

   Possess

   b. Look at the following three verses. What do they say about *professing* and *possessing* the righteousness of Christ?

   Romans 10:9–10

   Philippians 3:8–9

   2 Corinthians 5:21

LEARN ABOUT ...

6 Mute

No words will be sufficient when the God of the universe asks why we didn't accept His invitation or the saving sacrifice of His Son: "Now we know that ... it says to those who are under the law, that every mouth may be stopped, and all the world may become guilty before God" (Rom. 3:19).

---

7 Motive

The wedding garment represents those who truly accept our King's gift of salvation. If we accept that gift, we exchange our garment of unworthiness and sin for the glorious covering of Jesus Christ. There is a clear understanding that we can't come on our own terms or individual righteousness.

9. By refusing the king's garment, the wedding guest revealed his unwillingness to be truly changed. As you read the following statements, examine your life. If any of these phrases convey your attitude, confess it before the Lord. Underline the thought, and write a short prayer asking God to change your heart.

No, thank you. I have a new outfit—one I made myself.

I'm okay the way I am; I don't need to change.

I'm all yours, Lord, except for this one thing....

Compared to others, I think I'm good enough.

I'm more comfortable doing it my way.

○ ○ ● ○ ○

Weddings are a beautiful expression of love and devotion, commitment and promise. The vows state what is most important in the relationship between a man and wife and between God and His bride, the church. While the wedding ceremony may encompass all the proper elements, if the marriage is not strong and established on the proper foundation, the wedding is for naught.

Of the many British royal weddings that took place from 1936 to 1981, only three couples remained married: King Edward VIII (who married after abdicating his throne and giving up his title), Queen Elizabeth II, and Prince Edward. The other marriages dissolved in divorce. True commitment and sacrifice failed to develop in these marriages, and all the pomp, splendor, and tradition of the wedding ceremonies were not enough to sustain long-lasting marriages.

We see a similar situation in today's lesson. The improperly clad man accepted the invitation—but he came on his own terms, disregarding the appropriate preparation and honor. His heart was wrong. He neither submitted nor obeyed.

Regardless of our apparel and careful grooming, God sees our heart. Accept His invitation completely—He wants your heart and soul.

LISTEN TO ...

Exhalation is as necessary to life as inhalation. To accept Christ it is necessary that we reject whatever is contrary to Him.

—*A. W. Tozer*

DAY 5

Blacklisted

Anne Graham Lotz tells of a poor young boy living in London who heard that D. L. Moody would be preaching in a church on the other side of town. Determined to attend, the boy walked the long distance to the church.

As he entered, a doorman stopped him to inquire where he was going. The boy answered that he was going to hear Dr. Moody speak. The doorman blocked his entrance and replied, "Not you! You're too dirty to go inside."

The boy sat down on the steps. Tears streamed down his face. A gentleman approached him and asked why he was upset. The boy repeated the doorman's words. The gentleman extended his hand and said, "Come with me." Together they walked up the stairs, through the doors, and down the aisle to the front row. The boy took his seat, and the man walked up to the platform and began to preach. The man was D. L. Moody.[6]

In our lesson today, the man *refused* to trust and submit his heart to the king and suffered the consequences. We have a choice to make as well. Our admittance into God's kingdom depends solely upon our association with Him. The cost of ignoring or declining God's invitation is severe and forever, but acceptance places us in the front row for eternity.

LIFT UP ...

Lord, I want to be with You for eternity. Make me responsive to Your calling and obedient to Your will. Thank You for drawing me into Your family and Your kingdom. I want my presence to honor and glorify You. In Jesus' name. Amen.

LOOK AT ...

In today's text, we observe a change in the king's demeanor with his underdressed guest. When he first approached the man, the king addressed him as "friend"; today we read that the man was bound and cast away.

Hetairos is a Greek word translated as "a comrade, or companion." It implies association, but should not be confused with the word *philos*, which indicates a relationship of love and endearment.[7] Basically, the king allowed his guest an opportunity to explain himself and perhaps even confess his prideful action, but the guest was not repentant. Therefore, the king reacted quickly and decisively.

This lesson is difficult but poignant. The invitation is free, the requirements simple—but failure to comply results in prompt and everlasting punishment. This isn't the king's choice, but it is his promise.

READ MATTHEW 22:13–14.

Then the king said to the servants, "Bind him hand and foot, take him away, and cast him into outer darkness; there will be weeping and gnashing of teeth." For many are called, but few are chosen. Matthew 22:13–14

1. To whom was the king speaking in Matthew 22:13? How many assignments were the servants given in Matthew 22:1–14? What does this imply about their loyalty?

2. What were this man's transgressions (Matt. 22:11–12)?

3. What three actions were the servants instructed to take against the man?

    (1) _____ him

    (2) _____ him

    (3) _____ him

4. Where were they to cast him?

5. What kind of reactions would he have to this place?

6. How many were called?

7. How many were chosen?

Live Out ...

8. Count how many times the words *invite*, *call*, or *come* are used in Matthew 22:1–14.

   a. What does this tell you about the king's desire for his guests?

   b. Now consider 2 Peter 3:9: "The Lord is not slack concerning His promise, as some count slackness, but is longsuffering toward us, not willing that any should perish but that all should come to repentance." What does this tell you about God's desire for His people?

   c. Write the names of two people in your life who have not yet come to the Lord in repentance. Commit to pray for them.

9. a. Although the man without the proper wedding garment didn't refuse the king's invitation, he only pretended to accept it. God is not fooled by insincerity or deceit. How is this truth supported in the following verses?

   Galatians 6:7–8

   Romans 2:4–5

   Romans 12:3

LEARN ABOUT ...

10 Despair

The phrase *weeping and gnashing of teeth* is used to describe a place of separation and suffering. Weeping suggests the emotional agony experienced by the lost in hell, while gnashing of teeth represents the physical pain that will exist there.

b. Journal a short prayer asking the Lord to reveal any deceit, insincerity, or pride in your heart. Thank Him for His mercy and the hope of everlasting life found only in His grace.

10. The consequences of this man's actions were grave. He was cast into a place of judgment. What insights do these verses add to the description of this place?

SCRIPTURE	PLACE OF JUDGMENT
Matthew 13:41–42	
Matthew 13:49–50	
2 Thessalonians 1:8–9	
Luke 13:28	

11. There are so many things over which we have no control—but we *can* choose where we will spend eternity. The decision is ours. Journal about your thoughts regarding eternity in the King's presence, as opposed to eternity in outer darkness.

· · ● · ·

This parable focuses on a one-of-a-kind wedding. Other weddings may be royal or grand, but none compares to the wedding of the Lamb to His bride. God the Father will host a marriage feast to celebrate the union of His Son, Jesus Christ, to His bride, the redeemed sinners. Revelation says, "Let us be glad and rejoice and give Him glory, for the marriage of the Lamb has come, and His wife has made herself ready.... Blessed are those who are called to the marriage supper of the Lamb!" (Rev. 19:7, 9).

Although this unique invitation is extended to all humanity, it must be responded to individually. It requires private consideration and necessitates a timely, personal response. No other invitation offers such hope and promise. The King of Glory, our Lord, makes us clean and acceptable, clothes us in His righteousness, and invites us to spend eternity with Him. We do so by accepting the saving grace offered through a relationship with Jesus Christ.

Our lives are full of decisions, but this is the decision that truly matters. Don't hesitate. Accept the invitation now, embrace salvation as the bride of Christ, and choose eternal life! Anne Graham Lotz gives us the perfect prayer: "Just give me Jesus! He makes heaven available!"[8]

LISTEN TO ...

You may be deceived if you trust too much, but you will live in torment if you do not trust enough.

—*Frank Crane*

Baklava

Baklava dates back to travels through the Arabian Desert. Caravans carried baklava from one culture to the next because of its exquisite epicurean qualities. This delicacy of the rich and royal was prepared with layers of pastry stuffed with spiced nuts and drizzled with honey. The origin of baklava is as mired in controversy as the ancient kings and kingdoms were. As the dessert traveled the desert, successive cultures adapted it to their region with varying ingredients.

Historians trace baklava back to the eighth-century Assyrians, who baked it in their wood-burning ovens. Greek merchants frequented Mesopotamia and soon discovered the sweet treat. They carried it back to Athens and created paper-thin dough called *phyllo* that could be rolled into layers. The term means "leaf" in Greek and describes the delicate nature of the dough. From there baklava traveled to the Armenians, who added cinnamon and cloves. Arabs introduced rose water and cardamom to the recipe.

Most cultures served this expensive dish for special occasions like weddings or holidays. Also, most countries claim baklava as their own and believe that it possesses aphrodisiac properties.[9] Turks insist that pistachios bring fertility. Romans threw walnuts at their weddings as a way of wishing fruitfulness on the couple; they mixed walnuts in their baklava. Whatever your choice, you'll go nuts for baklava!

Ingredients:

    1 (16 ounce) package phyllo dough

    1 pound chopped nuts (walnut, pistachio, or pecan)

    1 cup butter

    1 teaspoon ground cinnamon

    1 cup water

    1 cup white sugar

    1 teaspoon vanilla extract

    1/2 cup honey

    2 cinnamon sticks

Instructions:

1. Preheat oven to 350 degrees. Butter the bottoms and sides of a thirteen-by-nine inch pan.

2. Chop nuts and toss with cinnamon. Set aside. Unroll phyllo dough. Cut whole stack in half to fit pan. Cover phyllo with a dampened cloth to keep from drying out as you work.

3. Place two sheets of dough in pan; butter thoroughly. Sprinkle two to three tablespoons of nut mixture on top. Top with two sheets of dough, butter, and nuts, layering as you go. Repeat until you have eight layered sheets. The finished product should be about six to eight sheets deep.

4. Using a sharp knife, cut into diamond or square shapes all the way to the bottom of the pan. You may cut into four long rows, then make diagonal cuts. Bake for about fifty minutes until baklava is golden and crisp.

5. While baking, make sauce by boiling sugar and water until sugar is melted. Add vanilla and honey. Simmer for about twenty minutes.

6. Place cinnamon sticks in a bowl and pour syrup over sticks.

7. Remove baklava from oven and immediately spoon sauce over it after removing the cinnamon sticks. Let cool. Serve in cupcake papers.

GRACE NOTE

Dear Lord,

We appreciate the nourishment of proteins and vegetables, but we also love the sweets! What a great variety of foods You have gifted us with during our short stay on earth. As we consider the sweet bounty of this world, we can only imagine the waiting delights of heaven. Thank You, sweet Jesus.

Farewell Feast
Mark 14:12–43

Scrapbooking is a multimillion-dollar industry and the fastest growing hobby in America. Gone are the days of the simple black pages and stick-on corners. Today, supplies encompass an unimaginable variety of papers, stickers, and equipment. Though technology has changed, this hobby has deep roots in our country. Even Thomas Jefferson kept albums containing newspaper clippings chronicling his presidency, as well as some of his favorite poems.

It seems we long to remember important passages in our lives. It's doubtful that utility bills or a grocery list would be found in a scrapbook, but you'd likely find wedding photos, baby pictures, holiday memories, prom mementos, concert tickets, and vacation photos.

When people consider the horrible scenario of evacuating their home in an emergency, photo books are almost always at the top of the list of things to save. Why? We yearn for reminders of the milestones and treasured moments of our lives.

Jesus understood the value of remembrance. At the farewell feast of the Last Supper, He wanted His disciples (including us) to remember Him for eternity. Facing His last days, He instituted one of our most sacred rituals: Communion. He wanted us to remember the somber time preceding His crucifixion and the wondrous times of His resurrection and transfiguration: "Do this in remembrance of Me" (Luke 22:19). And He left us something far better than a scrapbook: He left us His Word.

Day 1: Mark 14:12–16	**PARTY PLANNER**
Day 2: Mark 14:17–21	**GUILTY PARTY**
Day 3: Mark 14: 22–25	**PROPHETIC PARTY**
Day 4: Mark 14:26–31	**THE PARTY'S OVER**
Day 5: Mark 14:32–43	**SLUMBER PARTY**

Party Planner

LIFT UP ...

Lord, You are always prepared. What a comfort to know that nothing catches You by surprise. Increase my faith when things don't go as I expected, because I have put my trust in You. In Jesus' name. Amen.

LOOK AT ...

Last week we studied the parable of the wedding feast and learned how an unprepared wedding guest was removed from the celebration. Today we enter another celebration and consider the way Jesus prepared for it.

In observance of the Passover and the Feast of Unleavened Bread, Jerusalem pulsed with activity and anticipation. During this season, Jewish males were required to travel to Jerusalem to make an offering. Pilgrims filled the city, and citizens prepared to receive many travelers and help them with preparations for the Passover.

Earlier in the week, Jesus had entered the city in a royal procession, publicly presenting Himself to Israel as Messiah and King. Now He made preparations to meet privately with His disciples before He faced His accusers and the looming road to the cross.

Once again, our Lord anticipated the needs of His disciples. Aware of the current and impending circumstances, and respectful of tradition, Jesus prepared His followers for the future.

READ MARK 14:12–16.

Now on the first day of Unleavened Bread, when they killed the Passover lamb, His disciples said to Him, "Where do You want us to go and prepare, that You may eat the Passover?"

LEARN ABOUT ...

I Unleavened Bread

The Feast of Unleavened Bread marked the beginning of the barley harvest. It began on the fifteenth day of Nisan (the first month of the year) and continued for seven days. This celebration followed the Passover, which commemorated God's deliverance of Israel from bondage in Egypt (Lev. 23:4–8).

---

3 Passover

The Passover feast included roasted lamb, unleavened bread, and bitter herbs. The lamb was reminiscent of the sacrificed lamb whose blood marked the doorposts to prevent the angel of death from slaying the firstborn. The unleavened bread represented the haste with which the Israelites left Egypt, and the bitter herbs represented their suffering.

---

6 The Upper Room

Upper rooms were common in Jewish dwellings and were often made available to pilgrims who came to Jerusalem to celebrate the Passover and Feast of Unleavened Bread. It is believed that Mark may have lived at this home. This may also have been the same room later used by believers on the day of Pentecost.

And He sent out two of His disciples and said to them, "Go into the city, and a man will meet you carrying a pitcher of water; follow him. Wherever he goes in, say to the master of the house, 'The Teacher says, "Where is the guest room in which I may eat the Passover with My disciples?"' Then he will show you a large upper room, furnished and prepared; there make ready for us."

So His disciples went out, and came into the city, and found it just as He had said to them; and they prepared the Passover. Mark 14:12–16

1. What feast was celebrated? Underline the two traditions followed for this celebration.

2. What did the disciples ask Jesus? Why?

3. Read Luke 22:8. Which disciples did Jesus send to find a place to celebrate the Passover?

4. Describe where the disciples were sent and who they met.

5. What two things did the disciples do next?

6. In your own words, describe the guest room.

7. Read the last sentence in this passage. What conclusions can you draw about Jesus, based on this sentence?

LIVE OUT ...

8. Some people are naturally organized; others have to work hard at it. Jesus prepared for His last evening with His disciples. Are you organized about spending time with your Savior? Write a prayer asking God for His divine help.

9. After three years with Jesus, the disciples grew to trust Him at His word. Journal about a time in your life that required extraordinary trust in the Lord.

10. The owner of the upper room prepared for a celebration. He was uninvited, invisible—and indispensable! Is God asking you to work without receiving recognition? Place a check beside the way you can be a blessing:

❑ Helping a sick/needy friend

❑ Volunteering in your child's classroom

❑ Preparing a meal for another family

❑ Praying for others' needs

❑ Serving in the children's ministry

❑ Giving to a missionary

❑ Spending time with an elderly friend/relative

❑ Other

_____

· · ● · ·

LEARN ABOUT ...

8 Preparation

Jesus sent His disciples to get the donkey and colt in preparation for the triumphal entry (Matt. 21). He sent them again to secure the guest room for the Last Supper. But He alone went to prepare a place for us (John 14:2) so that we might be with Him forever.

10 Upper Room Host

The host of an event customarily washed the feet of his guests. Jesus was both the host and the guest of honor. In this most private celebration, Jesus washed His disciples' feet, knowing this would be their last shared meal together before His death (John 13:5).

As Jesus prepared for this monumental supper with His disciples, He understood all that lay ahead. Although it was a truly bittersweet time, He still planned a celebration with those He loved. The disciples had no idea Jesus faced betrayal, lies, false accusation, humiliation, torture, pain, and death. Jesus knew—but rather than retreating in solitude or self-pity, He focused on His friends. He did not want to leave them without hope. Instead, He planned a time for face-to-face farewells, to prepare them for the new form of their relationships. How kind. How loving.

Like the disciples, we tend to live with the illusion that all things remain the same. How about you? When hard times come, do you retreat? Do you smile and act like nothing is wrong? Jesus never put on a happy face. He was genuine with His followers even when they were baffled by what He said.

Only through truthfulness can we benefit from the strength of other believers. Jesus assured us, "In the world you will have tribulation; but be of good cheer, I have overcome the world" (John 16:33). He made preparations for us with as much love and attention as He planned for the last meal with His disciples. Worth remembering, isn't it?

LISTEN TO ...

One's philosophy is not best expressed in words; it is expressed in the choices one makes. In the long run, we shape our lives and we shape ourselves. The process never ends until we die. And the choices we make are ultimately our responsibility.

—*Eleanor Roosevelt*

DAY 2

Guilty Party

The Chronicles of Narnia by C. S. Lewis is a series of fantasy books written for children but embraced by children and adults alike. Considered classics, they've been translated into forty-seven languages and sold over a hundred million copies.

Lewis was a writer, scholar, intellectual—and former atheist. While he didn't set out to write an exact allegory of the gospel, some parallels are clear. In the second book of the series, *The Lion, the Witch and the Wardrobe*, four children find a way into a magical world of talking beasts, mythological creatures, and adventure. As events unfold, the youngest boy, Edmund, becomes vulnerable to the evil White Witch and leaves his brother and sisters to follow her. His siblings are devastated and confused by this betrayal.

When Lewis wrote this part of the story, he must have pondered Judas' betrayal of Christ. How could Judas betray the Lord? Wasn't he part of His family? Didn't he walk with Jesus, sit under His teachings, and stand by His side as He healed the sick and loved the unlovable? What an unimaginable sting. The Pharisees' behavior was consistent with their unbelief and hatred of the Man who opposed their self-righteousness—but Judas? Shocking!

Edmund's salvation takes the extraordinary sacrifice of Aslan, just as our salvation took the inconceivable sacrifice of our loving Savior.

LIFT UP ...

Lord, Your mercies are new every morning. I am so grateful because I often feel I've used up more than my fair share the day before. I want to be faithful. Strengthen my resolve to be diligent and deliberate in my pursuit to know You better. In Jesus' name. Amen.

LOOK AT ...

In yesterday's lesson, Jesus made plans to spend His last night on earth in fellowship with His disciples. Today, He painfully revealed His forthcoming betrayal and the betrayer from

LEARN ABOUT ...

I Evening

The evening was the period following sunset, when the Jewish Passover began. All preparations were made before sunset. Jesus was crucified and buried during the day—before sundown. He was the last Passover Lamb the world would ever need.

---

5 "Is it I?"

In Greek, this is a negative question that implies a negative answer. In other words they were saying, "It's not me, is it?" The New International Version translates it as, "Surely not I?" In the ISV, Matthew 26:25 reads, "I'm not the one, am I?" No one wanted to be the guilty party.

among His disciples. These men, who were called from their everyday lives to follow Jesus, saw proof upon proof that Jesus was no mere mortal. They received divine revelation and witnessed supernatural occurrences. Some even performed miracles in Jesus' name. How could one from this most select group of men betray the Lord?

It's interesting that while the disciples loved Jesus, each man considered the sorrowful possibility that he was the source of the betrayal. They all realized that in spite of their exposure to the Christ, they were weak. All but one: Judas. This passage marks the beginning of unparalleled sorrow for the disciples and unfathomable pain and sacrifice for the Savior.

READ MARK 14:17–21.

In the evening He came with the twelve. Now as they sat and ate, Jesus said, "Assuredly, I say to you, one of you who eats with Me will betray Me."

And they began to be sorrowful, and to say to Him one by one, "Is it I?" And another said, "Is it I?"

He answered and said to them, "It is one of the twelve, who dips with Me in the dish. The Son of Man indeed goes just as it is written of Him, but woe to that man by whom the Son of Man is betrayed! It would have been good for that man if he had never been born." Mark 14:17–21

1. When did this event take place?

2. Make a list of those who came with Jesus.

3. What statement did Jesus make that startled His disciples?

4. Describe how this statement made the disciples feel.

5. What question followed? By whom was it asked?

6. How did Jesus describe the betrayer?

7. What pronouncement did Jesus make about the betrayer?

Live Out ...

8. Have you ever been betrayed? Jesus knows exactly what you've gone through. Have you ever been the betrayer? He is willing to forgive. Confess your pain in a prayer, and accept His comfort or His forgiveness.

9. Look up the following Scriptures about the Passover Feast and the Lord's Supper, and list what they have in common: Exodus 12:14 and 1 Corinthians 11:23–26.

10. When Jesus said it would be better not to be born than to deny Him, He referred specifically to Judas. List three people you know who deny Christ. Then write a prayer for their salvation.

    a.

    b.

    c.

∘ ∘ ● ∘ ∘

Judas remains a controversial person among commentators. Some actually feel sorry for him and think he had no say in the role he played.

Learn About ...

6 The Betrayer

Mark did not disclose the betrayer, but both Matthew and John did. Matthew 26:25 says, "Then Judas, who was betraying Him, answered and said, 'Rabbi, is it I?' He said to him, 'You have said it.'" Judas allowed himself to be manipulated by Satan. He never experienced Jesus as his Savior.

8 Forgiveness

Whether we need to forgive or be forgiven, Scripture guides us: "If we confess our sins, He is faithful and just to forgive us our sins and to cleanse us from all unrighteousness" (1 John 1:9); "And be kind to one another, tenderhearted, forgiving one another, even as God in Christ forgave you" (Eph. 4:32).

9 Remembrance

The Passover Feast recalled Israel's deliverance from Egypt. Jesus instituted the Lord's Supper to commemorate His death and our deliverance from sin. Judas took part in the Passover only. As Jesus' betrayer, he was not included in the Last Supper.

Others, who presume that Jesus came primarily to fulfill an earthly reign, believe Judas did what he did in order to force Jesus' hand to establish His kingdom.

The fact is that Judas was lost for the same reasons many are lost today: He refused to confess his sins and receive forgiveness. Judas had opportunities to repent—for instance, when Jesus washed his feet! When the disciples were gathered in the upper room, Judas could have expressed remorse, confessed his sin, and returned the stolen money.

Until the very last hour in the company of the Lord, he could have turned away from his choice to betray. And a last opportunity: when he attempted to return the money. Three years in the company of the Savior and opportunity upon opportunity, yet Judas repeatedly made the choice to betray.

Today people are held captive by guilt, shame, or a sense of hopelessness, not unlike Judas. We know how the story ends for Judas, but it doesn't have to be the same for our friends and family—and certainly not for us. We have the awesome and humbling responsibility to offer hope and the promise of forgiveness to others through the Word of God.

Listen To ...

Bestow on me also, O Lord my God, understanding to know You, diligence to seek You, wisdom to find You, and a faithfulness that may finally embrace You.

—*Thomas Aquinas*

Prophetic Party

The memorial honoring our sixteenth president, Abraham Lincoln, stands at the west end of the National Mall in Washington DC. Lincoln was a pivotal figure in a time of crisis when our nation was torn by civil war. Through his leadership, the United States weathered one of the most difficult periods in its history. The massive statue of a contemplative President Lincoln sits on a ten-foot-high marble base surrounded by thirty-eight carved Grecian columns. Inscribed into the walls of the memorial are the Gettysburg Address and his Second Inaugural Address. The Lincoln Memorial is a deserving testament to a great man. Every year, millions of people come from all over the world to visit this and other historical monuments.[1]

Memorials are critical to our sense of national consciousness. They're a reminder of our roots and the cost paid for our freedoms by the men and women who came before us. Yet Jesus, the King of Kings and Lord of Lords, chose to leave no physical marker, no grand memorial, and no impressive structure that would bring a gasp of awe. Instead, He instituted a ritual that was both social and profoundly personal, one that helps us look back while urging us forward. The great men honored in Washington DC are gone. Jesus is alive.

Lift Up ...

Heavenly Father, You are worth thinking about, worth remembering, worth talking to, worth talking about, and so worth loving. Teach me the ways You want me to remember You in my life and in my heart. Thank You, Lord. Amen.

Look At ...

At this point Judas departed from the upper room, leaving the eleven alone with the Lord. Jesus then established an important memorial that reached forward through the ages, both observed and honored by believers.

LEARN ABOUT ...

I The Lord's Supper

Judas did not participate in the Lord's Supper. This event is reserved solely for believers. First Corinthians 11:26 says we are to eat the bread and drink the cup and proclaim the Lord's death till He comes. Only a believer would make known or declare the coming of the Lord.

2 His Body

The passing of the bread was a traditional part of the Passover meal. Jesus gave it new meaning by breaking it and saying it was His body about to be broken for us. Traditionally, Passover bread reminded them of their deliverance from Egypt; now it would remind them of their Messiah.

Despite the disturbing departure of Judas, the Lord's Supper proceeded according to God's plan. He characterized Himself with bread symbolizing His body, and wine symbolizing His blood. We first read about the sharing of bread and wine in Genesis 14 when Melchizedek celebrated Abram's deliverance from warring kings. In today's Scripture, the bread and wine are shared in celebration of the ultimate deliverance: the deliverance from eternal condemnation.

No more joyful celebrations with His disciples would occur until they were together again in the kingdom of God.

READ MARK 14:22–25.

And as they were eating, Jesus took bread, blessed and broke it, and gave it to them and said, "Take, eat; this is My body."

Then He took the cup, and when He had given thanks He gave it to them, and they all drank from it. And He said to them, "This is My blood of the new covenant, which is shed for many. Assuredly, I say to you, I will no longer drink of the fruit of the vine until that day when I drink it new in the kingdom of God." Mark 14:22–25

1. Describe what Jesus and the disciples were doing.

2. What does the bread represent?

3. List Jesus' actions with the cup:

   a.

   b.

   c.

4. In your own words, describe what the wine represented.

5. For whom did Jesus shed His blood? How does this make you feel?

6. Explain Jesus' decision regarding wine. When and where would He drink it? Why do you think this was the case?

Live Out ...

7. a. We are cautioned to take the Lord's Supper with the proper attitude. Read 1 Corinthians 11:27–34. Place a check by the attitudes that cloud Communion:

❑ A greedy spirit
❑ A judgmental attitude
❑ A desire to satisfy yourself at the expense of others
❑ A thoughtless performing of a ritual
❑ An unforgiving spirit

b. Journal a prayer asking God to free you from anything that interferes with your worship of Him.

8. Taking Communion provides a time for Christ's people to celebrate together. Fill in the following chart to discover the benefits of being united with fellow believers.

Scripture	Benefit(s)
Ecclesiastes 4:12	
Acts 2:46–47	
Romans 15:7	

Learn About ...

4 New Covenant

Moses sprinkled blood when he established the Mosaic covenant (Heb. 9:19–20). Jesus' blood established the new covenant promised in Jeremiah: "I will make a new covenant with the house of Israel and with the house of Judah" (Jer. 31:31). And later in verse 34 the Lord says, "For I will forgive their iniquity, and their sin I will remember no more."

7 Judgment (Chastening)

Taking the Lord's Supper in an unworthy manner invites His chastening. He will do what is necessary to bring about an attitude of honor and obedience: "My son, do not despise the chastening of the Lord, nor be discouraged when you are rebuked by Him; for whom the Lord loves He chastens" (Heb. 12:5–6).

8 Celebrate!

At Communion, self-reflection meets celebration! What better way to rejoice in our salvation and our Savior than with others in the body of Christ? Yes, we should come prepared to assess ourselves and ask God to forgive our sins—but we have a willing and forgiving Savior. We can celebrate that!

Galatians 6:2
1 Thessalonians 5:11
Hebrews 10:24

9. God prepared the disciples to remember Him with solemn and meaningful actions. Journal a prayer asking God to make you a reminder of Him for someone in need.

○ ○ ● ○ ○

The first words of Jesus recorded by Mark were: "The time is fulfilled, and the kingdom of God is at hand. Repent, and believe in the gospel" (1:15). Jesus began His ministry by announcing the kingdom of God. He concluded the Lord's Supper by pointing to the future, when He promised to neither eat the bread nor drink the wine again until the kingdom of God was established.

Daniel spoke of the coming kingdom:

And behold, One like the Son of Man,
Coming with the clouds of heaven!
He came to the Ancient of Days,
And they brought Him near before Him.
Then to Him was given dominion and glory and a kingdom,
That all peoples, nations, and languages should serve Him.
His dominion is an everlasting dominion,
Which shall not pass away,
And His kingdom the one
Which shall not be destroyed. (Dan. 7:13–14)

Talk about something to look forward to! How incredible that we serve a God who not only saw our need for salvation but was willing to pay the highest price. Knowing He also wants to be with us for eternity is almost more than we can comprehend.

Jesus is currently at the right hand of the Father. He thinks about you constantly and looks forward to being with you!

LISTEN TO ...

I will place no value on anything I have or possess unless it is in relationship to the kingdom of God.

—*David Livingstone*

DAY 4
The Party's Over

Japanese samurai warriors were professional soldiers who devoted their lives to prepare for warfare. They trained in mental and physical tactics to hone their skills for the battlefield. Although they trained with various weaponry that included bows and arrows, their primary focus was on the sword. Ethics and loyalty to one's master were of supreme importance. If that meant the sacrifice of thousands for their master's well-being, so be it. Each warrior took this charge so seriously that he mentally practiced dying before he engaged in battle. He knew that being overly concerned with living compromised his commitment to do what was necessary for victory. This freed him from the illusion that he could control outcomes and prepared him to give himself fully to fight the battle. For the samurai, neither life nor death was guaranteed: he simply did what he was trained to do.

Jesus always knew that our salvation would come at the price of His sacrificial death in our place. While the outcome of that Passover night was no surprise to Jesus, it didn't lessen the heartbreak of betrayal and the pain of His death. He was beaten, abandoned, insulted—and ultimately killed. He spent three years in ministry, telling people who He was, demonstrating love, offering forgiveness, and promising eternal life. Yet long before He entered the world, He knew it was necessary to take our punishment by dying for us.

LIFT UP ...

Lord Jesus, I can't fully understand Your love. Knowing that I am weak, like Peter, and inclined toward my own personal gain, like Judas, I can scarcely conceive of Your death in my place. I can never repay You, but it won't stop me from thanking You. In Jesus' name. Amen.

LEARN ABOUT ...

I Singing

It was traditional to sing psalms during Passover. It is likely they sang Psalms 113—118. These psalms speak of God's majesty (113), God's deliverance of Israel from Egypt (114), the trust God's people have in Him (115), deliverance from death (116), God's enduring truth (117), and God's everlasting mercy (118).

LOOK AT ...

Yesterday we saw how Jesus established the important practice of Communion, which is celebrated daily all over the world in various ways. Imagine His thoughts and the pain that surely pierced His heart. Although Judas gave Him up to His enemies, He established a sacrament that would be practiced for thousands of years to come. In the light of sorrow and dread, He demonstrated the strength to sing and celebrate.

Jesus realized that the pressures and horror of that night's events would take a toll on His disciples. They would not fare well. No mere man could handle the situation, knowing the horrors that lay ahead. But Jesus was no mere man. Ever true to His mission, He steadfastly prepared His followers by quoting Scripture to remind them that He is the Shepherd and they are His sheep.

READ MARK 14:26–31.

And when they had sung a hymn, they went out to the Mount of Olives. Then Jesus said to them, "All of you will be made to stumble because of Me this night, for it is written:

'I will strike the Shepherd,

And the sheep will be scattered.'

But after I have been raised, I will go before you to Galilee."

Peter said to Him, "Even if all are made to stumble, yet I will not be."

Jesus said to him, "Assuredly, I say to you that today, even this night, before the rooster crows twice, you will deny Me three times."

But he spoke more vehemently, "If I have to die with You, I will not deny You!"

And they all said likewise. Mark 14:26–31

1. What did Jesus and the disciples do next?

2. Where did they go next?

3. What did Jesus warn the disciples would happen? Why?

4. What metaphor did Jesus use to describe His relationship with His disciples? How do you think this made them feel?

5. Describe the promise Jesus made to the disciples. How could this have encouraged them?

6. What can you learn from the disparity between Peter's intentions and his behavior under stressful circumstances? Did this take Jesus by surprise?

7. What phrase makes you know that Peter wasn't alone in his feelings?

Live Out ...

8. Jesus knew a painful death awaited Him, yet He sang hymns. Are you dealing with a painful situation in your life? Sing a song of worship to God that reminds you of His greatness in the midst of your trial. Write down the lyrics.

9. Jesus said the sheep would be scattered. He would meet them later in Galilee. Do you ever feel scattered because of what's happening around you? Pray through the acronym ACTS:

   Adoration: Praise God because He is ultimately in control.
   Confession: Tell God about your fears, anxieties, and lack of faith.

LEARN ABOUT ...

2 Mount of Olives

The Mount of Olives is located east of Jerusalem. It is a significant location in Scripture. David fled there when he ran from Absalom (2 Sam. 15:30); Jesus entered triumphantly into Jerusalem from the Mount of Olives (Matt. 21:1); and following His resurrection, Jesus ascended to heaven from this mountain (Acts 1:9–12).

4 Scattered Sheep

Zechariah 13:7 says, "'Awake, O sword, against My Shepherd,' ... says the LORD of hosts." It is clear that Jesus' death was divinely destined—no accident. Without the constant tending of Jesus the Good Shepherd, the disciples were confused and scattered.

8 Singing through Sorrows

Paul and Silas were sitting in a jail cell when they began singing psalms at midnight (Acts 16:25). David wrote a song about the time Saul sent men to kill him (1 Sam. 19:11; Ps. 59). Worship through song is powerful because the focus changes from us and our circumstances to God.

LEARN ABOUT ...

9 Sheep

Shepherds in the Middle East don't herd their sheep like their counterparts in the West. Rather than using sheep dogs, the shepherds lead their flocks and call to them. Eventually, the sheep come to know their shepherd's voice. Even after Jesus was resurrected, the disciples recognized their Shepherd's voice.

Thanksgiving: Thank God that He has chosen this situation to deepen your faith.

Supplication: Ask God for strength, discernment, encouraging words, and peace.

10. Peter was overconfident about his loyalty to Jesus. Look at the following list, and check the ones that may be areas of overconfidence in your life:

❑ Your parenting approach
❑ Your skills at work
❑ Your financial situation
❑ Your abilities as a homemaker
❑ Your relationships and connections
❑ Your reputation

The solution to overconfidence is simple: give God the credit for the work He has accomplished. Cross out "your" from the list above and replace it with "Thank God for the blessing of my ..."

∘ ∘ ● ∘ ∘

The devastating nineteen-hour eruption of Mt. Vesuvius in AD 79 left the neighboring town of Pompeii completely overwhelmed with ash and lava. Unaware of the looming danger, many of the residents apparently took no escape actions. Buried in volcanic ash for 1700 years, those residents are immortalized in their horror and shock. One of the most indelible images discovered was of a mother and child who died side by side from the suffocating ash. No doubt the woman's maternal instincts propelled her toward a shelter never found in the panic.

Jesus knew well the horror He was about to experience, yet His protective instincts were for His disciples—not Himself. He made sure to leave them with instructions on where to meet Him after His resurrection. He even warned that they would be scattered for a time.

We don't know whether or not the disciples fully grasped the situation. In retrospect, it is easy for us to identify the many ways Jesus prepared and protected His disciples, but neither they nor Jesus were spared the inevitable pain that followed.

In the ruins of Pompeii, we can marvel at the brave efforts of a mother to protect her child. How much more do we marvel at the love of the God of the universe for His disciples. His actions to save them (and us) were not futile. We have only to gratefully receive His gift and inherit eternal life.

Listen To ...

In me there is darkness, but with Thee there is light. I am lonely, but Thou leavest me not; I am feeble in heart, but Thou leavest me not; I am restless, but with Thee there is peace; In me there is bitterness, but with Thee there is patience. Thy ways are past understanding, but Thou knowest the way for me.

—*Dietrich Bonhoeffer*

Slumber Party

In February 1944, the war in Europe still raged, and the soldiers' morale wavered. General George C. Marshall proposed that President Franklin D. Roosevelt institute a medal for heroic or meritorious achievement in the face of the armed enemy. The name of the medal? The Bronze Star. Roosevelt liked the proposal and implemented the medal the following day. Although poor records were kept, it is believed that several thousand men received the medal during World War II. Bravery and heroism in dangerous circumstances have always fostered feelings of pride, satisfaction, and inspiration.[2]

Soldiers are trained for battle and aware that danger and challenge are parts of daily life. But for the common person, defenses and readiness tend to lie untried and dormant.

Although the disciples (Peter in particular) talked about loyalty and heroism, they had no idea how to walk out that bravado. Jesus knew what He faced and prepared for the coming agony by turning to His Father in prayer.

For the small squadron of Jesus' followers, loyalty, vigilance, and obedient discipline went AWOL at this critical time. There were no acts of heroism or selfless bravery or achievement above and beyond the call of duty. Instead, the men privileged to be led and loved by the greatest Man in history responded to His command to "sit here," "stay here," "watch," and "pray" … by sleeping.

LIFT UP …

Lord Jesus, I can scarcely understand the selflessness of Your sacrifice for me. Awaken me to be vigilant and ready to lead a life of faith and loyalty. Like the disciples, I fall into the sleepiness of apathy without Your Holy Spirit. Fill me, Lord, with Your Spirit. In Jesus' name. Amen.

LOOK AT ...

Yesterday, we saw that Jesus prepared His disciples for the evening's events by warning that they would wander from their commitment to Him. Today, they've fled from the city to the Mount of Olives in a garden called Gethsemane. Here Jesus shifts His focus from preparing the disciples to bracing Himself for coming events. He prays for the Father's help and guidance during this agonizing time.

While the dread of a violent and painful death was certainly on His mind, the inevitable separation from His Father as He atoned for our sin brought Him to His knees. Ultimately, His obedient strength and love for us overcame His dread and pain.

READ MARK 14:32–43.

Then they came to a place which was named Gethsemane; and He said to His disciples, "Sit here while I pray." And He took Peter, James, and John with Him, and He began to be troubled and deeply distressed. Then He said to them, "My soul is exceedingly sorrowful, even to death. Stay here and watch."

He went a little farther, and fell on the ground, and prayed that if it were possible, the hour might pass from Him. And He said, "Abba, Father, all things are possible for You. Take this cup away from Me; nevertheless, not what I will, but what You will."

Then He came and found them sleeping, and said to Peter, "Simon, are you sleeping? Could you not watch one hour? Watch and pray, lest you enter into temptation. The spirit indeed is willing, but the flesh is weak."

Again He went away and prayed, and spoke the same words. And when He returned, He found them asleep again, for their eyes were heavy; and they did not know what to answer Him.

Then He came the third time and said to them, "Are you still sleeping and resting? It is enough! The hour has come; behold, the Son of Man is being betrayed into the hands of sinners. Rise, let us be going. See, My betrayer is at hand."

And immediately, while He was still speaking, Judas, one of the twelve, with a great multitude with swords and clubs, came from the chief priests and the scribes and the elders.

Mark 14:32–43

1. What did Jesus ask His disciples to do when they reached Gethsemane?

2. Who did Jesus pull aside? Why?

3. Describe the Lord's position in prayer and the condition of His heart.

4. In His prayer to the Father:

   a. What did Jesus recognize about the Father?

   b. What did He request of the Father?

   c. What did He relinquish to the Father?

5. What were the disciples doing while Jesus prayed? How many times did this happen?

6. What personal admonition did Jesus give to Peter? Why?

7. After Jesus finished praying, what event did He alert them was about to happen?

8. List those who arrived "immediately." What was their intent?

LIVE OUT ...

9. Jesus chose three of the disciples to stand by Him at this most difficult time. Do you have an inner circle of friends who share in hard times? List their names, and ask God to bless each one.

LEARN ABOUT ...

I Gethsemane

The word *Gethsemane* means "oil press." The garden was an orchard of olive trees. Jesus and His disciples often visited this place. While it may have been a familiar and comforting spot during His ministry, it is most remembered for being the place where Jesus endured great agony in preparation for the cross.

4 Abba

Abba is an Aramaic word that means "papa" or "daddy." The relationship Jesus had with His Father was like the tenderness of a child who trusts the goodness of a loving parent. In Romans 8:15 Paul told believers that we could also have an intimate relationship with our "Abba, Father."

6 "Watch and Pray"

This is a familiar admonition in Scripture. Jesus told His disciples to watch and pray because they did not know the hour of His return (Mark 13:33). Paul similarly instructs believers after talking about the armor of God (Eph. 6:18). We are warned to keep our eyes open because the Enemy is near.

LEARN ABOUT ...

9 Peter, James, and John
This is not the first time that Jesus singled out these three disciples. He chose them to be with Him during His transfiguration (Matt. 17:1–13). The transfiguration was a visible manifestation of Jesus' inner glory. Both Moses (the lawgiver) and Elijah (the prophet) appeared and spoke with Jesus.

11 Time
We must make choices about what we do with our time. The psalmists prayed: "So teach us to number our days, that we may gain a heart of wisdom" (Ps. 90:12) and, "Show me, O LORD, my life's end and the number of my days; let me know how fleeting is my life" (Ps. 39:4 NIV).

10. The intimate relationship Jesus had with His Father was anchored in trust. Fill in the chart to discover the results of trusting God.

SCRIPTURE	TRUSTING GOD
Psalm 36:7	
Psalm 64:10	
Psalm 112:7	
Isaiah 26:3	
Jeremiah 17:7	

11. So many things compete for our time to "watch and pray." For the disciples, it was sleep. What is getting in your way?

❑ Lack of time management
❑ Too busy with volunteer work
❑ Too much time watching TV
❑ Too tired
❑ Too busy at work
❑ Poor physical condition
❑ Too busy with family activities
❑ Other _____

Whether or not your excuse is valid, it's still an obstacle. Determine to change your priorities and make time to "watch and pray." Journal about your personal plan to "watch and pray" (time, place, frequency, etc.).

∘ ∘ ● ∘ ∘

A preacher recovering from a near-death illness conversed with a close friend. The friend expressed concern that the preacher's long recovery kept him from his calling from God to be in the pulpit. The minister responded by saying, "You are mistaken, my friend; for this six weeks' illness has taught me more divinity than all my past studies and all my ten years' ministry put together. God only knows what temptation I avoided by being constrained to watch and pray as we are instructed to do."[3]

"Watch and pray": These are the antidotes to falling into temptation and apathy. To watch is more than merely glancing up from our current activity—it's a constant vigil against the Enemy. And prayer is our lifeline to God in all seasons—whether in sadness, joy, loneliness, need, or blessing.

Jesus cautioned Peter with these words, and we are given the same admonition. Jesus Himself found it necessary to go to His Father in prayer. Our prayers are heard not because they are heartfelt, but because of the agony suffered by our Lord in the garden of Gethsemane and on the cross at Calvary. Prayers should never be regarded as holy, saintly work—they are a divine privilege wrapped in our gratitude and wonder.

Listen To ...

There is no way that Christians in a private capacity can do so much to promote the work of God, and advance the kingdom of Christ, as by prayer.

—Jonathan Edwards

Hummus

Nobody knows the exact origin of hummus. The word is Arabic for "chickpea." The Spanish call chickpeas garbanzo beans. The dish is served throughout the Middle East from the Mediterranean to India. The ancients gathered the chickpea for nearly seven thousand years. The Phoenicians are credited for bringing the chickpea to western Europe. The Romans included them in their Iberian diet.[4] To this day a war regarding the origin of hummus exists between Lebanon and Israel.

As Americans love peanut butter and Australians adore Vegemite, the Israelis love the spreadable side dish of hummus. This pureed chickpea dip is eaten by sopping pita bread into the mixture, like a tortilla chip into salsa. A variety of toppings can be added to hummus, like broad beans called *ful*, mushrooms, pine nuts, and meat. Every Israeli has a favorite place to enjoy hummus and argue that theirs is the best. My favorite hummus purveyor is Lina's Restaurant, found down the winding streets of Old Jerusalem.

Preparation Time: 10 minutes
Ingredients:

> 1 (16 ounce) can of chickpeas or garbanzo beans
>
> 1/4 cup liquid from can of chickpeas
>
> 3–5 tablespoons lemon juice (to taste)
>
> 1 1/2 tablespoons tahini
>
> 2 cloves garlic, crushed
>
> 1/2 teaspoon salt
>
> 2 tablespoons olive oil
>
> 1 teaspoon sumac or parsley for garnish

Instructions:

1. Drain chickpeas and set aside liquid from can. Combine remaining ingredients in blender or food processor. Add a quarter cup of liquid from chickpeas. Blend for three to five minutes on low until thoroughly mixed and smooth.

2. Place in serving bowl, and create a shallow well in the center of the hummus.

3. Add a small amount (one to two tablespoons) of olive oil in the well. Garnish with sumac or parsley (optional).

Serve immediately with warm or toasted pita bread, or cover and refrigerate.

GRACE NOTE

Lord,

As we consider the humble chickpea, we are reminded of Your transformative work in our lives. Sometimes we need to be combined with others, pressed out of ourselves, garnished with the flavor of Your Word, seasoned with salt and light. Please impart in Your children the desire to be used generously for Your glory. In Jesus' name. Amen.

Roadside Picnic
Luke 24:13–35

The word *picnic* sounds so very 1950s America. Can't you just picture dad and mom with kids in tow, traveling across the country in their Rambler station wagon? As they pull into a wooded rest stop, out comes the wicker basket abounding with sandwiches, chips, Hostess Twinkies, and lemonade.

Even the cartoons of the day echoed our love of picnics. Yogi Bear's catchphrase, "Hey there, Boo Boo, let's get us some pic-a-nic baskets," proved that he was indeed "smarter than the average bear."

Skip and I often escape to the Sandia Mountains with basket in hand. We pull into a wooded state park, find a quiet picnic table, and spread out a colorful tablecloth. Our basket, a treasured wedding gift, brims with homemade chicken, potato salad, cookies, and sparkling apple juice served in crystal goblets. It's a romantic getaway on a budget.

Interestingly, it is believed the word *picnic* came from the fifteenth-century French word *piquenique*, which depicts an elegant repast served alfresco rather than a peasant's meal during harvest. In the 1800s, the English added entertainment and games to the gathering.[1]

This week we discover that picnics existed long before the American, French, or English traditions. Ancient Middle Easterners knew all about rest stops to enjoy food and fellowship along their journeys. In fact, Ruth and Boaz met at a picnic during the barley harvest. In this study, we'll see that two of the Lord's disciples unwittingly invited Jesus to join them for a roadside picnic.

Day 1: Luke 24:13–17   **PICKING UP HITCHHIKERS**

Day 2: Luke 24:18–24   **CURRENT EVENTS**

Day 3: Luke 24:25–27   **GETTING PERSPECTIVE**

Day 4: Luke 24:28–32   **SAYING GRACE**

Day 5: Luke 24:33–35   **HEART BURN**

DAY 1
Picking Up Hitchhikers

LIFT UP ...

Risen Savior, awaken my senses that I might know the opportunities You place before me. I pray that I will be quick to recognize Your presence and faithful to spread the good news of Your coming. In Jesus' name. Amen.

LOOK AT ...

This story took place on a Sunday, "the first day of the week" (Luke 24:1). The Jewish Sabbath fell on the last day of the week, Saturday. So what distinguished this first day? It was Resurrection Day! On this first Christian Sunday, some women gathered at the Savior's tomb to find it was empty. After encountering an angel who announced the Lord's resurrection, the women ran to tell the disciples. Sadly, the men refused to believe their extraordinary report. But Peter's curiosity was piqued. He ran to verify the incredible news and left the scene "marveling to himself" (Luke 24:12).

Isn't it wonderful that women were the first to believe? They were (dare I say?) the first Christians: the last at the cross and the first at the grave. Be encouraged. If you're the first believer in your family, never give up proclaiming our risen Lord. Perhaps they will eventually believe—just like Peter.

READ LUKE 24:13–17.

Now behold, two of them were traveling that same day to a village called Emmaus, which was seven miles from Jerusalem. And they talked together of all these things which had happened. So it was, while they conversed and reasoned, that Jesus Himself drew near and went with them. But their eyes were restrained, so that they did not know Him.

LEARN ABOUT ...

I Dawning Day

Emmaus lay west of Jerusalem, so the men were journeying into the setting sun. Perhaps the men's eyes were restrained due to the glare of the sunset. Or maybe it was because they walked toward the *Sonshine*. The unknown man who fell into step with them was none other than the glorified Savior.

---

5 Drawing Near

The Lord loves to hear His followers talk about Him. In fact Malachi wrote, "Then those who feared the LORD talked with each other, and the LORD listened and heard" (Mal. 3:16 NIV). If you want Jesus to draw near, find a friend and talk about the Lord. Jesus will join in.

---

7 Drawing Out

Jesus noticed they were sad. Imagine a countenance so downcast a stranger could easily detect it. Unable to reconcile the notion of a dead Savior, they were engaged in a loud and animated conversation. The miraculous Messiah crucified? How could this be? Jesus eavesdropped and then asked a kind question.

And He said to them, "What kind of conversation is this that you have with one another as you walk and are sad?" Luke 24:13–17

1. Underline the phrase that describes the timing of this event. Read Luke 24:1–12, and describe what else happened during this time span.

2. Describe their place of origin and destination.

3. How far was this journey? How long do you think this might have taken on foot?

4. In your own words, recount the topic of their conversation.

5. Who joined them on the journey?

6. Why didn't the disciples recognize the sojourner?

7. What did the sojourner ask, and why?

LIVE OUT ...

8. Jesus turns sunsets into *Sonrises*. What the travelers thought was the end turned out to be the beginning of a new era. Fill in the following columns with your dusks that Jesus turned into dawn.

DUSK	DAWN

9. Jesus drew near to those traveling the Emmaus road. Fill in the following chart to discover others who drew near.

SCRIPTURE	THOSE WHO DREW NEAR
Exodus 20:21	
Lamentations 3:56–57	
Psalm 73:28	
Luke 15:1	
Hebrews 10:22–23	

10. Jesus responded to the sadness of His people. What makes you sad? Rewrite the following Scripture into a personal plea to God:

Hear my cry, O God;
    Attend to my prayer.
From the end of the earth I will cry to You,
    When my heart is overwhelmed;
    Lead me to the rock that is higher than I.

For You have been a shelter for me,
    A strong tower from the enemy. (Ps. 61:1–3)

○ ○ ● ○ ○

I love the beautiful poem by Robert Browning Hamilton:

I walked a mile with Pleasure
She chatted all the way;
And left me none the wiser
For all she had to say.
I walked a mile with Sorrow

LEARN ABOUT …

9 Developing Intimacy

It takes two to develop intimacy. Jesus drew near to the disciples on their journey. James said, "Draw near to God and He will draw near to you" (James 4:8). More than a religion, Christianity is a relationship in which God's people both initiate and respond. Pursue God as He pursues you.

10 Drying Tears

Brokenness attracts God—He can't resist a crushed spirit. David, the psalmist, wrote, "The LORD is close to the brokenhearted and saves those who are crushed in spirit" (Ps. 34:18 NIV). The Savior is not drawn to puffed-up people but to humble humans. When you're hurt, He helps!

And ne'er a word said she;

But, oh, the things I learned from her

When Sorrow walked with me.[2]

Little is known of the two sad men traveling the road to Emmaus. They were not from among the twelve apostles, and nothing further is mentioned about them either on the day of Pentecost or in the book of Acts. Their encounter with the risen Lord was more intense than that of the women who saw Him at the tomb and more radiant than a joint visitation in the upper room. These two privileged men walked and talked with the Lord on their road of sorrow. Jesus even lingered long enough to dine with them. They were all the more blessed for this encounter.

LISTEN TO ...

Authentic [people] aren't afraid to show affection, release their feelings, hug their children, cry when they're sad, admit it when they're wrong, and ask for help when they need it.

—Charles R. Swindoll

DAY 2
Current Events

What is your news source? I've met people who cite late-night comedians as their source of current events. In 2008, according to a Pew Survey, most Americans received more of their news from the Internet, via email or social networks, than from newspapers or radio.[3]

The word *news* has its origins in "word of mouth." In eighteenth-century England, the town crier, an official of the court, dressed in a red coat, white wig, and tri-cornered hat, proclaimed the news to eager townsfolk. While ringing a bell, the crier shouted, "Oyez, oyez, oyez"—which means, "Hear ye, hear ye, hear ye"—before announcing court decisions, local news, market days, and royal decrees.

During the biblical era, news traveled by word of mouth and usually originated at the city gates, which served as the courthouse, civic center, and news outlet.

As we observe the two sojourners on the road to Emmaus sharing the news about Jesus (to Jesus!), we discover that many Jerusalemites believed Him to be a prophet from Nazareth whose words and works were miraculous.

When Jesus wanted the gospel spread throughout the world, He confirmed the precedence of "word of mouth." His disciples were to "go into all the world and preach the gospel to every creature" (Mark 16:15). To this day, sharing the gospel from person to person is the most effective method of evangelism. How did you hear about Jesus? Are you telling others, too?

LIFT UP ...

Lord, I consider how eagerly I share good news of impending marriages, new babies, and other worldly successes. Yet at times I am hesitant to share the good news of the Savior who died for our sins. Help me to be so heavenly minded that I am quick to proclaim the gospel. In Jesus' name. Amen.

LEARN ABOUT ...

I Puzzled

Jesus' question stopped the
travelers in their tracks.
They were puzzled that
a resident of—or even a
visitor to—Jerusalem missed
the news about the arrest,
death, and resurrection
of Jesus. Perhaps Jesus
retained His Galilean accent
and appeared to be from
the country rather than the
city of Jerusalem.

LOOK AT ...

Yesterday we met two sorrowful sojourners embarking on a two-hour
walk from Jerusalem to Emmaus. We don't know if they were headed
toward business or family. Perhaps Emmaus was their home. Some
believe Emmaus served as a rest spot on the way to Galilee—their final
destination. Maybe they ran from controversy or persecution, because
they had clearly followed Jesus. Regardless, they attempted to escape a
past in which they *had* hoped in the Messiah.

Have you ever tried to flee from the past instead of running toward
the future? You don't really care where you go as long as you get out
of Dodge, right? None of us escapes our problems; instead, they dog us
wherever we go. Perhaps that's why Jesus joined these characters on their
journey. He wanted them to either go back and face their pasts or move
into the future with confidence. Where are you headed, and why?

READ LUKE 24:18–24.

*Then the one whose name was Cleopas answered and said to Him, "Are
You the only stranger in Jerusalem, and have You not known the things
which happened there in these days?"*

*And He said to them, "What things?" So they said to Him, "The things
concerning Jesus of Nazareth, who was a Prophet mighty in deed and word
before God and all the people, and how the chief priests and our rulers delivered Him to be condemned to death, and crucified Him. But we were hoping
that it was He who was going to redeem Israel. Indeed, besides all this, today is
the third day since these things happened. Yes, and certain women of our company, who arrived at the tomb early, astonished us. When they did not find His
body, they came saying that they had also seen a vision of angels who said He
was alive. And certain of those who were with us went to the tomb and found
it just as the women had said; but Him they did not see." Luke 24:18–24*

1. Who responded to the stranger's question, and how?

2. How did Jesus respond? Why?

3. How did they describe the Lord and the actions of their leaders?

   LORD   LEADERS

4. Explain how the travelers previously felt about Jesus. Circle the verbs they used. In what tense were they written?

5. Underline and then list the three key witnesses. Recount the perplexing news they shared on the "third day."

   a.

   b.

   c.

LIVE OUT ...

6. The conversation in today's lesson began with a question from Jesus. Read Matthew 16:13–17.

   a. Describe the setting and those who were present (v. 13).

   b. In your own words, recount the Savior's first question and how the disciples answered it (vv. 13–14).

   c. What was the Lord's second question, and how did it differ from the first (v. 15)?

LEARN ABOUT ...

4 Past Tense

NIV translates "we were hoping" into "we had hoped." Either way their hope was in the past tense—a dream dashed. Many of Jesus' followers anticipated that the Messiah would deliver them from Roman rule. Instead, He broke sin's power and Satan's hold over the world. Spiritual deliverance precedes the political deliverance He will establish with His second coming.

5 Perplexed

They had perplexed minds but passionate hearts. G. H. Morrison wrote, "They never understood how much they needed Him until the day when they thought that He was gone. They never understood how much they loved Him, till the shadow of parting had fallen on their love."

6 Poignant

Jesus asked questions that exposed either faith or fear. He asked the rich young ruler, "Why do you call Me good?" (Mark 10:18). At the feeding of the five thousand, He queried, "How many loaves do you have?" (Mark 6:38). What is the Lord asking you? Will you respond in faith or fear?

d. How did Simon Peter respond to the question (v. 16)?

e. What did Jesus bestow upon the disciple? What was the source of Peter's knowledge (v. 17)?

7. The travelers mourned that Jesus "was going to redeem Israel." Fill in the following chart to discover how we are redeemed.

SCRIPTURE	REDEEMED
Galatians 3:13	
Titus 2:13–14	
1 Peter 1:18–19	
Revelation 5:9	

8. Review question 5 to remember the three witnesses to the resurrection. Read 1 John 5:5–10.

a. List the three witnesses from heaven.

b. List the three witnesses on earth.

c. Whose witness is the greatest? Explain why.

∘ ∘ ● ∘ ∘

Most remember Norman Vincent Peale as a man who walked an uplifting path of hope. He once shared about a time when he strolled Hong Kong's busy streets and stumbled upon a tattoo studio. The window displayed colorful renderings—everything from hearts to hula girls and anchors to airplanes. Included in the array were slogans in fancy fonts. One negative tattoo slogan hit the positive-thinking author abruptly. It read: "Born to lose."

Drawn inside the shop by this peculiar phrase, he questioned the Chinese tattoo artist if anyone ever permanently inked those desperate words onto his or her body. The Chinese man confirmed that some did. Incredulous, Norman asked why.

The tattoo artist pointed to his head and replied with a thick accent, "Before tattoo on body, tattoo on mind."[4]

Likewise, the men on their way to Emmaus wore their hopeless mind-sets like tattoos. Did they hang their heads? Were their eyes swollen and red? Perhaps they scowled or shook their fists. All we know is that Jesus read them like a book, determined to change their minds in order to transform their visage.

Proverbs warns, "For as he thinks in his heart, so is he" (Prov. 23:7). Like the disciples, your greatest battles will be fought in your mind. If the enemy gains a foothold in your mind, it won't be long before your actions will lead to defeat.

Listen To ...

There are no hopeless situations. There are only people who have grown hopeless about them.

—Clare Boothe

Getting Perspective

We all need a perspective check from time to time. Think about it. We complain about traffic—but forget to thank God for our transportation. We grumble about screaming children—forgetting the infertile women who long for noisy children underfoot. I heard a saying that begins, "I cried because I had no shoes until I met a man who had no feet." It's taught me to look at life more optimistically. At any given time, it could be worse. Cat Stevens epitomized this poem into the lyrics of his 1970s song "Moonshadow":

> And if I ever lose my legs
> I won't moan and I won't beg
> Oh if I ever lose my legs …
> I won't have to walk no more.[5]

Scripture provides a better perspective check than '70s pop songs. When David felt depressed, he cried, "Why are you cast down, O my soul? … Hope in God, for I shall yet praise Him for the help of His countenance" (Ps. 42:5). Paul had lost hope because of physical ailments, but the Lord reminded him, "My grace is sufficient for you, for My strength is made perfect in weakness" (2 Cor. 12:9).

What have you been complaining about? Your husband or home? Your career or clothes? Your looks or lot in life? I challenge you to transform these moanings into melodies. Write your own Scripture-based lyric or psalm to gain a perspective check. Before you know it, you'll be humming instead of grumbling.

LIFT UP ...

Heavenly Father, help me transform my difficult circumstances into a song of Your grace and compassion. You have entrusted me with my situation to grow me into a woman who uniquely expresses a mind held captive by love for You. In Jesus' name. Amen.

LEARN ABOUT ...

1 Foolish Fellas

Christ called them "fools" to describe their weakness, not their wickedness. They had heard three witnesses testify to the Lord's resurrection, but these men refused to be comforted. Perhaps they expected a grand public display. Jesus said, "Blessed are those who have not seen and yet have believed" (John 20:29).

---

5 Suffering Savior

Many New Testament Jews (and Orthodox Jews today) believed the Messiah would come as a conquering king establishing peace on earth. They missed His first coming as the suffering Savior according to Isaiah 53 and Psalm 22. At the Lord's Second Coming, they'll recognize too late "the one they have pierced" (John 19:37 NIV).

LOOK AT ...

The tumultuous thinking of the travelers to Emmaus bounced between bragging about the miraculous Messiah and doubting the Savior who suffered. Finally they shared stories that pointed toward the Lord's resurrection. James warned, "A double minded man is unstable in all his ways" (James 1:8 KJV).

Jesus, aware of their sorrowful hearts, initially approached the travelers with a compassionate question. Today we'll see how the Lord changed tactics and reprimanded them for harboring unbelief. Thankfully, Jesus knows just what we need—whether it's pity or a push. Sometimes it's a gentle word; on another occasion, it's a firm rebuke. Paul reminded Timothy, "Preach the word! Be ready in season and out of season. Convince, rebuke, exhort, with all longsuffering and teaching" (2 Tim. 4:2). What do you need most: a kick in the pants or a pat on the back?

READ LUKE 24:25–27.

Then He said to them, "O foolish ones, and slow of heart to believe in all that the prophets have spoken! Ought not the Christ to have suffered these things and to enter into His glory?" And beginning at Moses and all the Prophets, He expounded to them in all the Scriptures the things concerning Himself. Luke 24:25–27

1. What is the first description Jesus gave for the men traveling to Emmaus? How do you think this made them feel?

2. How did Jesus describe them next? What do you think this phrase meant?

3. What was the source of their unbelief?

4. What rhetorical question did Jesus ask?

5. Where did Jesus begin His defense for a suffering Savior?

6. How far did He expound His teaching, and what was the central topic?

LIVE OUT ...

7. The travelers were guilty of "unbelieving hearts," despite ample evidence to the contrary.

   Journal about a situation that caused you to doubt God.

   Make a list of promises and proofs to trust in God despite your circumstances.

8. Jesus understood that His pain brought gain. Using these two words as acrostics, list some of the ways Jesus suffered and ultimately received glory.

   P   G
   A   A
   I   I
   N   N

9. Jesus expounded about Himself "in all the Scripture." Recall one of the many Old Testament prophecies concerning the Messiah. Research the chapter and verse, and then write about what was predicted and how it was fulfilled.

LEARN ABOUT ...

6 Searching Scripture

This may be Jesus' most comprehensive teaching. He taught the plan of redemption from Genesis to Malachi, revealed Moses' portrayal of Jesus as the Passover lamb, referred to the psalmist's graphic description of the crucifixion, and pointed out the prophets' prediction of the virgin birth. The New Testament reveals what the Old Testament concealed.

7 Foolish or Faithful?

Jesus called these men foolish because of their unbelieving hearts. Faith is the polar opposite of foolishness. The psalmist wrote, "The fool has said in his heart, 'There is no God'" (Ps. 14:1). Or, "The fool has said, 'NO, God!'" It's not that people can't believe; it's that they won't.

8 Grief before Glory

For Jesus, grief preceded glory. Scripture teaches that we are cursed with sin, and the wages of sin is death. Jesus took our place and bore our shame, our sin, and our sorrow: "Christ has redeemed us from the curse of the law, having become a curse for us" (Gal. 3:13).

○ ○ ● ○ ○

Anyone can make future predictions, from weather forecasters to astrologists. The proof lies in clearly describing the event in advance and seeing it actually come to pass. You might predict the sun rising tomorrow, but could you predict the exact birthplace of a future US president just a few years in advance? The prophet Micah did just that when he foretold the Messiah would be born in Bethlehem (Mic. 5:2)—seven hundred years in advance. Then there's Jeremiah, he predicted that Jesus' family tree would spring from tribe of Judah. Both Matthew and Luke confirm that Jesus' ancestry follow this royal line that also included King David.

There are over three hundred prophecies concerning the Messiah in the Old Testament. Skeptics may challenge that such an outcome could be rigged—but could death by crucifixion, or being hung between two criminals with soldiers gambling for His garments? Could Jesus conspire or conjure up miracles like healing the blind and deaf or making the lame walk as Isaiah foretold? The Gospels tell us that Jesus, indeed, performed all of these miracles to His own detriment. As a result, the religious and political leaders of His day rejected and persecuted the Messiah.

You don't have to be a math whiz or a theologian to know that the evidence adds up. Jesus is the King of Kings, the long awaited Messiah.

LISTEN TO ...

No one ever graduates from Bible study until he meets the author face-to-face.

—Everett Harris

DAY 4

Saying Grace

In the atheist household where I grew up, our family never said grace at mealtime unless it was in jest. I remember my stepfather's flippant prayer: "Good food, good meat. Good God, let's eat." But when I ate at my friend Julie Miller's house, as my fork plunged into the spaghetti, I was abruptly interrupted by her dad saying grace. I awkwardly set down my fork and bowed my head. I learned that in some families, prayers were sincere, and thankfulness for food was basic. I am still grateful for their quiet example.

Most Westerners call this prayer before eating "saying grace." Many religions, from Catholics to Lutherans, repeat a memorized prayer at mealtimes. Interestingly, the Jews say grace *after* they eat. The precedence is found in Deuteronomy 8:10: "When you *have eaten and are full,* then you shall bless the LORD your God for the good land which He has given you." I don't know about you, but I feel more grateful on a full belly than an empty one. In our home, we sometimes say grace before, during, *and* after a meal.

Before Jesus partook of dinner at the invitation of His traveling companions, He stopped to "bless" the food. Think about this. Jesus was God, yet He thanked God for the bread provided by the Father. Does that make you feel a bit ashamed for the times you dived into a salad before thanking the Lord? Resolve to regularly "say grace" and give God glory for providing your daily bread.

LIFT UP ...

Lord, I confess that I have often recited a prayer without truly feeling grateful or acknowledging Your provision. At every meal, awaken me to the opportunity to appreciate Your steadfast grace in my life. Thank You. In Jesus' name. Amen.

LEARN ABOUT ...

2 Beckon

Without an invitation, gentleman Jesus intended to travel on. He beckons, "Behold, I stand at the door and knock. If anyone hears My voice and opens the door, I will come in to him and dine with him, and he with Me" (Rev. 3:20). Have you invited Him to join you?

LOOK AT ...

As Jesus unveiled the many Old Testament prophecies pertaining to Himself, His traveling companions wanted to extend their time with Him. Their two-hour journey probably felt like mere minutes. Too soon it was sunset, and they arrived at their destination. Clearly, they did not want their time with the Lord to end. Jesus indicated He would have walked farther, but they compelled Him to stay longer with them. How did they entice Jesus to stay? They invited Him to dinner! As He blessed the bread and talked about the truths of Scripture, the scales on their eyes were shed, and they *saw* the Savior. How interesting that at that moment of revelation, Jesus vanished from their midst. Was His mission accomplished with their recognition of His deity? Now the men who had been called "slow of heart" experienced racing hearts. Today, we'll observe God's table manners.

READ LUKE 24:28–32.

Then they drew near to the village where they were going, and He indicated that He would have gone farther. But they constrained Him, saying, "Abide with us, for it is toward evening, and the day is far spent." And He went in to stay with them.

Now it came to pass, as He sat at the table with them, that He took bread, blessed and broke it, and gave it to them. Then their eyes were opened and they knew Him; and He vanished from their sight.

And they said to one another, "Did not our heart burn within us while He talked with us on the road, and while He opened the Scriptures to us?"
Luke 24:28–32

1. Where did this event take place?

2. How did Jesus respond upon arriving at the village? Why?

3. Describe how the two men responded. Underline the word that suggests they were persuasive.

4. How did Jesus respond to their compelling invitation?

5. Circle the things Jesus did, and list your findings.

6. Describe how the two men responded. Why do you think they responded like this?

7. What did Jesus do next? How did this further affect the two men?

8. Explain how the men felt and why.

Live Out ...

9. The disciples refused to let Jesus leave, and Ruth refused to leave Naomi's side when returning to Bethlehem. Rewrite Ruth's plea into a personal prayer refusing to ever leave Jesus' side:

> Entreat me not to leave you,
> Or to turn back from following after you;
> For wherever you go, I will go;
> And wherever you lodge, I will lodge;
> Your people shall be my people,
> And your God, my God.
>
> Where you die, I will die,
> And there will I be buried.
> The LORD do so to me, and more also,
> If anything but death parts you and me. (Ruth 1:16–17)

Learn About ...

5 Bread

In the style of the Lord's Supper, Jesus offered the blessing and broke the bread. Perhaps the disciples had told them about the upper room where Jesus "took bread, gave thanks and broke it, and gave it to them, saying, 'This is My body which is given for you'" (Luke 22:19).

8 Burned

The weary travelers' spiritual heartburn wasn't from spicy food, but scriptural fire. When Jeremiah refused to share God's Word, he said, "'I will not make mention of Him, nor speak anymore in His name.' But His word was in my heart like a burning fire shut up in my bones" (Jer. 20:9).

9 Beg

When Jesus indicated He wanted to continue on His journey, the disciples "constrained" Him to stay. The word *constrain* carries the idea of begging, entreating, or compelling. It can also mean to force against one's nature. The disciples couldn't force God to do anything. Instead they compelled Him with courteous words.

LEARN ABOUT ...

10 Broken

Jesus introduced the Lord's Supper at His last Passover feast with the disciples. As He broke the bread and shared the wine, He encouraged them to repeat this "often" as a remembrance. The earliest believers met "daily with one accord in the temple, ... breaking bread from house to house" (Acts 2:46).

10. Jesus broke bread with the men traveling to Emmaus. Communion can be taken anywhere—not just in church. Take time now to find the elements for Communion, and enjoy breaking bread with Jesus. Journal about your experience.

11. The words of Jesus made the disciples' hearts burn. List some of the Scripture passages that have made your heart burn and why.

· · ● · ·

Innovation and creativity are often borne from necessity. For Ken Taylor, the problem was: *How can I help my children understand the Bible?* Taylor, who was raised on the King James Bible by his pastor-father, began paraphrasing Scripture into understandable passages during his train commute to Chicago. By 1962 he'd finished paraphrasing the epistles, which he called Living Letters, and in 1971 he published the complete Living Bible. Initially, no publisher acknowledged the achievement until Billy Graham printed half a million copies of Living Letters to distribute at his crusades. Ken Taylor birthed Tyndale Publishing out of his home into a humble business with the goal of making God's Word accessible to all. The New Living Translation, Tyndale's most recent Bible version, has now reached every continent in the world.[6]

In 1994, creativity came into play in Moscow when a sixty-year ban on Bible distribution was lifted. Christian missionaries arrived in Stavropol, Russia, with freshly printed Bibles, but the Bibles languished in customs. Meanwhile, the team learned of a warehouse where old confiscated Bibles were stored. Gaining permission from authorities, they hired a team to spread the good news.

An agnostic man hired to help distribute the Bibles decided to steal one for himself. When he opened it, he was stunned to discover his grandmother's familiar signature on the front page. He was found sobbing with the worn Book cradled in his hands.[7] Whether on the road to Emmaus, on a commuter train in Chicago, or in a warehouse in Stavropol, God's Word burns brightly!

LISTEN TO ...

I know the Bible is inspired because it finds me at a greater depth of my being than any other book.

—*Samuel Taylor Coleridge*

DAY 5

Heart Burn

Did you know that heartburn has nothing to do with the heart? Although the symptoms are similar to those of a heart attack, the two ailments vary greatly. One stems from the cardiovascular system while the other attacks the gastrointestinal tract. Heartburn does cause chest pain along with other telltale symptoms like difficulty swallowing; a burning sensation in the throat; a sour, bitter taste; and sometimes shortness of breath. Most causes are curable and avoidable. These include smoking, stress, snug clothing, and supersizing your meals.

Right after supper, our travelers to Emmaus experienced heartburn that kept them up throughout the night. Rich foods were not the culprits. Instead, God's revelation of truths gave them burning hearts. The only antidote for this kind of spiritual aching comes from changed lives. They had to act quickly on the new revelation of the risen Lord and exercise true faith by sharing the good news with their brethren. When they passed along the amazing truths, scriptural heartburn spread to Jerusalem and beyond. Oh, that our hearts would burn as brightly and obediently as with these faithful men!

LIFT UP ...

Lord, You constantly appear before me through Your Word. I pray to be quick to recognize Your voice and eager to share with others the message of the risen Savior. Time deceives and distracts me. Prompt me to get up and go where You would lead me. In Jesus' name. Amen.

LOOK AT ...

Out of nowhere, the mysterious traveler appeared to the two men on the road to Emmaus. Just as they recognized it was Jesus in their midst, He disappeared—vanished into thin air. Why do you suppose Jesus frequently appeared incognito? On the road to Damascus, Saul heard the voice of Jesus from the midst of a bright light. His companions heard the voice but saw no one (Acts 9:7). At the tomb, Mary mistook Jesus for a gardener until He called

LEARN ABOUT ...

I Rose Up!

These men went from men who "had hoped" to men who "rose up" to testify of Christ's resurrection. They left their supper and retraced their steps to share their revelation. As Jesus told Peter to "strengthen your brethren" (Luke 22:32), these men returned to do the same.

---

3 Reached Out!

After His resurrection, Jesus first reached out to the women—Mary specifically. Second, to Peter, the betrayer. Third, He joined two hopeless travelers to Emmaus. When Jesus appeared to the eleven disciples, He singled out Thomas, the doubter. What word describes you when you first recognized the resurrection?

---

6 Reaffirm

While the disciples discussed recent developments, two men ran in to bear witness. They cited chapter and verse from their Bible study with Jesus, strongly testifying of their encounter with the risen Lord. The seemingly inconsequential Emmaus travelers comforted the "mighty" apostles. Paul wrote, "Comfort one another" (I Thess. 4:18).

---

her by name (John 20:15–16). Did hearing His voice make her do a double take?

Perhaps something similar has happened to you. Maybe a good idea turned out to be God-inspired. Or a random act revealed God's right hand of favor. Begin to look for Jesus in some of your familiar places. He may be hiding in plain sight.

READ LUKE 24:33–35.

So they rose up that very hour and returned to Jerusalem, and found the eleven and those who were with them gathered together, saying, "The Lord is risen indeed, and has appeared to Simon!" And they told about the things that had happened on the road, and how He was known to them in the breaking of bread. Luke 24:33–35

1. Review yesterday's lesson. What miraculous event preceded this passage?

2. What phrase indicates that the men responded immediately?

3. Where did they go? Why do you think they went?

4. What two groups did they encounter?

5. In your own words, describe the topic of conversation.

6. What was the first thing the travelers shared?

7. Explain how they recognized Jesus.

LIVE OUT ...

8. a. The resurrection caused the hopeless travelers to rise up and testify. Write the name of someone you know who needs to believe in the risen Lord.

    b. Where does he or she live? How will you reach that individual with the good news?

    c. After making contact, record how the encounter went.

9. Jesus first appeared to those who seemed to need it most. Read 1 Corinthians 15:5–10.

    a. Which disciple first saw Jesus (v. 5)? Why do you think this was the case?

    b. How many saw Jesus next (v. 6)? Why do you think this was important?

    c. Who received a repeat appearance (v. 7)? Why do you think he did?

    d. Who was the last eyewitness of the risen Lord, and how did it affect his life (vv. 8–10)?

10. Sometimes our witness is not to the sinner but to the errant saint. Peter was called to strengthen his brethren. Journal about the ways you can strengthen the faith of someone who is wavering.

LEARN ABOUT ...

8 Resurrection

Salvation hinges on the reality of the resurrection of Jesus. Paul asserted that without the resurrection, Christianity has no meaning: "And if Christ has not been raised, our preaching is useless and so is your faith" (I Cor. 15:14 NIV). God's plan from eternity past crystallizes at the cross and the empty tomb.

10 Rebuild

Christians are humans too. Life deals blows to believers and unbelievers alike. Still, the psalmist promised that though we may stumble, we are never down for the count: "Though they stumble, they will never fall, for the LORD holds them by the hand" (Ps. 37:24 NLT). Let God lift you up!

○ ○ ● ○ ○

Broken bread. Jesus says He is "the bread of life." Why is the symbol of our Savior broken-ness? Can't the bread remain whole like a French baguette, an Italian ciabatta, or a Jewish challah? While delicious, these breads need yeast to make them rise. In Scripture, yeast often represents sin's nature to spread and permeate all it touches. Jesus warned His disciples, "Beware of the leaven of the Pharisees and the Sadducees" (Matt. 16:6). Could it be that Jesus needed no leavening agent or earthly element to rise again? Or that Jesus, God made flesh, remained untainted during His tenure among us?

Perhaps the reason unleavened bread best depicts Jesus lies in the fact that it breaks so easily. Isaiah prophesied, "He was wounded ... [and] bruised" for our sins (Isa. 53:5). Today we call unleavened bread *matzo*, which is similar in consistency to a saltine cracker. Have you noticed that crackers crumble more than the proverbial cookie? Jesus may have understood this when, during the Last Supper, He broke the unleavened bread and said, "Take, eat; this is My body which is broken for you; do this in remembrance of Me" (1 Cor. 11:24).

Any way you slice it, Jesus came to die. He was born to be bruised. It's impossible to receive the Communion wafer or cracker or matzo without remembering that the Bread *had* to be broken.

Listen To ...

The hands of Christ
Seem very frail
For they were broken
By a nail.
But only they
Reach heaven at last
Whom these frail, broken
Hands hold fast.

—*John Richard Moreland*

Barley Cake

Like wheat, barley grew abundantly in Middle Eastern regions. In ancient days, barley cost half the price of wheat, making it affordable even to the poor. As a method of welfare, the poor were allowed to glean from the edges of the field during the harvest. Barley was also used as fodder for livestock, which may explain why the prodigal filled himself on pig slop. As we learned from the story of the famine of Gideon's day, barley was a staple during times of famine. One of Gideon's men had a dream of a round loaf of barley bread that came tumbling into the Midianite camp (Judg. 7:13).

Barley grains were eaten raw or roasted over a fire and seasoned. Flour from barley came either coarse or fine. The coarse type produced rustic, chewy bread as eaten by Ezekiel the prophet (Ezek. 4:9). The fine flour added to honey created a delicious cake.

Preparation Time: 10 minutes
Cook Time: 10–15 minutes

Ingredients:

> 1 1/2 cups barley flour
>
> 1/2 cup wheat flour
>
> 1 teaspoon baking powder
>
> 1 cup whole milk
>
> 1 egg
>
> 1 cup liquefied honey
>
> Salt to taste

Instructions:

1. Preheat oven to 425 degrees. Sift flours and salt together.

2. In separate bowl, whisk together the milk and egg, constantly stirring; add the honey.

3. Make a trench in flour mixture, then add liquids and stir until evenly blended and moist. Do not overstir.

4. Scoop into spoonfuls (about a tablespoon) and drop on greased cookie sheet, leaving even spacing for cakes to spread. Bake for ten to fifteen minutes or until done.

GRACE NOTE

Heavenly Father,
*   When times are lean, we hunger for basic and accessible nourishment*
rather than delicacies and frivolous recipes. Often, it's more difficult to tune in
to our own spiritual famine. Let us think on the basics of our beliefs as we enjoy
this basic food. In Jesus' name. Amen.

Breakfast of Champions
John 21:1–25

Sport fishing is one of America's most popular outdoor activities, with a reported thirty million "anglers" and $45 billion in retail sales in 2006.[1] According to a report by The Recreational Boating and Fishing Foundation, "Boaters and anglers are significantly more satisfied with their marriages, relationships and friendships—and are more likely to have a close relationship with their children—than those who don't boat or fish."[2] Not only is fishing a recreational activity enjoyed for its relaxing atmosphere out in nature, but it's also an industry that contributes to the United States economy. The report goes on to say, "One in eight American adults—more than 30 million—fish, as do some eight million children ages six to fifteen. In 2006, they fished 517 million days and took 403 million trips."[3]

Twice in the book of John, the disciples saw the resurrected Lord. After that, they might have wanted a little relaxation and rest on their familiar Sea of Galilee. Instead, they were about to witness Jesus' final miracle before His ascension. This week we will study a fishing trip that left the disciples speechless and left Simon Peter forgiven.

Day 1: John 21:1–3	I'D RATHER BE FISHING
Day 2: John 21:4–8	SOUNDS FAMILIAR
Day 3: John 21:9–14	FILET OF SOUL
Day 4: John 21:15–19	DO YOU LOVE ME?
Day 5: John 21:20–25	NO COMPARISONS

DAY 1
I'd Rather Be Fishing

LIFT UP ...

Lord, when I am confused and trying to find my way, help me keep my eyes on You and the things of Your kingdom. Help me always to look for You on the shoreline. In Jesus' name. Amen.

LOOK AT ...

This week we see the third meeting of the disciples and Jesus following the resurrection. Earlier, Jesus instructed the disciples to meet Him in Galilee (Mark 14:28). Believing they had arrived first, they did what they usually did—went fishing. Some commentators believe this was disobedience, because they were told to meet Jesus in the mountains. Maybe it was difficult to resist Galilee in the springtime—the hills green and scattered with flowers, and warm ripples from the sea lapping on the shore. Either way, it wouldn't be long before the Savior appeared and the disciples once again learned that, although Jesus had been crucified and raised from the dead, He still provided for their needs. Once again He invited them to "come."

READ JOHN 21:1–3.

After these things Jesus showed Himself again to the disciples at the Sea of Tiberias, and in this way He showed Himself: Simon Peter, Thomas called the Twin, Nathanael of Cana in Galilee, the sons of Zebedee, and two others of His disciples were together. Simon Peter said to them, "I am going fishing."

They said to him, "We are going with you also." They went out and immediately got into the boat, and that night they caught nothing. John 21:1–3

LEARN ABOUT ...

2 Sea of Galilee

The Sea of Tiberias, also known as the Sea of Galilee, was where Jesus walked on water and calmed the storm. It is Israel's largest freshwater lake and is about thirty-three miles around, thirteen miles long, and eight miles wide. It is partly fed by underground springs, but the Jordan River is its main source.

---

3 Sea of Trouble

J. Vernon McGee called this group "the convention of the problem children ... Simon Peter, fervent but failing ... Thomas, that magnificent skeptic ... Nathanael, the wisecracker ... and the sons of thunder, James and John. Perhaps they represent you and me."

---

5 Sea of Men

Seven of the twelve disciples were fishermen. Fishermen were known for their courage and dedication and obedience to orders. They never quit, stayed focused on the task at hand, and knew how to work together. It makes sense that Jesus filled His inner circle with committed followers.

1. We begin today with the phrase *after these things*. Quickly review John 20 and note what "these things" refer to.

2. Where did this event take place?

3. Who witnessed this event?

4. What declaration did Simon Peter make? Why do you think he did this?

5. How did the rest of the men respond?

6. Describe how their adventure ended. Why do you think this was the case?

LIVE OUT ...

7. Review the events in John 20. How do you think the disciples were feeling? How do you think you would feel seeing the resurrected Jesus after watching Him die on the cross?

8. The disciples didn't know what to do after seeing Jesus resurrected, so they did the thing that came naturally—they went fishing. From the list below, mark some of the things you do when you need to work something out in your mind.

❑ Go fishing   ❑ Listen to music
❑ Read your Bible   ❑ Clean
❑ Talk to friends   ❑ Exercise
❑ Sing worship music   ❑ Sleep
❑ Read   ❑ Watch TV
❑ Pray   ❑ Other _____

9. If you regularly find yourself seeking solace in worldly things, make a commitment to seek comfort in the things of the Lord. Rewrite Psalm 63:1–5 into a prayer request to the Lord:

> O God, You are my God;
> > Early will I seek You;
> > My soul thirsts for You;
> > My flesh longs for You
> > In a dry and thirsty land
> > Where there is no water.
> So I have looked for You in the sanctuary,
> > To see Your power and Your glory.
>
> Because Your lovingkindness is better than life,
> > My lips shall praise You.
> Thus I will bless You while I live;
> > I will lift up my hands in Your name.
> My soul shall be satisfied as with marrow and fatness,
> > And my mouth shall praise You with joyful lips.

10. Jesus previously told His disciples He would make them "fishers of men." Fill in the chart below to find out what other "I will make" statements are in Scripture.

SCRIPTURE	I WILL MAKE ...
Genesis 12:2	
Genesis 17:6	
Isaiah 60:15	
Jeremiah 15:20	
Ezekiel 26:14	
Matthew 25:23	

LEARN ABOUT ...

8 Fishing for Peace

The word *peace* appears over three hundred times in the Bible. The disciples may have been seeking peace for their souls amid the familiar waves of Galilee, but they should have been seeking the One who gives peace: "Peace I leave with you, My peace I give to you" (John 14:27).

---

10 Fishing for Men

As fishers of men, we should seek unbelievers and catch them with the truth of the gospel. Fishermen make their living catching fish, but once caught, the fish dies. As believers, we should seek to catch those who are dead in their trespasses (Eph. 2:1) in order that they may be made alive in Christ.

· · ● · ·

An old joke is told about rogue pirates attempting to board a ship. "Bring me my red shirt!" bellowed the ship's captain to his anxious crew. The first mate quickly did the captain's bidding. The captain donned the shirt, and the fighting commenced. Victory! Later, as the crew rehashed the victory, one of them asked the captain, "Sir, why did you call for your red shirt before battle?" The captain replied, "If I'm wounded, the shirt will not show my blood, and thus, you men would continue to resist, unafraid." The captain knew his crew would fiercely fight on as long as he did.[4]

The disciples might have felt alone without Christ, but they knew He had given them the command to "go therefore and make disciples of all the nations" (Matt. 28:19). Jesus Christ put on the scarlet blood of salvation, which allowed His children to continue with this commission unafraid while resisting the Devil.

LISTEN TO ...

Hope is like the sun, which, as we journey toward it, casts the shadow of our burden behind us.

—*Samuel Smiles*

DAY 2
Sounds Familiar

The term *déjà vu* means "already seen"—it's the feeling that one has already encountered a current situation, even though the exact circumstances of the previous encounter aren't clear.[5] This feeling is often accompanied by a compelling sense of familiarity, strangeness, weirdness, or the uncanny. Most people can't recall when they first encountered the situation, but there is a strong sense of identification with the sights, sounds, smells, or feeling of the situation. Such experiences can be traced back as far as AD 400 in the writings of St. Augustine, who wrote of *falsae memoriae*. Authors like Sir Walter Scott, Dickens, Tolstoy, and Proust explored this phenomenon in one way or another in their writing.[6]

This is such a common experience that an Internet search for *déjà vu* yields dozens of sites where people post experiences like, "I once had a dream that I lost my tooth. I remember it was the tooth next to my buckteeth. Next week I lost the exact same tooth!" This may fall more in the category of premonition, but a repeated experience tends to chill us.

Did the disciples feel a similar sense on the Sea of Galilee early in the morning in these very familiar surroundings? They had been there before—with Jesus, in what must have seemed to have been another life.

LIFT UP ...

Lord, help me eagerly reach for You through Your Word. Remind me daily of Your familiar presence and Your past touches in my life. In Jesus' name. Amen.

LOOK AT ...

In yesterday's passage, the disciples took a fishing trip that yielded no fish. Today we find them receiving instruction from the Savior—and with their nets overflowing with fish. When the disciples saw the sun rising over the Galilean waters, all they could see was an empty boat. Jesus told them to cast their nets again, but they had toiled all night without

LEARN ABOUT ...

2 Occupied

The disciples might not have recognized Jesus because they had been up all night fishing and it was early morning on the Sea of Galilee. Maybe they were preoccupied with the task at hand. But the sheep know their Shepherd: "My sheep hear my voice, and I know them, and they follow Me" (John 10:27).

---

3 Offspring

Believers are often referred to as "children" in Scripture. We are heirs to the throne of God because of the sacrifice of His Son: "The Spirit Himself bears witness with our spirit that we are children of God, and if children, then heirs—heirs of God and joint heirs with Christ" (Rom. 8:16–17).

---

4 Overboard

Jesus provided a catch far greater than the disciples expected. Matthew Henry said, "Jesus manifests himself to His people by doing for them what no one else can do, and by doing things which they look not for."

---

success and were doubtful. The Lord filled their boats with fish to the point of sinking. Similarly, when Jesus called Simon Peter to ministry, Peter was in the same type of boat, on the same sea with not a fish in sight (Luke 5:1–11).

In John 20 the disciples had their first two interactions with the risen Lord. Today we see those same "fishers of men" as the Lord revealed His extraordinary hand in their lives: once again they met Jesus face-to-face.

READ JOHN 21:4–8.

But when the morning had now come, Jesus stood on the shore; yet the disciples did not know that it was Jesus. Then Jesus said to them, "Children, have you any food?" They answered Him, "No."

And He said to them, "Cast the net on the right side of the boat, and you will find some." So they cast, and now they were not able to draw it in because of the multitude of fish.

Therefore that disciple whom Jesus loved said to Peter, "It is the Lord!" Now when Simon Peter heard that it was the Lord, he put on his outer garment (for he had removed it), and plunged into the sea. But the other disciples came in the little boat (for they were not far from land, but about two hundred cubits), dragging the net with fish. John 21:4–8

1. How long were the disciples out on the boat?

2. Why do you think the disciples didn't recognize Jesus?

3. In what way did Jesus refer to the disciples? Do you think this tipped them off? Explain.

4. What did He instruct them to do? What were the results?

5. How do you think this affected the disciples?

6. Who recognized Jesus first? How did Simon Peter react?

7. Describe how the others responded.

Live Out ...

8. Simon Peter was zealous in all he did. What do you think your reaction would be in these circumstances?

9. In what other ways do people react to Jesus and His miracles?

10. John ("the disciple whom Jesus loved") was the first to recognize Jesus, but Simon Peter was the first to act. Fill in the following columns with the ways you see Jesus in your daily life and how you react.

I See Jesus In	I Act/React

11. Journal a prayer asking to know more of Jesus in your daily walk with Him. If you act/react in a way that is ungodly, ask Him to reveal how you can change those actions.

∘ ∘ ● ∘ ∘

Infatuation with oceans and seas is woven through cultures all over the world. From the worship of gods and goddesses of water, to worship of water itself, there is a vibrant fascination with taming and exploring

Learn About ...

8 Swimming

Peter jumped headfirst into the water in order to reach his Lord. Two hundred cubits is about three hundred feet from the shore. It would not have been a long swim, but it was too far to wade. Getting to Jesus always requires an effort. At the least, we must consider and believe.

---

9 Sensation

This is the last recorded miracle Jesus performed, and it is the only known miracle after the resurrection. Jesus performed over thirty miracles during His ministry on earth, but not all people believed: "Then Jesus said to him, 'Unless you people see signs and wonders, you will by no means believe'" (John 4:48).

the unknown deep. The Greek myths speak of Orion, who supposedly was gifted with the ability to walk on water by his father, Poseidon. Leonardo da Vinci sketched and described a way to walk on water using a set of floats on the feet. A countless number of gods and goddesses were associated in some way with water. Although there are not many stories of people obsessed with water itself, the *Urban Dictionary* defines a hydromaniac as "a person who is fascinated by water, intensely attracted by water, or loves to play in the water."[7]

As Christians, our fascination with water comes from a deeply spiritual place. We know that God created the sea (Gen. 1:9); He is also known as the fountain of life (Ps. 36:9), and Jesus offers living water (John 7:38). It's likely that fishermen had a fond connection to the water and no reservations about jumping in. Simon Peter was so zealous to get to the Lord, he didn't settle for treading water.

LISTEN TO ...

Faith expects from God what is beyond all expectation.

—*Andrew Murray*

DAY 3

Filet of Soul

There is a lengthy process and protocol for White House state dinners. Coordination begins with setting a date that works with the White House, the State Department, and the country being honored. The State Dining Room seats 140 guests, but in recent years a hangar-like tent has been erected on the South Lawn to allow for additional guests. Formal invitations are designed and calligraphed by the White House chief calligrapher.

At the event, each guest finds his or her name handwritten on a place card at the table, along with a copy of the evening's menu. The First Lady works closely with the White House executive chef and pastry chef to create a four- to five-course meal tailored to the theme of the visiting country. She also coordinates with the chief floral designer to ensure that tables are set with aromatic arrangements representing the two cultures—the United States and the visiting country.[8] It's said the only acceptable reason for failing to accept a presidential invitation is death or serious illness.

If Jesus had required such pomp and circumstance surrounding a meal with the disciples, the conversation would have been very different. Instead, Jesus offered a humble and simple request: "Come."

LIFT UP ...

Lord, the invitation to come to You will not arrive in the mail as an engraved invitation. Help me shed the busyness of life and sit down to dine with You. In Jesus' name. Amen.

LOOK AT ...

Today we read of the Savior's simple invitation to the disciples: "Come and dine." From the boat, the disciples saw Jesus on the shore. They made a dash to get to land while hauling in a huge catch of fish.

LEARN ABOUT ...

2 Combine

Jesus beckoned the disciples to add some of their catch to what He was preparing. This was the same meal Jesus provided for the five thousand (John 6:1–13). Once again the disciples saw what happened when they trusted the Son of God.

3 Caught

Jesus still provided for the needs of the disciples. By giving them 153 fish, He supplied far more than they could eat by themselves. God promised to provide *according* to His riches: "And my God shall supply all your need according to His riches in glory by Christ Jesus" (Phil. 4:19).

4 Come

This was the third time Jesus urged them to "come." The Savior bids us to "come and see" in John 1:39 and to "come to Me and drink" in John 7:37. Here He told the disciples to "come and eat." He also beckons all who labor and are heavy laden us to "come" to Him, and He will give rest (Matt. 11:28).

They may have rubbed their eyes to make certain it was really Jesus waiting for them with a seaside breakfast sizzling on the coals. Did they recall the last meal they shared with Him just before His crucifixion? Could they believe their eyes and their blessings to share yet another meal and conversation with Jesus? This meal would fill more than empty stomachs.

Now we step into the intimate setting Jesus arranged for the disciples in this early morning feast of fish and bread.

READ JOHN 21:9–14.

Then, as soon as they had come to land, they saw a fire of coals there, and fish laid on it, and bread. Jesus said to them, "Bring some of the fish which you have just caught."

Simon Peter went up and dragged the net to land, full of large fish, one hundred and fifty-three; and although there were so many, the net was not broken. Jesus said to them, "Come and eat breakfast." Yet none of the disciples dared ask Him, "Who are You?"—knowing that it was the Lord. Jesus then came and took the bread and gave it to them, and likewise the fish.

This is now the third time Jesus showed Himself to His disciples after He was raised from the dead. John 21:9–14

1. Describe what the disciples saw when they arrived at the shore.

2. What did He tell them to do? Why do you think this was His request?

3. How many fish did they catch? Why do you think the exact amount was important?

4. What did Jesus invite them to do?

5. None of the disciples asked who Jesus was. Why do you think this was so?

6. Why do you think the number of times Jesus showed Himself to the disciples is noteworthy?

LIVE OUT ...

7. Recount some of the other times Jesus gave bread and fish to the disciples.

8. Imagine what it would be like to sit down and have a meal with Jesus. Describe how you would respond. Would you be too nervous to eat, become speechless, or fear talking too much?

9. Today, Jesus invited the disciples to come and dine. Using the acrostic COME below, describe ways Jesus invites you to come to Him.

   C

   O

   M

   E

10. Sometimes it's hard to pursue a relationship with an unseen Savior. To help you think about Him in a more concrete way, you might set aside a time to have a "Jesus date." Arrange a meal, and set two places. Talk with the Savior over dinner. Sit in a park with your sack lunch. Send your family out for a meal while you have a quiet time with Jesus. Journal about your experience.

LEARN ABOUT ...

8 To Dine

Jesus continually calls us to be still and spend time with Him. He extends this invitation to all mankind: "Behold, I stand at the door and knock. If anyone hears My voice and opens the door, I will come in to him and dine with him, and he with Me" (Rev. 3:20).

9 To Die

Jesus urged us to come to Him. He also told us His purpose in coming to us. He came to seek and save the lost and pay the price and penalty for our sins: "God has sent His only begotten Son into the world ... to be the propitiation for our sins" (I John 4:9–10).

○ ○ ● ○ ○

In 2009 there was media frenzy over the infamous couple that crashed the White House State Dinner for visiting dignitaries from India. Michaele and Tareq Salahi attended the State Dinner but were not invited guests. The married couple from Virginia made it past *two* security checkpoints—including one that required positive photo identification by security. They were able to enter the White House and even meet the president.[9] They were photographed with Vice President Joe Biden; the White House Marines; the mayor of Washington DC, Adrian Fenty; and Katie Couric from CBS.[10]

Since that incident, a formal investigation was conducted to determine the breach of security at the White House. The Salahis have been dubbed "losers" by 70 percent of adults in the US according to a poll of 1,025 people by USA Today/Gallup.[11]

Today we see Jesus invite the disciples to "come and dine." They didn't need a written invitation or their names to be found on a security list. They had a personal invitation from the One hosting the gathering. Jesus bade them to come and share in the intimate friendship He offered. What does it feels like to dine with the Savior? Let's come to Him and "taste and see that the LORD is good" (Ps. 34:8).

LISTEN TO ...

Human fellowship can go to great lengths, but not all the way. Fellowship with God can go to all lengths.

—*Oswald Chambers*

DAY 4
Do You Love Me?

As a little girl, did you ever play "he loves me, he loves me not"? After you plucked the petals off a flower, the last remaining petal revealed if the boy in question loved you or loved you not. This test of affection crosses thirty languages. There is even a more positive version that says, "he loves me, he loves me lots."

Our culture is infatuated with love. However, the word *love* is shamefully misused. People use the word interchangeably to describe their fondness for pizza and their affection for their spouse. In English, there is only one word for love. On the other hand, Greek has several distinct words. Even if you really like pizza, you probably don't love it unconditionally—as in the *agape* love Christ has for us.

Outside of English and Greek, words for love can be found in many languages, and all are used differently, depending on context. No matter what the language, people everywhere seek love.

The disciples knew Jesus loved them, but today's conversation was about Simon Peter's love for Jesus. In the first three gospel accounts, Peter boasted he would *never* deny Jesus—and later each gospel sadly records Simon Peter's denial of the Lord. Just as the resurrection followed the crucifixion, we see that forgiveness followed Peter's denial.

LIFT UP ...

Lord, if You ask me, "Do you love Me?" I pray my answer will always be a resounding, "Yes, Lord, You know all things; You know that I love You." I pray that no words could fully describe my ever-deepening love for You. In Jesus' name. Amen.

Look At ...

Peter was impulsive and zealous. I understand his eagerness to run ahead of the Lord and his emotional loyalty that led him to blurt, "Lord, not so!" These actions got him into trouble at times.

Today, however, we read of an encounter with a much different Simon Peter. Following the Lord's crucifixion and resurrection, Peter's heart ached because of his betrayal of the Lord he loved. Confronted with the painful realization that his actions didn't match his words, he learned he should weigh his words and control his will. Jesus, in His grace and mercy, offered Simon Peter another chance—in fact, three chances—to verify his love.

Read John 21:15–19.

So when they had eaten breakfast, Jesus said to Simon Peter, "Simon, son of Jonah, do you love Me more than these?" He said to Him, "Yes, Lord; You know that I love You."

He said to him, "Feed My lambs."

He said to him again a second time, "Simon, son of Jonah, do you love Me?"

He said to Him, "Yes, Lord; You know that I love You."

He said to him, "Tend My sheep."

He said to him the third time, "Simon, son of Jonah, do you love Me?" Peter was grieved because He said to him the third time, "Do you love Me?"

And he said to Him, "Lord, You know all things; You know that I love You."

Jesus said to him, "Feed My sheep. Most assuredly, I say to you, when you were younger, you girded yourself and walked where you wished; but when you are old, you will stretch out your hands, and another will gird you and carry you where you do not wish." This He spoke, signifying by what death he would glorify God. And when He had spoken this, He said to him, "Follow Me." John 21:15–19

1. Describe what Jesus and the disciples did first.

2. To whom did Jesus turn His attention? What did He ask?

3. How did Simon reply?

4. How did Jesus encourage Peter to express his love? Why?

5. Underline how many times Jesus asked the same question, and record your findings here.

6. What was Simon's final response? What does it say about how he was feeling?

7. Recount the prediction Jesus made about Simon Peter's future. What do you think this referred to?

8. What final command did Jesus give to Simon Peter?

9. Count the number of times the word *love* is used in today's Scripture. Fill in the chart below to learn of others throughout Scripture that Jesus loved.

SCRIPTURE	THOSE JESUS LOVED
Mark 10:21	
John 11:5	
John 13:1	
John 13:23	

LEARN ABOUT ...

3 Humbling the Sinner

Previously, Simon Peter had boasted of his faith and service to the Lord. In Matthew 26:33 he compared himself to other disciples, saying *they* might stumble but *he* never would. In John 21, he humbly sought forgiveness from Jesus and learned, "He scorns the scornful, but gives grace to the humble" (Prov. 3:34).

4 Heeding the Shepherd

If Simon Peter loved Jesus, he would heed His instruction and take care of the flock. Lambs, like babies, need to be fed. Sheep need to be tended and led and protected. Jesus asked Simon Peter to love the diverse people of this world—just as He did.

6 Hearing the Savior

Simon Peter denied the Lord three times and wept bitterly. Here he wept again because the Lord allowed him to offset those denials with three affirmations of his love. Peter came to know the true love of God. "Yes, I have loved you with an everlasting love" (Jer. 31:3).

LIVE OUT ...

10. Jesus instructed Simon Peter to tend His sheep. In any position of life, there are always sheep in our care. Journal about who is in your flock. What do you think it means to tend them? Have you done a good job as a shepherd, or have you let your sheep wander?

Learn About ...

10 Peter the Shepherd

Only those who love the Good Shepherd and follow Him are qualified to tend the flock. The word for "tend" in the Greek is *poimaino*, meaning, "to shepherd." "He will feed His flock like a shepherd; He will gather the lambs with His arm, and carry them in His bosom" (Isa. 40:11).

---

11 Peter the Servant

Peter, who denied the Lord, was restored to serve, sacrifice, and speak the truth of the Lord Jesus. Nothing distracted him from service. Empowered by the Holy Spirit, Simon Peter was an under-shepherd who continued the work of shepherding the flock, even when he was in chains (Acts 12:6).

11. Upon his restoration, Jesus told Simon Peter that his job was to tend the sheep. This task would not be without trials. What trials have you faced when given a task by the Lord? Journal about them.

○ ○ ● ○ ○

Throughout the Bible we read stories of redemption. People who were headed down a path of destruction or a path of the unknown are turned around by the One who leads the way—Jesus. Saul, on the road to Damascus, was turned around and then given a new name: Paul. He became one of the greatest evangelists in the Bible. The adulteress, about to be stoned by the hostile mob, was redeemed by the challenging words of Jesus as He wrote in the sand. Joseph was sold into slavery by his jealous brothers but would later become second-in-command and save the very ones who betrayed him. Ruth, a Moabite widow who swore to take care of her mother-in-law, found love and preservation in the arms of Boaz, her kinsman-redeemer.

Our God is a God of redemption. He gives us "beauty for ashes, the oil of joy for mourning, the garment of praise for the spirit of heaviness" (Isa. 61:3). Today we see this promise come to life again as Peter, who had denied the Lord, was given another chance to serve and love Him. Webster's defines *redeem* as "to free from what distresses or harms. To release from blame or debt."[12] What sweet words those were to Peter. Although the prediction of his death soon followed his commission, he knew he was redeemed by the God who saves.

Listen To ...

I find the doing of the will of God leaves me no time for disputing about His plans.

—*George MacDonald*

No Comparisons

Making comparisons can sometimes get us into trouble, yet we are routinely inclined to "compare and contrast" in our daily lives. This might be helpful when comparing two apples—choosing the one without the worm makes total sense. But if we are comparing apples to oranges, the fundamental difference between them negates a valid conclusion.

But there is nothing that compares to the living God. God said in Isaiah 46:5–9:

> To whom will you liken Me, and make Me equal
> And compare Me, that we should be alike?
> They lavish gold out of the bag,
> And weigh silver on the scales;
> They hire a goldsmith, and he makes it a god;
> They prostrate themselves, yes, they worship.
> They bear it on the shoulder, they carry it
> And set it in its place, and it stands;
> From its place it shall not move.
> Though one cries out to it, yet it cannot answer
> Nor save him out of his trouble.
> Remember this, and show yourselves men;
> Recall to mind, O you transgressors.
> Remember the former things of old,
> For I am God, and there is no other;
> I am God, and there is none like Me.

When we compare ourselves to others, we are setting the stage for jealousy and pride: *Lord, why does she have good health, while I'm sick? Why do You bless my neighbor financially, while I'm struggling? Lord, it looks like You love her more than You love me!*

God looks at us singularly. He sees our strengths, weaknesses, potential, and limitations. He loves us so much that He will discipline us when we wander into foolish comparisons. You are uniquely you—like no one else—and He loves you.

LIFT UP ...

Lord, I get in trouble when I compare myself to others. I either fall short and feel badly, or I am swelled up with pride. Help me keep my eyes on You to ponder Your incomparable greatness and uniqueness. In Jesus' name. Amen.

LOOK AT ...

The Lord no sooner humbled Simon Peter and commissioned him to shepherd the flock than Peter once again took his eyes off the Lord. He began to compare himself to John. In the past, Peter often boasted that he would die for the Lord. Finally, he humbled himself to do the Lord's work when Jesus told him he would be bound in chains and taken to a place he didn't want to go. It's easy to keep your focus when you are doing the work of the Lord—much harder when you find yourself in chains. Are you commissioned to work for the Lord but feel as though you are bound in chains? Like Simon Peter you can take hold of God's promise: "The LORD gives freedom to the prisoners" (Ps. 146:7).

READ JOHN 21:20–25.

Then Peter, turning around, saw the disciple whom Jesus loved following, who also had leaned on His breast at the supper, and said, "Lord, who is the one who betrays You?" Peter, seeing him, said to Jesus, "But Lord, what about this man?"

Jesus said to him, "If I will that he remain till I come, what is that to you? You follow Me."

Then this saying went out among the brethren that this disciple would not die. Yet Jesus did not say to him that he would not die, but, "If I will that he remain till I come, what is that to you?"

This is the disciple who testifies of these things, and wrote these things; and we know that his testimony is true.

And there are also many other things that Jesus did, which if they were written one by one, I suppose that even the world itself could not contain the books that would be written. Amen. John 21:20–25

LEARN ABOUT ...

1. Who did Simon Peter see when he turned around? What did he ask Jesus?

2. How did Jesus respond to Peter's question? What did He command?

3. How was this comment misinterpreted? How did John clarify this?

4. How did John describe himself?

5. What did John know to be true? How did he know it?

6. What did John say would be the result if each thing about Jesus were written down?

7. When you think of the miracles of Jesus, what do you think of?

LIVE OUT ...

8. Proverbs 4:27 tells us, "Do not turn to the right or the left." We are commanded to keep our eyes straight ahead on God. Fill in the columns with the things that either clear or confuse your focus.

CLEAR FOCUS   **CONFUSE FOCUS**

1 Boasting

Previously, Peter boasted that he would die for the Lord. Now Jesus told him that his boast would be a reality. He learned that the only thing worth boasting in is Christ: "But God forbid that I should boast except in the cross of our Lord Jesus Christ" (Gal. 6:14).

2 Following

Jesus told us not to worry about ourselves, but to stay focused on Him. Romans 14:8–10 says all we do should be for the Lord, not for praise from our brother: "For if we live, we live to the Lord; and if we die, we die to the Lord" (Rom. 14:8).

5 Bearing

Greco-Roman and Jewish legal documents typically ended with an attestation by a witness or witnesses. John ended his book attesting that he personally bore witness to these things, validating the works of the Lord: "To bear witness of the Light, that all through him might believe" (John 1:7).

8 Running

It's tempting to look around us as we run the race. Jesus wants us to keep our eyes on the prize: heaven. Matthew Henry said, "If we attend to the duty of following Christ, we shall find neither heart nor time to meddle with that which does not belong to us."

LEARN ABOUT ...

10 Testifying

God does not want us to
testify to the things of this
world, but rather to His
presence in our lives: "So
that I may finish my race
with joy, and the ministry
which I received from the
Lord Jesus, to testify to the
gospel of the grace of God"
(Acts 20:24).

9. Twice Jesus told Peter to "follow Me." Fill in the chart below to find other times He gave this command.

SCRIPTURE	FOLLOW ME
Matthew 16:24	
Matthew 19:21	
John 10:27	
John 12:26	

10. John said if all that Jesus did was written down, all the books in the world could not contain the accounts of them. Below write a handful of the things Jesus has done for you. Making this a practice in your life might one day fill a book—or a library of books!

○ ○ ● ○ ○

Inside St. Peter's Basilica in Rome is a pieta by Michelangelo. *Pietà* is Italian for "pity," and a pieta is a type of artwork that depicts Mary holding the dead body of the crucified Jesus. The sculpture in the Basilica was originally commissioned for the French Cardinal Jean de Bilheres, a representative in Rome. It took two years to carve and is the only piece Michelangelo ever signed. In 1972 the statue sustained considerable damage at the hand of a mentally disturbed man, Laszlo Toth, who entered the Basilica and struck the statue fifteen times with a hammer while shouting, "I am Jesus Christ!" Damage to Mary's face included the loss of part of her nose and a chipped eyelid. Her head, neck, and veil were damaged and her fingers and arm were broken off. Tourists took many of the marble pieces of the statue, and some were later returned. It was a painstaking task to restore the image, but today there is little evidence of the damage.[13]

This is a metaphor of the restoration our Savior offers to us. He takes the damaged pieces and replaces them with pieces of Himself to restore us. He polishes and repairs us, knowing the cracks and damage from our past. He makes us new.

LISTEN TO ...

By a Carpenter mankind was made, and only by that Carpenter can mankind be remade.

—*Desiderius Erasmus*

Grilled St. Peter's Fish

"A rose by any other name would smell as sweet," said William Shakespeare. In other words, changing the name of a thing does not alter the thing itself. The Sea of Galilee in northern Galilee bears three names. In the Old Testament, people knew this bountiful body of water as *Kinneret*, which originated from the Hebrew word for harp. The word perfectly suits the shape of this lake. By the New Testament era, Peter and the sons of Zebedee fished from the Sea of Tiberias, which bore the same name as that region's capital. Whatever the name, this body of freshwater is the largest lake in Israel.[14]

The sea with three names yields a fish with three names too. Most famously, we know this species as *St. Peter's fish*, named after the salty apostle. Before Peter arrived on the scene, the Hebrews called this fish *musht*. Today we know this tender, moist, mild-tasting fish as *tilapia*.[15] This fish has been a staple for the Israeli diet throughout the ages. Most often the fish is grilled whole from head to tail. Sometimes restaurants present it with a coin in its mouth, recalling how God provided money for taxes in the mouth of a fish. I suggest serving it with this lovely chervil sauce.

Ingredients:

> 1 1/4 cup fresh chervil, chopped coarsely
> 2 cloves garlic, chopped
> Juice and zest of 1 lemon
> Salt and pepper to taste
> 4 St. Peter's fish (tilapia) fillets
> 3 tablespoons flour
> 1/2 cup olive oil
> 1/4 cup onion, chopped

Instructions:

1. In a food processor, combine the chervil and garlic with two tablespoons of water and blend until the mixture is completely smooth. Adding another two tablespoons of water, mix well to thin the mixture. Add the lemon juice and salt and pepper to taste. Set aside, covered.

2. On a flat plate, combine the flour with about a half teaspoon each of salt and pepper, and mix well. Into this, dip the fillets, coating well and shaking off whatever excess adheres. In a large, heavy skillet, heat the oil and fry the fish until well browned on both sides. Transfer the fish to a preheated serving platter, and set aside to keep warm.

3. Discard about half of the oil. In the remaining oil, sauté the onions until golden brown. Add the remaining flour, and cook over a low flame until the mixture is light brown, stirring constantly. Add the chervil mixture and cook, continuing to stir, for two to three minutes longer. Pour the sauce over the fish, and serve immediately.

GRACE NOTE

Heavenly Father,

We know that a rose by any other name is still a sweet-smelling and beautiful flower. You, too, are known by other names—the Father, the Son, and the Holy Spirit—and yet You are One God: singular, fragrant, beautiful, and pure. In the name of the Father, the Son, and the Holy Spirit. Amen.

Bibliography

The author has used the following books and electronic sources in preparing the illustrations and sidebar material for this book.

The American Heritage® Dictionary of the English Language, 4th ed.

Arnold, Clinton E. *Zondervan Illustrated Bible Backgrounds Commentary: Matthew, Mark, Luke.* Grand Rapids: 2002.

Barclay, William. *The Gospel of Luke.* Louisville, KY: Westminster John Knox Press, 2001.

————. *The New Daily Study Bible, The Gospel of Matthew Volume Two.* Louisville, KY: Westminster John Knox, 2001.

Batmanglij, Najmieh. *Food of Life: Ancient Persian and Modern Iranian Cooking and Ceremonies.* Waldorf, MD: Mage, 1986.

Benge, Janet and Geoff. *George Müller.* Seattle: YWAM Publishing, 1998.

Bible Illustrator for Windows, version 3.0F. Parsons Technology, 1998. Illustrations copyright © 1998 by Christianity Today, Inc.

Blue Letter Bible, www.blueletterbible.org.

Bock, Darrell L. *The NIV Application Commentary: Luke.* Grand Rapids, MI: Zondervan, 1996.

Boice, James Montgomery. *The Gospel of John.* Grand Rapids: Zondervan, 1985.

Bromiley, Geoffrey W. *International Standard Bible Encyclopedia.* Vol. 2. Grand Rapids: Eerdmans, 1982.

Clark, Cynthia L. *The American Economy: A Historical Encyclopedia, Volume 1.* Santa Barbara, CA: ABC-CLIO, LLC, 2011.

Coleridge, Samuel. *The Rime of the Ancient Mariner.* London: Sampson Low, Son & Co., 1857.

Easton's Bible Dictionary. In PC Study Bible. Seattle, Biblesoft: 2003, 2006.

Encyclopædia Britannica Online. Encyclopædia Britannica, 2011.

Fausset's Bible Dictionary. Electronic Database. Seattle: Biblesoft, 1998, 2003, 2006.

Freeman, James M. *The New Manners and Customs of the Bible.* Alachua: Bridge-Logos, 1998.

Geldenhuys, Norval. *Commentary on the Gospel of Luke.* Grand Rapids: Eerdmans, 1966.

Gladwell, Malcolm. *Outliers.* New York: Little Brown, 2008.

Griffin, John Howard. *Black Like Me.* New York: Penguin, 1963.

Guest, Edgar Albert. "Be a Friend," *A Heap O' Livin'.* Chicago: The Reilly & Britton Co., 1916.

Henry, Matthew. *Matthew Henry's Commentary on the Whole Bible: One Volume Edition, Complete and Unabridged.* Peabody, MA: Hendrickson, 1991.

Hewett, James. *Illustrations Unlimited.* Carol Stream, IL: Tyndale, 1988.

INFOsearch™. Illustrations data and database. The Communicator's Companion™. P.O. Box 171749, Arlington, Texas 76003. www.infosearch.com.

International Standard Bible Encyclopaedia. Electronic Database. Seattle: Biblesoft, 1996.

Keener, Craig S. *IVP Bible Background Commentary: New Testament.* Downer's Grove, IL: InterVarsity Press, 1993.

Keeven, Ronald P. *A Joke, a Quote, and the Word.* Mustang, OK: Tate Publishing, 2006.

Kempis, Thomas à. *The Imitation of Christ.* Peabody, MA: Hendrickson, 2004.

Lockyer, Herbert. *Nelson's Illustrated Bible Dictionary.* In *PC Study Bible,* version 4.2b. Seattle: Biblesoft, 2004.

Lotz, Anne Graham. *Just Give Me Jesus.* Nashville: Thomas Nelson, 2000.

MacArthur, John. *The MacArthur Study Bible.* Nashville: Thomas Nelson, 1997.

Mackay, Charles. *Selected Poems and Songs.* London: Whittaker and Co., 1888.

McGee, J. Vernon. *John III.* Nashville: Thomas Nelson, 1995.

McClintock and Strong Encyclopedia. Electronic Database. Seattle: Biblesoft, 2000.

Merriam-Webster's Collegiate Dictionary, 11th ed.

Morrison, G. H. *Morrison on Luke.* Chattanooga, TN: AMG Publishers, 1978.

Müller, George. *George Müller's Narratives.* Mobi Classics, 2010.

Nelson's Quick Reference Topical Bible Index. Nashville: Thomas Nelson, 1996.

The Nelson Study Bible. Nashville: Thomas Nelson, 1997.

New Exhaustive Strong's Numbers and Concordance with Expanded Greek-Hebrew Dictionary. Seattle: Biblesoft and International Bible Translators, Inc., 1994.

Phillips, John. *Exploring the Gospel of Matthew.* Grand Rapids: Kregel, 1999.

Phillips, Rachael. *Well With My Soul.* Uhrichsville, OH: Barbour Publishing, 2003.

Piven, Frances Fox, and Richard Cloward. *Poor People's Movements.* New York: Vantage Books, 1979.

Salt for Sermons, http://www.saltforsermons.org.uk.

SermonCentral.com, http://www.sermoncentral.com.

"Sermon Illustrations," Net Bible, http://www.sabda.org/netbible5/illustration.php.

Sermon Illustrations, http://www.sermonillustrations.com.

Smith, Chuck, and Tal Brooke. *Harvest.* Costa Mesa, CA: Chosen Books, 1987.

Steel, Jr., Richard A., and Evelyn Stoner. *Bible Illustrations, Book 3: Practical Bible Illustrations from Yesterday and Today.* Chattanooga, TN: AMG Publishers.

St. James Encyclopedia of Popular Culture. Detroit: St. James Press, 2005–2006.

Stoner, Peter, and Robert Newman. *Science Speaks.* Chicago: Moody Press, 1976. Revised and HTML formatted by Don W. Stoner, 2005.

Strathern, Paul. *Mendeleyev's Dream.* New York: St. Martin's Press, 2000.

Strong's Complete Word Study Concordance. Chattanooga, TN: AMG, 2004.

Swindoll, Charles. *The Tale of the Tardy Oxcart.* Nashville: Thomas Nelson, 1998.

Tenney, Merrill C. *John: The Gospel of Belief.* Grand Rapids: Eerdmans, 1976.

Thompson, C. J. S. *Mystery and Lure of Perfume.* Whitefish, MT: Kessinger Publishing, 2003.

Trumbull, H. C. *The Biblical Illustrator.* Seattle: Ages Software and Biblesoft, 2006.

Uldrich, Jack. *Soldier, Statesman, Peacemaker.* New York: AMACOM, 2005.

Unger, Merrill F., and R. K. Harrison, eds., *The New Unger's Bible Dictionary.* Chicago: Moody Press, 1988.

———. *The Unger's Bible Dictionary.* In *PC Study Bible,* version 4.2b. Seattle: Biblesoft, 2004.

Vine, W. E. *Vine's Expository Dictionary of New Testament Words.* In *PC Study Bible,* version 4.2b. Seattle: Biblesoft, 2004.

———, Merrill F. Unger, and William White Jr. *Vines' Complete Expository Dictionary of Old and New Testament Words.* Nashville: Thomas Nelson, 1984, 1996.

Walvoord, John F., and Roy B. Zuck. *The Bible Knowledge Commentary: New Testament.* Colorado Springs: David C Cook, 1983.

Wiersbe, Warren. *The Bible Exposition Commentary: New Testament, Volume 1.* Colorado Springs: David C Cook, 2001.

Youngblood, Ronald F. *Nelson's Bible Dictionary.* In *PC Study Bible,* version 4.2b. Seattle: Biblesoft, 2004.

Notes

INTRODUCTION

1. Merrill F. Unger, *The New Unger's Bible Dictionary*. Originally published by Moody Press, Chicago, Illinois, 1988. In PC Study Bible, version 4.2b (Seattle: Biblesoft, 2004).

LESSON ONE: THE BEST IS YET TO COME

1. Frank Sinatra, "The Best Is Yet to Come," *It Might as Well Be Swing* © 1964 Sonny Burke.
2. Merrill C. Tenney, *John: The Gospel of Belief* (Grand Rapids: Eerdmans, 1976), 83.
3. "How to Make a Wedding Guest List," posted by tbolin728, eHow.com, http://www.ehow.com/how_2183225_weddingguestlist.html#ixzz0uGH3BJ2s, accessed October 10, 2011.
4. Robin Turner, "Hotel Bug Ruined Dream Wedding," *South Wales Echo,* January 15, 2009, http://www.walesonline.co.uk/news/wales-news/2009/01/15/hotel-bug-ruined-dream-wedding-91466-22695762/.
5. James Montgomery Boice, *The Gospel of John* (Grand Rapids: Zondervan, 1985), 143.
6. "Preparations for Friday Prayer," The 30-Days Prayer Network, http://www.30-days.net/islam/basics/preparations-for-friday-prayer/, adapted.
7. *McClintock and Strong Encyclopedia*, Electronic Database (Seattle: Biblesoft, 2000).
8. George Müller, "Orphanages," *George Müller's Narratives* (Mobi Classics, 2010), e-book.
9. Janet and Geoff Benge, *George Müller* (Seattle: YWAM Publishing, 1998), 166–68.
10. Mary Stevenson, "Footprints in the Sand," 1939, http://www.footprints-inthe-sand.com/index.php?page=Poem/Poem.php. Used with permission.
11. Ronit Treatman, "Rosh Hashanah Wishes Bundled in a Grape Leaf," http://blog.pjvoice.com/diary/663/rosh-hashanah-wishes-bundled-in-a-grape-leaf (accessed November 28, 2011).

LESSON TWO: HAPPY HOUR

1. *St. James Encyclopedia of Popular Culture* 2005–2006, s.v. "happy hour."

2. Charles Swindoll, *The Tale of the Tardy Oxcart* (Nashville: Thomas Nelson, 1998), 21, 626.

3. "The Water in You," U.S. Geological Survey, http://ga.water.usgs.gov/edu/propertyyou. html, last modified June 20, 2011.

4. Samuel Coleridge, *The Rime of the Ancient Mariner* (London: Sampson Low, Son & Co., 1857), 50.

5. R. G. Kirk, "Would Ancient Egyptians Worship Your Pet Cat?" October 2, 2007, http:// www.articlesbase.com/pets-articles/would-ancient-egyptians-worship-your-pet-cat-225044. html.

6. Vikas Kamat, "Indian Culture: Worship of Vehicles—Car Puja," Kamat's Potpourri, http://www.kamat.com/indica/culture/sub-cultures/car_puja.htm, last modified October 9, 2011.

7. Thomas à Kempis, *The Imitation of Christ* (Peabody, MA: Hendrickson, 2004), 18.

8. Rachael Phillips, *Well With My Soul* (Uhrichsville, OH: Barbour Publishing, 2003), 41.

9. Kenneth W. Osbeck, *101 Hymn Stories* (Grand Rapids: Kregel, 1982), 126–27.

10. Claudia Reinhart and Bill Ganzel, "Rural Life in the 1940s," Wessel's Living History Farm, http://www.livinghistoryfarm.org/farminginthe40s/life_01.html, last modified May 19, 2010.

LESSON THREE: IN KNEAD OF BREAD

1. Sue Forrester, "Ready-Sliced Bread Favored," *New York Times*, January 26, 1943, http:// select.nytimes.com/gst/abstract.html?res=FA0D15F63D59147B93C4AB178AD85F478 485F9.

2. Matthew Henry, *Matthew Henry's Commentary on the Whole Bible: New Modern Edition*, Electronic Database (Hendrickson, 1991).

3. Cynthia L. Clark, *The American Economy: A Historical Encyclopedia, Volume 1* (Santa Barbara, CA: ABC-CLIO, LLC, 2011), 384.

4. Frances Fox Piven and Richard Cloward, *Poor People's Movements* (New York: Vantage Books, 1979), 43, 52.

5. "Never Too Old to Serve," Index #3895, *Bible Illustrator For Windows*, version 3.0 F (Parson Technology, 1998), adapted.

6. Tony Phillips, David Noever, "Planets in a Bottle—More about Yeast," NASA Science: Science News, http://science.nasa.gov/newhome/headlines/msad16mar99_1b.htm, last modified April 6, 2011.

7. *Wikipedia,* s.v. "Pita," http://en.wikipedia.org/wiki/Pita, last modified October 10, 2011.

LESSON FOUR: GOOD COMPANY CORRECTS BAD MORALS

1. Edgar Albert Guest, "Be a Friend," *A Heap O' Livin'* (Chicago: The Reilly & Britton Co., 1916), 97.

2. "Feeding America: Hunger in America," Hunger & Poverty Statistics, U.S. Census Bureau. Carmen DeNavas Walt, B. Proctor, C. Lee. Income, Poverty, and Heath Insurance Coverage in the United States: 2009, http://feedingamerica.org/hunger-in-america/hunger-facts/hunger-and-poverty-statistics.aspx, accessed December 28, 2001.

3. "Feeding America: Hunger in America," U.S. Census Bureau.

4. Silas Shotwell, *Homemade*, September 1987.

5. "The Origin of Tabouli," Sabra Foods, http://www.sabrafoods.com/Tabouli_Origin.htm, last modified April 25, 2009.

LESSON FIVE: BUSY OR BLESSED?

1. Malcolm Gladwell, *Outliers* (New York: Little Brown, 2008).

2. "St. Mary's Church," Fairford History Society, http://www.fairfordhistory.org.uk/Topics/StMarys.html, last modified July 20, 2010.

3. Herbert Lockyer, *Nelson's Illustrated Bible Dictionary* (Nashville: Thomas Nelson, 1986).

4. *McClintock and Strong Encyclopedia*, Electronic Database (Seattle: Biblesoft, 2000).

5. C. J. S. Thompson, *Mystery and Lure of Perfume* (Whitefish, MT: Kessinger Publishing, 2003), 12.

6. *Merriam-Webster's Collegiate Dictionary,* 11th ed., s.v. "perfume."

7. Paul Strathern, *Mendeleyev's Dream* (New York: St. Martin's Press, 2000), 19.

8. Tabitha Morgan, "Bronze Age Perfume 'Discovered,'" BBC News, March 19, 2005, http://news.bbc.co.uk/2/hi/europe/4364469.stm.

9. Office of Technology Assessment, *Who Goes There: Friend or Foe?* (Washington, DC: US Government Printing Office, June 1993), 38.

10. Craig Brian Larson, "Strong to the Finish," Preaching Today, Tape No. 155, 1997.

11. "Judas Burning," *BBC,* April 12, 2006, http://www.bbc.co.uk/liverpool/content/articles/2006/04/12/faith_judas_burning_feature.shtml.

12. Orin Philip Gifford (B. 1847), Topic: Riches, Index # 2805-2815, *Bible Illustrator For Windows*, version 3.0 F (Parson Technology, 1998).

13. O. Henry, "The Gift of the Magi," 1906, Project Gutenberg, http://www.gutenberg.org/dirs/etext05/magi10h.htm.

LESSON SIX: GUESS WHO'S COMING TO DINNER?

1. John Howard Griffin, *Black Like Me* (New York: Penguin, 1963).

2. Rebecca Winters Keegan, "The Top 10 Everything of 2008," *TIME,* November 3, 2008, http://www.time.com/time/specials/packages/article/0,28804,1855948_1864014,00.html.

3. *McClintock and Strong's Encyclopedia*, Electronic Database (Seattle: Biblesoft, 2000).

4. William Barclay, *The Gospel of Luke* (Louisville, KY: Westminster John Knox Press, 2001), 282.

5. Norval Geldenhuys, *Commentary on the Gospel of Luke* (Grand Rapids: Eerdmans, 1966), 475.

6. Charles Mackay, *Selected Poems and Songs* (London: Whittaker and Co., 1888), 159–60.

7. Najmieh Batmanglij, *Food of Life: Ancient Persian and Modern Iranian Cooking and Ceremonies* (Waldorf, MD: Mage, 1986), as quoted on *Cooking Books,* November 17, 2008, http://cooking-books.blogspot.com/2008/11/veal-stew.html?utm_source=feedburner&utm_medium=feed&utm_campaign=Feed%3A+CookingBooks+%28Cooking+Books%29.

LESSON SEVEN: WEDDING FIT FOR A KING

1. Adapted from "The Acceptable Time," Topic: Salvation, Practical Illustrations from Yesterday and Today, Quick Verse SermonBuilder, version 4.0, ©2005.

2. Emily, "The 10 Most Expensive Weddings of All Time," Leftos the Blog, May 28, 2010, http://leftos.com/blog/the-ten-most-expensive-weddings-of-all-time.

3. Chuck Smith and Tal Brooke, *Harvest* (Costa Mesa, CA: Chosen Books, 1987), 49.

4. "The Wedding Report," Bridal Association of America, http://www.bridalassociationofamerica.com/Wedding_Statistics/.

5. John Phillips, *Exploring The Gospel of Matthew* (Grand Rapids, MI: Kregel, 1999), 419.

6. Anne Graham Lotz, *Just Give Me Jesus* (Nashville: Thomas Nelson, 2000), 286–88.

7. W. E. Vine, Merrill F. Unger, William White Jr., *Vines Complete Expository Dictionary of Old and New Testament Words* (Nashville: Thomas Nelson, 1984, 1996), 256.

8. Lotz, *Just Give Me Jesus,* 285.

9. Debopriya Bose, "Baklava History," February 6, 2010, http://www.buzzle.com/articles/baklava-history.html.

LESSON EIGHT: FAREWELL FEAST

1. "Lincoln Memorial," National Park Service, http://www.nps.gov/nr/travel/wash/dc71.htm, last modified June 30, 2011.

2. Jack Uldrich, *Soldier, Statesman, Peacemaker* (New York: AMACOM, 2005), 213.

3. Richard A. Steele, Jr., and Evelyn Stoner, *Bible Illustrations, Book 3: Practical Bible Illustrations from Yesterday and Today* (Chattanooga, TN: AMG Publishers), accessed January 2011.

4. Dex, "Who Invented Hummus?" The Straight Dope, March 21, 2001, http://www.straightdope.com/columns/read/1898/who-invented-hummus.

LESSON NINE: ROADSIDE PICNIC

1. "What Is the Origin of the Word Picnic?" All About History, http://www.allabouthistory.org/origin-of-the-word-picnic-faq.htm, last modified September 28, 2011. Published by AllAboutGOD.com Ministries. Used by permission.

2. Robert Browning Hamilton, "Along the Road," *Journal of Education* 81 (1915): 76. Public domain.

3. "Internet Overtakes Newspapers as News Outlet," Pew Research Center Publications, December 23, 2008, http://pewresearch.org/pubs/1066/internet-overtakes-newspapers-as-news-source.

4. "Self-Fulfilling Prophecy," Index #1694, *Bible Illustrator For Windows*, version 3.0 F (Parson Technology, 1998), adapted.

5. Cat Stevens, "Moonshadow," *Teaser & The Firecat* © 1971 A&M.

6. "Kenneth N. Taylor," Tyndale House Publishers, http://www.tyndale.com/50_Company/dr_taylor_story.php.

7. "God's Word Does Not Return Void," Bible.org, April 1995, http://bible.org/illustration/god%E2%80%99s-word-does-not-return-void.

8. Venkat Mohan, ed., "Understanding Heartburn—The Basics," WebMD, http://www.webmd.com/heartburn-gerd/guide/understanding-heartburn-basics, last reviewed November 2, 2010.

LESSON TEN: BREAKFAST OF CHAMPIONS

1. Rob Southwick, "Sportfishing in America," American Sportfishing Association, 5, http://www.asafishing.org/images/statistics/resources/Sportfishing%20in%20America%20Rev.%207%2008.pdf, 5, last revised January 2008.

2. Mueller Writing, "Background," Recreational Boating and Fishing Foundation, 2011, http://www.muellerwriting.com/wp-content/uploads/2010/11/MediaKit-RBFF.pdf, 4.

3. Mueller Writing, "Background," 4.

4. Ronald P. Keeven, *A Joke, a Quote, and the Word* (Mustang, OK: Tate Publishing, 2006), 117.

5. *Merriam-Webster's Collegiate Dictionary,* 11th ed., s.v. "déjà vu."

6. Evan Ratliff, "Déjà Vu, Again and Again," *New York Times*, July 2, 2006. http://www.nytimes.com/2006/07/02/magazine/02dejavu.html?pagewanted=3.

7. Robert Paul Singleton, "Hydromaniac," May 29, 2006, http://www.urbandictionary.com/define.php?term=Hydromaniac.

8. "The White House State Dinner," The White House Historical Association, http://www.

whitehousehistory.org/whha_features/features_media/whha_history-background-state-dinners.pdf, last modified June 23, 2011.

9. Jason Horowitz, Roxanne Roberts, and Michael Shear, "Secret Service Apologizes for Ticketless Couple's Access," *Washington Post,* November 28, 2009, http://www.washingtonpost.com/wp-dyn/content/article/2009/11/27/AR2009112702650_pf.html.

10. Associated Press, "Washington Couple Crashed State Dinner," CBS News, December 1, 2009, http://www.cbsnews.com/stories/2009/11/25/national/main5780325.shtml.

11. Lydia Saad, "'Political Winners' Circle Filled by Figures Close to Obama," Gallup, December 28, 2009, http://www.gallup.com/poll/124790/Political-Winners-Circle-Filled-Figures-Close-Obama.aspx.

12. *Merriam-Webster's Collegiate Dictionary*, 11th ed., s.v. "redeem."

13. "Chapel of the Pieta," St. Peter's Basilia.org, http://saintpetersbasilica.org/Altars/Pieta/Pieta.htm, last modified February 5, 2010.

14. Geoffrey W. Bromiley, *International Standard Bible Encyclopedia*, vol. 2 (Grand Rapids: Eerdmans, 1982), 391, s.v. Galilee, Sea of.

15. Clinton E. Arnold, *Zondervan Illustrated Bible Backgrounds Commentary: Matthew, Mark, Luke* (Grand Rapids: 2002), 111.

About the Author

Born in a small town on the shores of Lake Michigan, Lenya Heitzig moved to beach cities in California and Hawaii before settling into the mountainous terrain of Albuquerque, New Mexico, where she now resides. Whether majoring in fashion merchandising, serving as a missionary with YWAM, or being a cancer survivor, Lenya thrives on adventure. As executive director of *she* Ministries of Albuquerque and coauthor of two Bible study series—the Pathway series published by Tyndale, and the Fresh Life series, published by David C Cook—she delights in seeing God's Word resulting in God's work in the lives of women. Her first book, *Pathway to God's Treasure: Ephesians*, received the Gold Medallion Award. She also contributed a number of devotionals to *The New Women's Devotional Bible*, which was a finalist in the 2007 Christian Book Awards. Her semiautobiographical book, *Holy Moments*, published by Regal, enlightens readers to see God's hand of providence move miraculously in daily life. Her husband, Skip Heitzig, is senior pastor of the fourteen-thousand–member congregation at Calvary of Albuquerque. Their son, Nathan, and his wife, Janaé, have two children, Seth Nathaniel and Kadence Joy.

Also by the author:

Holy Moments: Recognizing God's Fingerprints in Your Life with Regal Books from Gospel Light

Live Abundantly: A Study in the Book of Ephesians with David C Cook

Live Deeply: A Study in the Parables of Jesus with David C Cook

Live Faithfully: A Study in the Book of James with David C Cook, due November 2012

Live Fearlessly: A Study in the Book of Joshua with David C Cook

Live Intimately: Lessons from the Upper Room with David C Cook

Live Beautifully: A Study in the Books of Ruth and Esther with David C Cook

Live Reflectively: Lessons from the Watershed Moments with Moses with David C Cook

Live Relationally: Lessons from the Women of Genesis with David C Cook

Contributor:

A Passion For Jesus with Calvary Distribution

Decision Magazine

Redeemed and Restored with Calvary Distribution

The New Women's Devotional Bible with Zondervan